One language for the world

Mario Pei

BOOKS BY MARIO PEI

Language for Everybody (1957)
All About Language (1954)
Swords of Anjou (1953)
The Story of English (1952)
The Story of Language (1949)
The World's Chief Languages (1946)
The American Road to Peace (1945)
The Italian Language (1941)
The Language of the Eighth-Century Texts in Northern France (1932)

Mario Pei:

1958

THE DEVIN-ADAIR COMPANY: *New York*

One language for the world

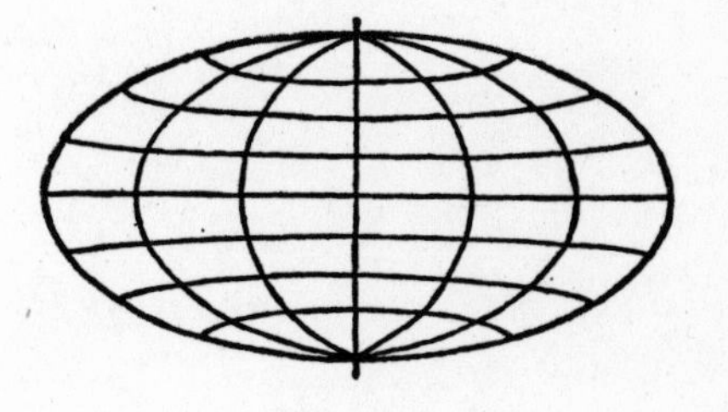

Canadian Agents: Thomas Nelson & Sons, Toronto
Library of Congress Catalog Card Number: 58-8818
Designed by Marshall Lee
Manufactured in the United States of America by H. Wolff, New York

CONTENTS

2

THE PROBLEM IN THE PAST: THE ATTEMPTS

3

THE PROBLEM IN THE FUTURE: THE SOLUTION

INTRODUCTION

What would happen if all the children in the world learned another language along with their own? Not just *another* language, but *the same* language?

In thirty years there would be no need for interpreters. Our children could travel around the world and learn the customs and thoughts of other people in foreign lands first hand, easily and naturally.

One of the greatest needs in the world of today is *a* language spoken and understood by everybody. But this need will be far, far greater in the world of tomorrow, the world of our children and their descendants.

Does this common language of the future have to be a constructed, artificial one, like Esperanto? Does it have to be one of the big national tongues, like English, French, or Russian? Not necessarily. It merely has to be *whatever language,* national or constructed, may be selected, in common accord, by the nations of the world.

To be effective, the teaching of this language should start in the first grade, side by side with the national language; better yet, in kindergarten.

Why is all this so necessary? For a very simple reason.

There was a time when very few people left their homes, or, at the most, their own countries; when the individual's chances of coming in contact with the speakers of another language were slim indeed. The last fifty years have changed all that. Today, the probabilities that you, whatever be your walk of life, will be called upon at some time or other to travel abroad are at least one out of ten, as against one out of a hundred in the nineteenth century. The chances that you will want to communicate with a non-English speaker on your own home soil are practically one hundred per cent even now.

For your children, the chances of foreign travel and foreign contacts are at least double yours. For their children, they will be fourfold. Within a century, the man or woman who has no occasion to travel abroad will be as rare as is today the man or woman who has never left his home town.

This casts a new light upon what was for centuries a pleasant intellectual exercise—the creation or selection of an international, universal language, a tongue for everybody, to be spoken, understood, read, and written by all the peoples of this earth.

The problem was not urgent back in the seventeenth century, when it was first given some conscious thought. It became immediate only in the nineteenth, when modern means of communication and transportation began to appear. Today, when the jet plane brings all countries of the earth to within a few hours of one another, it is almost as imperative as is the problem of survival in the face of nuclear weapons.

The only real difficulty lies in the *method* for choosing *a* language, national or constructed, that will serve as the international tongue. Once this hurdle is surmounted, the educational resources of the modern world will be ample to insure the success of the project.

The question is often asked: "Who wants an international language?" To this query, the word "anyway" is occasionally appended, in token of skepticism. The answer is: "Practically everybody."

Everyone knows about the troubles encountered by UN diplomats, with their complicated systems of simultaneous translations, by scientists who attend international congresses, by students and visiting professors, by tourists and sightseers, by missionaries and technicians, by people engaged in international trade, by immigrants and emigrants. That all these people would favor an international language is self-evident.

Far more to the point is the response of populations at large. A Gallup poll conducted a few years ago in the United States, Canada, Norway, and the Netherlands revealed that nearly eighty per cent of those polled, in each of the four countries, favored an international tongue, to be taught in the elementary schools of the world on a basis of complete parity with the national languages, with the implication that the children of each country would grow up speaking two languages, the national and the international tongue, with equal fluency.

Surprisingly, in a country like the United States, where interest in foreign languages is supposed to be far from pronounced, there was no noticeable difference in feeling about this issue from what existed in lands widely exposed to international currents, like Norway and Holland.

This popular interest takes the question out of the academic realms and brings it squarely before the bar of public opinion. It is not merely a few diplomats and government people concerned with translation problems who want an international tongue, or a few million tourists worrying about the location of a hotel. It is not even a large number of migrants concerned with the vital problem of seeking a job in a foreign land. It is the rank and file of the population. It is fathers and mothers thinking of their children's future welfare and happiness, young people who want to communicate with other young people in other lands. People in all walks of life who have at some time or other been up against the blank wall that the lack of a common language produces want to tear down that wall.

There is a big difference between voting "yes" on a Gallup

poll question and undertaking to do something about it. The majority of the world's people are too busy with their own concerns, with the everyday job of making a living and filling their places in their own limited social group, to go out into the streets and agitate for an international language the way the suffragettes agitated for women's right to vote back in the early days of this century.

But this, if anything, makes the point even more overwhelming. Without the support of any great, concerted movement, without open and flamboyant agitation, without picket lines or demonstrations or brick-throwing or Congressional lobbies, the international language is accepted in principle by four-fifths of those who are asked their opinion about it.

It is therefore high time to go into this question in detail once more, not on the basis of advocating any one particular solution (something that goes on all the time), but on the basis of an informative study of the entire issue.

What is the need? Why does it exist? In which fields of human activity is it most keenly felt? When did people first become aware of it? What steps did they take? What unconscious, partial solutions had previously been worked out? What languages served through history as tongues of common intercourse for groups speaking two or more different languages? At what point did the idea of a constructed, artificial language begin to take hold, and how was it received? In the light of present-day conditions, what solutions are feasible? Could a national, natural language be used? Could it be modified to serve the purpose? Could a combination of languages work? What is the status of "neutral," constructed tongues today? What machinery would have to be set up to select a world language? What machinery would be needed to impart it? What would be its fruits, and how soon would they mature?

As this book unfolds, we may see the answers to some of these questions.

1

THE PROBLEM IN THE PRESENT: THE NEED

1. The jigsaw puzzle of language

The Existing Languages—How They Are Distributed—What Appeal They Make—Inequalities Among Languages—The Thirteen Leaders

A tool is seldom missed save when you want it and it isn't there. We seldom miss language, because it is so readily available. It is only when we find ourselves faced with someone whose linguistic tool does not mesh with ours that we become acutely conscious of language.

Language is by far the most important of the tools we use. It serves the purpose of communication with our fellow men, and without it no coordinated activity is possible. It is in use practically every waking moment of our lives. Without language, we tend to lose some of our human qualities and sink to the level of the animals.

But normally we are not aware of this. Language is there for us to use, like the water gushing from the tap of a kitchen sink in an apartment house. Who worries about water, save on the very rare occasions when the mains are under repair, and we turn on the faucet only to be rewarded with a gurgle?

When things go wrong with language, the gurgle we get in the place of the steady flow may be a gesture, a broken phrase, a word that fails to carry a complete message. Or we may get a flow of something we can't use, as though our water faucet suddenly started spurting ammonia instead of water.

At any rate, we quickly feel lost. Our power of communication is drastically curtailed, and so is our activity. There are a million things we would like to say, but we can't say them.

There are a thousand things we would like to do which involve the participation of the other person. We can't call for that participation, so we can't do them. We don't merely *feel* lost. We *are* lost.

How often have you found yourself in this situation? Perhaps you were a soldier in one of our recent wars, and found that you could not communicate with an enemy, or an ally, or a neutral, that you couldn't question a prisoner, call upon a trapped foe to surrender, ask for food, or directions, or medical help. Perhaps you have been a tourist abroad, trying to tell a taxi driver who spoke only French, or German, or Spanish, where to take you, trying to find out where the restroom was, or the elevator, or the museum, or at what time your train was scheduled to leave. Perhaps you have tried, here or elsewhere, to do business with people who did not speak your language, to show them the advantages of what you had to sell, inquire about the things you wanted to buy. Even without leaving the continental United States, you may have been approached by someone struggling with a penciled address and the intricacies of the New York subway system, and you recall the feeling of helplessness as you vainly tried to impart the needed directions to one who could not understand them.

Take all these situations, multiply them by the two and a half billion people now living on the globe, and you have a picture of what the lack of a common language does to the people of the world today. To get the picture of what it will do a hundred years hence, when travel, trade, and general international intercourse will probably be ten times what they are today, multiply again by ten.

If you are intellectually inclined, there is also the matter of books, magazines, and newspapers published abroad that you may be interested in reading, of foreign radio or television broadcasts that you may want to listen to, of foreign movies or plays that you may want to see. For all these things, stemming from our twentieth-century civilization, as well as for the more vital matter of direct spoken-language communication, there is one stock answer: "Learn foreign languages!"

It is a good answer, and one well worth considering. But there is one big drawback. The foreign languages are many in number. Whether you learn one, or two, or a dozen, you are still up against the basic problem. You cannot foresee what your specific language needs are going to be ten years, or even one year, from now. Of what practical use to have learned perfect French and then be shipped to China, or to have mastered Russian and then find yourself in Mexico?

The world's activities, cultural, scientific, commercial, and even military, now proceed on a more or less integrated basis, not piecemeal, country by country, or continent by continent, as they once did. This means that the complete answer to the language question can only be an integrated, global one. The leisurely language learning that well served chosen segments of previous generations is today at best only a stopgap. Language learning has drastic limitations, both for the individual and the community, when one considers the infinite amount of new factual material that both individual and community have to assimilate, in widely unrelated fields, in order to keep abreast of modern progress. We cannot spend all our lives learning foreign languages. Even if we did, a lifetime would be insufficient to give us what we want in the way of full, easy, untrammeled communication with our fellow men.

There are in spoken use throughout the world today, according to our most reliable linguists, 2,796 separate languages, exclusive of dialects. This is far more than any man could master in a hundred lifetimes.

It is quite true that the majority of these languages belong to small groups, numbering fewer than a million speakers and having little practical importance. But even after we have assigned over two thousand tongues to North and South American Indian tribes, African Negro groups, clans of Australian and Papuan aborigines, and sparse populations of remote Asiatic regions and South Pacific islands, we are still faced with over a hundred languages used by large and civilized groups, numbering from one million to five hundred million people, and living in continents and countries with which we have broad contacts. Millions of them have come, are coming or will come to our shores. Millions of us have traveled or will travel to the lands where these languages are spoken. The products of their culture, their spoken, written, radioed, televised words, are forever with us, in international discussions, in books, magazines, and newspapers, in science and commerce and advertising. There is now almost no way to avoid them, and as time and the swift march of modern technological progress advance, there will be even less.

There are big, well-known, widely studied languages that range far beyond their homelands, like English, French, and Spanish. There are medium-sized tongues like Polish, Dutch, and Tamil, that are spoken by populations in the tens of millions. There are smaller tongues, like Danish, Hungarian, modern Greek, and the Singhalese of Ceylon, which may not reach ten million speakers, but are the regular medium of linguistic exchange in their own well-defined areas. It is conceivable that any one of us, individually, may come in contact with any one of them, and with dozens of others besides. The possibility of such contact, once quite remote, is now commonplace, and if present trends continue will become far more extensive.

In the Western Hemisphere alone, disregarding the American Indian languages, which are over a thousand in number, and of which some, like the Quichua of Peru and the Nahuatl of Mexico, have millions of speakers, we find four widely spoken languages. These are the English of the United States and Canada, the Portuguese of Brazil, the Spanish of a score of nations ranging in population from Mexico's 30 million and Argentina's 20 million to the 900,000 of Panama, and the French of Quebec, Haiti, French Guiana, and some insular French possessions—not to mention the Dutch of Surinam and the Danish of Greenland.

In practice, this means that a Western Hemisphere traveler who wishes to be linguistically at home wherever he goes, for whatever purposes he may have in mind, would have to possess a fairly fluent knowledge of four languages, English, French, Spanish, and Portuguese, obviously a major, though not an unattainable, achievement. Even so, he might find himself at a loss in Dutch Guiana, in Greenland, and in parts of Mexico and Central or South America where the native languages prevail almost to the exclusion of Spanish and Portuguese.

The world traveler wishing to make his way about western Europe would be faced with a far more serious language problem. English would carry him through the British Isles (though he might run into Welsh, Irish, and Scots Gaelic areas where not all the inhabitants speak English). On the continent, it would be a question of knowing French, Spanish, Portuguese, Italian, German, Dutch, Swedish, Norwegian, Danish, Finnish, Serbo-Croatian, modern Greek, and Turkish. This impressive list still leaves out the Breton of northwestern France, the Basque and Catalan of the Pyrenees, the Rumansh of Switzerland, the Flemish of Belgium, the Slovenian of Yugoslavia, languages for which substitutions can normally be effected, since their speakers are almost all bilingual.

In eastern Europe would be found Polish, Czech and Slovak, Hungarian, Albanian, Bulgarian, Rumanian, plus whatever may be left of Lithuanian, Lettish, and Estonian, plus the Russian of the Soviet homeland with its closely allied sister tongues, Ukrainian and Byelorussian.

Even before reaching the Asiatic portion of the Soviet

Union, our traveler would come in contact with numerous other Soviet tongues: some, like Armenian, of the Indo-European family; some, like Georgian, of the Caucasian group; others of the same family as Finnish and Hungarian, still others related to Turkish. Numerous tongues of the Finnish or Turkic stock occupy the northern half of Asia, but they are by no means the major Asiatic languages. This distinction pertains to Chinese and Japanese and Korean, the Vietnamese of Indochina, the Malay and Javanese of Indonesia, Tibetan, Burmese, and Thai, the Hindustani and Bengali of northern India, the Tamil and Telugu of southern India, the Pushtu of Afghanistan, the Persian of Iran, the Arabic of Syria, Lebanon, Jordan, Iraq, Yemen, and the domains of Ibn Sa'ud, as well as the modern Hebrew of Israel. There are many dozens of additional languages spoken by large populations in India, Indonesia, and southeastern Asia.

The westerner who has mastered even one of these Asiatic tongues is viewed as exceptional. The specialist who has three or four of them at his command is a seven-day wonder. Yet these tongues are becoming more important every day as Asia begins to rival Europe and America in the international picture.

In Africa we find Arabic north of the Sahara, but we also find Berber and Kushitic tongues intermingled with Arabic. Other languages of the Semito-Hamitic family appear in Ethiopia, Eritrea, and Somaliland. Then there are the very numerous languages of the African Negroes, some of which, like the Hausa of Nigeria and the Swahili of East Africa, have several million speakers. There is the Malagasy of the island of Madagascar, related to the Malay of Indonesia and the languages of Hawaii and Tahiti. There are the European tongues of colonization, English, French, Spanish, Portuguese, Italian; the Afrikaans of the Union of South Africa, which is an offshoot of Dutch; even a faint memory, in Tanganyika and Southwest Africa, of German from the days that preceded the First World War.

The chances that the average American, unless he is a missionary or an African trader, would require an African language are small. Yet during the Second World War people who knew anything at all about the native languages of French Equatorial and West Africa were desperately needed for military and propaganda purposes.

Australia and the Pacific Islands present a picture not too unlike that of Africa—the tongues of European settlers, English, French, Dutch, Portuguese, a sprinkling of former tongues of colonization, like Spanish, German, and Japanese, and then hundreds of native tongues, some linked to Malay, others, especially in Australia and New Guinea, of unrelated families.

No one knows all the languages of even a corner of the globe. People who have business in a certain area normally undertake to do something about communicating with the people around them. They acquire a smattering of one or several languages, teach the natives elements of their own language, in pidgin form if necessary, or, most often, procure the services of translators and interpreters. Whatever is done along these lines in one area is normally of no value in another. H. Rider Haggard's character Alan Quatermain, who was familiar with many of the languages of South and East Africa, would have found himself as completely lost as you or I if he had been suddenly transplanted to the jungles of Borneo or the mountains of Burma. No satisfactory way has been yet devised of solving the problem of language differences save at the purely local level.

There is, however, this to be said. On the basis of speaking population, geographical distribution and location, commercial, scientific, cultural, and military-political importance, some languages have a greater practical appeal than others.

This practical appeal forms the basis of our language-study. It also forms the basis of such internationality in language as has so far been achieved. Certain languages offer certain advantages—a large speaking population, widespread distribution due to colonization or other historical factors, and commercial or cultural merits.

In our search for a tongue that may serve the entire human race these leading tongues possess tremendous advantages. They are already established as partially international tongues, covering large areas of the earth and being well known beyond their own boundaries. This same feature, however, also acts as a handicap. It causes such languages to be regarded as peculiarly the vehicles of certain cultures, of certain patterns of civilization, of certain types of mental activity, and so offends the speakers of other languages and renders them suspicious. The situation is not too different from that prevailing at a political convention where there are many strong candidates in the field. It may resolve itself into a stalemate, with the ultimate emergence of a comparatively unknown "dark horse" candidate whom nobody really wants, but who at least has the merit of not offending anyone's susceptibilities.

The population factor is by no means the only one that makes a language great or outstanding. At the same time, it is the one which can be most simply and objectively reckoned. Using this simple yardstick as a first means of establishing class distinctions among the world's 2796 languages, we find that there are only thirteen which top the mark of fifty million speakers. They are, in numerical order, and in very round numbers:

Chinese	600,000,000
English	250,000,000
Hindustani (including Hindi and Urdu)	200,000,000

Russian (including Ukrainian and Byelorussian)	150,000,000
Spanish	120,000,000
German	100,000,000
Japanese	100,000,000
Malay (including Indonesian)	80,000,000
French	80,000,000
Portuguese	60,000,000
Bengali	60,000,000
Italian	60,000,000
Arabic	50,000,000

Let us by all means stress the fact, which will be brought out in later chapters, that these figures are very far from telling the entire story; that by reason of imperfect census figures, some doubt attaches to certain of the totals; that the totals themselves do not reflect the very important factor of greater or lesser dialectalization within what is classified as a single language.

At the same time, these two facts are indisputable: 1. None of these languages has fewer than fifty million speakers; 2. No other languages pass the fifty million mark.

In what light these figures are to be viewed, and what other factors enter the picture of language hierarchy, will appear shortly.

2. What you can do with each language

The Population Factor—The Distribution Factor—The Military-Political Factor—The Economic Factor—The Cultural Factor

On a scientifically linguistic basis, all languages are equal. They all consist of meaningful, distinctive sounds (sometimes called phonemes); of grammatical devices, which include prefixes, suffixes, changes within the individual word, and word arrangements; of words, conveying separate partial meanings; and of sentences, or complete utterances, conveying minimal units of complete meaning. In spoken (though not in written) form, they are all equally easy and clear to their own speakers, the people who have heard them and practiced them from babyhood, no matter how outlandish or complicated they may seem to the outsider. They all serve the same purpose, which is that of transferring thought and meaning from one person to another. They all have within themselves the machinery to become vehicles of literature, philosophy, science, political thought. Like human beings, they are endowed with an individuality, a complete set of physiological features, and an intellectual or spiritual quality which distinguishes them from the lower orders of creation.

But just as all men, though created equal and endowed with basic equality in the eyes of God, are not endowed with all faculties, powers, and gifts to the same degree, or even if so endowed, have not had equal opportunity to develop them, so languages have marked differences of a purely external, nonlinguistic nature, which make them far from equal in size, importance, use, and general practical desirability. Men faced with a choice between English, the language of one tenth of the earth's population, with its infinite possibilities of use throughout the globe, and Kwakiutl, the tongue of a few thousand North American Indians, will almost invariably prefer to learn and possess English. They will base this choice on external factors—population, distribution, cultural, political, and economic importance. These factors are nonlinguistic, but they are far from unimportant. In a practical sense, they come close to being paramount, just as the possession of wealth, education, social prestige, and influence are tremendously important in the affairs of the individual, though not inherent to his nature and far more subject to change than those more permanent physiological, mental, and spiritual qualities which make up the true essence of a man.

The population factor is to a language much as wealth is to the individual. It can be rather easily gained or lost. It does not particularly enhance its possessor, save insofar as he may make good and socially advantageous use of his increased opportunities. To say that English has 250 million speakers while Greek, in modern times, has fewer than ten million, is not to claim superiority of English over Greek, but only to state an incontrovertible, objective fact, like saying that Winthrop Rockefeller has more money than Albert Schweitzer.

From a practical standpoint, the fact that the thirteen leading languages have over fifty million speakers each gives them a tremendous objective advantage. But other factors come into play. One, which is almost equally subject to empirical observation and enumeration, is that of distribution throughout the globe. Speakers of Chinese outnumber those of English two to one, but they are rather inconveniently located within the boundaries of China, a large and important country, but one which constitutes only a fraction of one continent. English, on the other hand, enjoys widespread distribution throughout the globe. It is found on the North American continent, in the United States, Canada, and Alaska; in Europe, in the British Isles; in Australia, New Zealand and South Africa; in the innumerable possessions and former possessions of the British Empire, scattered over the world, from Malta, Gibraltar, and Cyprus in Europe to British Honduras and British Guiana in America, from India and Pakistan in Asia to Egypt and Kenya in Africa. It is a language that has been learned by many who do not have it as a native tongue, so that you find people who speak it almost everywhere you may travel. This distributional advantage more than offsets the numerical superiority of Chinese.

Second only to English in distributional power is French. Though endowed with only about 80 million native speakers, it is practically as widespread as English. It is not only the official language of France and one of the official languages of Belgium and Switzerland, but it is spoken in Europe by large numbers of educated people of all countries. In the Western Hemisphere it is official only in Canada, Haiti, and the few French possessions that are left, but it is widely spoken by the educated classes of Latin America. In Africa it is one of the great colonizing languages. Madagascar and Indochina, Samoa and Tahiti, the formerly French-held cities on the Indian coast and numerous scattered islands in the Pacific and Indian oceans recognize French as an official language. Like English, French can be used almost anywhere.

Spanish, by way of contrast, is largely limited to the Western Hemisphere, though its homeland is in Europe. Relatively few Spanish speakers are to be found in Europe outside of Spain. Spanish possessions in Africa are few. In the East, with the exception of the Philippines, where large numbers of Spanish speakers were inherited from pre-Spanish–American War days, Spanish is practically nonexistent. But in our own hemisphere, Spanish vies with English in distributional strength. It is heard from the Rio Grande to Cape Horn, and is the official language of eighteen of the twenty-two independent American nations.

Portuguese is also primarily a Western Hemisphere language, with Brazil, a country larger than the United States, as its western preserve. But Portuguese still holds sway in a fairly widespread Portuguese empire (continental Portugal and the Azores in Europe; Angola and Mozambique in Africa; Goa, Diu, and Damau in India; Timor in the Indonesian islands).

The distributional force of German is largely limited to central Europe, since Germany's bid to become a world imperial power failed in two world wars. But the German language's position in the heart of the European continent gives it an irradiating power that is felt as far north as

Sweden, as far east as Russia, as far south as Yugoslavia, and as far west as France and Belgium. Similar, though somewhat lesser, advantages are enjoyed by Italian, which makes its force felt throughout the Mediterranean basin. In addition, both German and Italian have large masses of transoceanic speakers who impart their own flavor to the Western Hemisphere countries to which they have emigrated—the United States, Argentina, Brazil, Chile, Uruguay.

Russian, which until recently was a restricted language, has now embarked upon a wide career of expansion. It not only dominates the Soviet Union, which covers one sixth of the earth's land surface, but infiltrates the countries of central Europe and the Balkans. To the east it presses upon China, Manchuria, and Mongolia, though it seems to be meeting with resistance from the Chinese. Still, Russian, like Chinese, Hindustani, and Bengali, is landlocked. A landlocked language, as long as it remains so, cannot be a world language.

Hindustani, surrounded by minor languages and further split into the Hindi of India and the Urdu of Pakistan, is an important and growing tongue. The day will probably dawn when it will serve as a common linguistic medium for all of the subcontinent's four hundred million or more people, but for the time it must be remembered that it is known to less than half that population. Bengali, despite the number of its speakers and its literary merits, may be regarded as a local tongue of northeast India and East Pakistan.

Japanese, Malay, and Arabic are languages of some pretensions. The first made a bid for world power during the recent war. That bid failed, and Japanese is today the language of Japan's 90 million, and little more. The predominant tongue of Indonesia is Indonesian, based on the Malay which served as a lingua franca throughout the Dutch East Indies even before they gained their independence. But it is a language superimposed upon countless minor languages and dialects of the same family—Javanese, Madurese, Balinese, and a host of others. It has little currency outside of Indonesia and Malaya.

This leaves Arabic as the only Asiatic language whose spread permits it to rank in distribution with the great languages of the west. Arabic dominates the African continent from the Mediterranean to the Sahara, and from Morocco to Egypt. It covers most countries of the Middle East–Arabia, Yemen, Syria, Jordan, Lebanon, Iraq. In addition, Arabic is the vehicle of Islamic civilization, and its influence is felt wherever there are Moslems. It is safe to say that it affects, directly or indirectly, at least 300 million persons, among whom are African Negroes and East Indians, Indonesians and Turks, Chinese and Albanians.

Is it possible to establish a hierarchy of distribution, as we established one of numbers? In such a hierarchy, we would have to list English and French at the very top, then arrange Arabic, Spanish, Russian, Portuguese, German in a second division, and end up with the more localized tongues, Chinese, Indonesian, Italian, Hindustani, Japanese, Bengali.

But here other factors come in to interfere with our distributional values. What are the economic forces that underlie each language? What political and military elements enter each picture? What scientific realizations and cultural traditions does each language represent?

Here we are forced to depart from the realm of the purely objective. Statistics concerning the production of steel, coal, oil, the number of telephones or radio stations or automobiles are partly or totally available. But it is no more desirable that a language should dominate the world by reason of these purely material factors than that the individual or family that owns half the township property should control the local elections. The military-political and even the scientific elements in modern times closely follow the economic pattern, so that the languages used in countries of vast industrial and economic potential, like the United States, the British Commonwealth, and the Soviet Union, are the ones most likely to have the backing of big guns and atom bombs. These advantages, however, are largely illusory, since in the absence of complete world domination by one power, the large national units, so far as language is concerned, tend to cancel one another out. If English speakers refuse under any and all circumstances to accept the tongue of their Soviet rivals, and the latter in turn reject English, one of three things is likely to happen: in the event of an armed clash, one language will emerge triumphant; or, in the absence of war, the two languages will withdraw each to its own sphere, and become dominant there; or a third, compromise, "dark horse" candidate may replace them both.

The cultural factor remains, but that is so shadowy, so subjective, so dependent upon individual interpretation and taste, that it is doubtful whether it will ever play a very serious role in the choice of a language for the world.

Each group considers its own culture paramount. At the most, a grudging measure of respect may be paid by some of the more enlightened members of one culture to another culture, as when English speakers admit that French is a language well suited for diplomacy, or cookery, or women's fashions, or that Italian works out best for opera singing.

Each of the thirteen leading languages is in a position to advance serious cultural claims, at least from its own viewpoint. We may point out to the speakers of Japanese that their culture stems largely from China, but they can counter that we of the English language have inherited an originally alien, Judaeo-Graeco-Roman civilization, on which we have superimposed a medieval and Renaissance structure that came largely from France and Italy. Speakers of Hindustani, Bengali, even Indonesian, can proudly point to the stemming of their cultures from Sanskrit, earliest of the Indo-European languages on record. Speakers of Arabic can remind us of the mighty Islamic civilization that gathered to itself some of the best elements of Judaism and Christianity, along with the philosophy and science of the ancient Greek world, and went on to build a great cultural empire that for centuries was in advance of anything produced by the west. The antiquity of Chinese civilization, and its direct and indirect contributions to the west are too well known to bear repetition. As for the cultural claims of western languages like French, Italian, German, Spanish, anyone who has attended a foreign-language-choice session in an American high school is familiar with them. The Russians claim not only to have had a share in developing the civilizations of both east and west, but also to have made a modern political contribution to the welfare of mankind, the validity of which is very much disputed by many in the western world.

Perhaps we should learn to regard culture as something world-wide rather than as a mosaic of different parts, and begin to realize that it is precisely this world-wide aspect of culture and civilization that lends itself to the proposition that mankind is fundamentally one. No civilization has grown to truly great stature without copious contributions and admixtures from countless foreign sources.

One aspect of culture, perhaps, is directly and easily measurable in terms of language, and that is literacy; or, to put it another way, the extent to which education in that particular culture has pervaded the speakers of the language can be determined. Here we find vast differences, ranging from the almost 100 per cent literacy of English speakers to the 90 per cent illiteracy of the people of India. But illiteracy may be described as a passing phase in the history of modern cultures. Its aspects are purely temporary and remediable.

How temporary or permanent, how remediable or irremediable are some of the other factors we have discussed? How stable are population, distribution, economic and political and military prestige? Does the status quo have to endure?

Is it desirable that it should? For the answers to these questions, we shall have to look at the reverse of the medal.

3. What you can't do with each language

Negative Side of Each Factor—Factors Not Everlasting—The Changing Geographical Picture—The Changing Pattern Within Each Language—Dialects—The Factor of Future Uncertainty

The population factor in language has been described as among the most objective and stable. While there is no doubt about its objectivity (provided reliable statistics are available for a given country at a given period), stability is something else.

There is, of course, no absolute stability in language or in anything else in the world. The earth's population is subject to shift and change. During the last few centuries the tendency has been for populations to grow in numbers, to the point where some scientists are beginning to wonder about the problem of food and living space. Even this trend, however, may be reversible. Atomic warfare on a large scale may bring the world's population down to more manageable proportions, to cite one spectacular possibility. But population decrease has occurred before in history without the benefit of atomic fission or planned birth control. The Black Death that cut Europe's population to half its former numbers, and the Thirty Years' War that saw the population of Germany shrink to one third its original size, are two examples. There is no guarantee that something of this nature may not occur again.

In connection with language, it is, rather, relative population trends that are of interest, and here history presents some significant episodes.

Among the major western languages, English, which around the year 1100 A.D. seems to have been spoken by no more than 1½ million (French at that time had a speaking population of about 8 million), had gone up to 5 million by the year 1500. At that period our most reliable figures indicate 12 million for French, 10 million for German, 9½ million for Italian, 8½ million for Spanish.

By 1700 English had grown to about 8 million, but in the next two centuries, mainly by reason of expansion in the North American and Australian continents, it rose to 123 million, outstripping French, which in 1900 showed 52 million, German with 80 million, Spanish with 58 million, Italian with 54 million, and Russian with 80 million. By 1952 the approximate figures were: English, 250 million; Russian, 150 million; Spanish, 120 million; German, 100 million; French, 80 million; Italian, 60 million. Anyone evaluating the status of the western languages in 1500 would have concluded that French would remain forever in the lead, and that English would forever trail its four major European competitors.

China's population of an estimated 140 million in 1741 (the first year for which tentative Chinese statistics are available), representing the practical totality of Chinese speakers, had risen to 300 million by 1800, to 440 million by 1900, and is estimated today at 600 million. Here a projection into the future would have worked out more correctly, but the percentage of growth of English speakers, from the 10 to 15 million of 1741 to the 250 million of today, is seen to exceed even the rate of growth of Chinese.

No one viewing the few thousand speakers of Latin at the time of the founding of Rome around 500 B.C., would have been able to foretell that by the time of Christ the Latin language would have spread over the entire Mediterranean basin and far to the north and east, encompassing a population of at least 100 million persons.

The truth is that not only languages, but the populations speaking them, rise and fall in accordance with historical conditions which are largely unpredictable. It is not merely a case of populations of individual countries rising and falling at different rates. It is also a case of wholesale language shifts on the part of individuals and masses. If the speakers of Imperial Latin had been only the descendants of the early Romans who founded the City on the Tiber, and not the children of the Oscans, Etruscans, Greeks, Carthaginians, Iberians, and Gauls conquered by Rome, Latin would have remained an obscure language. If only the descendants of the original English settlers spoke English in America, at least half of our American population would not be speaking English. But the prestige of Imperial Latin and American English were such that most of those who came in contact with them learned and spoke them, with a foreign accent in the first generation or two, as native speakers in the following generations.

Accepting the lessons of the past for the future, we may safely assert that the present hierarchy of language populations is by no means fixed and everlasting. Some of the thirteen leading languages may drop into a lower classification with the passing of time, while other languages may come up to replace them. Even if this does not happen, the order of the thirteen leaders may be quite changed by the year 2000.

Changes in the geographical distribution of language go on under our own eyes. We see, for example, that while English gains ground in certain areas, by reason of economic or financial penetration, it loses ground in others. India, Pakistan, Ceylon, and the Philippines, four countries where English was till recently used for all official government purposes, now tend to replace it with native languages. Russian, not English, or French, or German, is the foreign tongue most studied in eastern European states and, probably, in Red China. But English makes giant strides in Japan, western Europe, and Latin America, displacing even German and French. Chinese in North Korea, English in South Korea, replace an earlier Japanese influence. In North Vietnam Chinese tends to displace French. Everywhere, language distribution follows the pattern of military conquest or economic penetration. The world's linguistic picture is extremely unstable.

Living people who in their earlier years studied French and German because those were, along with English, the great world languages are now advising their children to take up the study of Russian and Chinese. Spanish at the time of the First, and Portuguese at the time of the Second World War had considerable vogue on grounds of Latin-American trade. The world's language picture is an extremely confusing one for the person who does not have an absolutely precise purpose in mind. The oil engineer who learns a little Arabic because he is being sent to the oil wells of Iraq, the businessman whose agency in Rio calls for a Portuguese speaker and who accordingly takes a course in Portuguese, are on comparatively safe ground. But what of the man whose plans are not yet formulated? What of the high-school or college student who is faced with the conflicting claims of a dozen modern foreign languages? The picture that unfolds before his eyes is not merely confused, but unstable. Selecting a language, or two or three languages, is somewhat on a par with picking a winning horse at the races.

It is this confusion and uncertainty as much as anything else that has contributed to the decline of language study in American high schools and colleges. Were there *a* language which the American student could embrace with full confidence that it would take care of all, or at any rate most, of the foreign problems that might confront him in later life, he would embrace it with enthusiasm. As matters stand, he is supposed to gamble so many hours for so many years of his limited lifetime, on the chance that the French, or Spanish, or German, or Italian, or Russian that he is taking up will be the language he may need later.

Matters are not eased by what we may describe as the changing pattern within each language, or, to put it another way, the different facets or aspects of the same tongue. It has been customary in the past to impart foreign languages in their purest and most grammatical literary form, on the supposition that they would be used primarily for the purpose of enjoying the literary culture of the country from which they stemmed. Recently there has been a spectacular reversal in this point of view, with the spoken tongue in its most colloquial vernacular form, including even slang and vulgarisms, presented as the *summum bonum*. This has led to bigger and better confusion. When you are already taking a gamble on a given foreign tongue, you are further required to gamble on one of its aspects. Are you learning French for the purpose of reading Molière, or French for the purpose of arguing with a Paris taxi driver? It is not at all the same thing, nor does it involve the same processes.

Even where some sort of compromise is effected between the written and the spoken language, along comes a question of dialects to complicate the matter further. Foreigners learning English are often faced with a very difficult choice: shall it be British or American English? Both are important. Knowledge of one does not automatically imply full command of the other, particularly in the colloquial realm. If you undertake to learn Chinese or Arabic, you will have a universal written tongue, but many widely diverging vernacular dialects, almost mutually incomprehensible. Even in standardized western European languages, like French, Italian, and German, you may run up against dialectal differences. It is all very well for the pedant to say: "Learn the standard, official tongue—Parisian French, Castilian Spanish, Florentine Italian, North Mandarin Chinese"! What happens if you encounter a speaker of Provençal, or a Puerto Rican, or a Sicilian, or a Cantonese? And what of those languages, like English and Arabic, that have no true official spoken standard, because each locality sets up its own standards of pronunciation?

The facts of language are harsh, but it is best to face them, and even to repeat them. Language is divided into numerous varieties, of which thirteen can be described as major tongues, and of the thirteen only seven or eight have, at the present moment, broad international diffusion coupled with all the other factors, economic, political, and cultural, that make a language of paramount importance.

But——there is no guarantee that the language picture will remain the same, even within our own lifetime. Population, distribution, as well as economic, political, and military factors, are all subject to sudden and startling change.

Languages are subject to drastic change and variation not only externally, but internally—in their forms, in their vocabularies, and above all, in their class and local distinctions, so that learning any one of them, even your own, means subjecting yourself to a constant process of check and recheck, of additional language learning, of acceptance, or at least recognition, of a variety of words, constructions, usages, accents, and intonations.

From the standpoint of selecting a national language for world use, if such be our purpose, this means not only a choice among the languages, but also a choice among the individual forms of a language (British or American, Mandarin or Cantonese, Castilian or Argentine usage).

4. The immediate need: political and diplomatic

The Languages of Diplomacy—UN and UNESCO—The Language of National Politics—The Language of International Politics

At the Congress of Vienna, which closed the cycle of the Napoleonic Wars, French was the sole official language; at Versailles, which ended the First World War, French and English were used interchangeably and on a basis of parity; while at the UN, which continues the traditions of San Francisco and Dumbarton Oaks, five languages are in official use: English, French, Spanish, Russian, and Chinese.

The world, far from tending to become a linguistic unit, is spreading farther and farther apart so far as language is concerned.

One might argue that while Vienna reflected a purely cultural state of affairs (French was, after all, the language of the defeated nation), Versailles and the UN were and are rather reflections of power politics thrown into the language field. One could easily go on from that to moralize upon the lowering of cultural standards and ideals that has marked the transition from the early nineteenth to the middle of the twentieth century. One might even go further, and claim that the progression from one to five languages is a symbol not of progress, but of intellectual retrogression and growing ignorance.

In 1815, anyone who was engaged in diplomacy spoke,

understood, read, and wrote French, easily and fluently, whether his name was Talleyrand or Metternich, Castlereagh or von Hardenberg or Alexander of Russia. In 1919, the Lloyd Georges and Wilsons had succumbed to the forces of linguistic isolationism and linguistic nationalism. In 1958, the use of five official languages points to the growth and spreading of those forces, coupled with a relentless insistence on the part of each major linguistic group upon the separate recognition of its own culture and an absolute unwillingness to defer to the culture of others, or even to what might be defined as a world culture. The Russians have actually had to compile a glossary of diplomatic terms, which they almost completely lacked, because of the fact that in the old days French was their one and only diplomatic language. The Chinese Reds, rejecting the English favored by the Chinese Nationalists, are now said to be grimly engaged in a similar project.

There is a reverse to the medal, to be sure. One could argue with some plausibility that the use of many languages is an indication of the working of modern democratic processes, which grant recognition to everyone. There is no good reason, spokesmen for this viewpoint will say, why the speakers of Spanish, Russian, or Chinese should have to defer to a hypothetically superior French or Anglo-American culture.

Unfortunately, there are some grounds for the rejection of this "modern democratic" explanation of the phenomenon. If it was desired to bring in other languages than the French of Vienna or the French and English of Versailles, why did the choice have to fall upon Spanish, Russian, and Chinese? The two other great languages of western culture, German and Italian, were perhaps temporarily excluded because they were the languages of defeated countries. But why was recognition not granted to Arabic, a language of vast extension and distribution, and the vehicle of a separate culture and mode of thought? (Note, in this connection, that the Arab states, in desperation, have finally sponsored a vast translation project into Arabic of the documents of the General Assembly.) Should not some provision have been made for Hindustani, Japanese, Portuguese, the tongues of vast masses of people? Too many languages for practical purposes? But then, aren't five too many?

The use of five official languages by the UN points up the inherent difficulty of a situation wherein all major addresses have to be interpreted from the language in which they are made into four other tongues, and all important documents have to come out in quintuplicate, at the cost of enormous amounts of time, labor, and money.

The UN still has a backlog of official records to be translated into Russian, Spanish, and Chinese that goes back to the years 1946–1949; this in spite of the fact that a force of about five hundred expert translators handles, yearly, material equal to some fifty million pages.

Confusion, of course, abounds. One episode reported by the press dealt with a Molotov proposal to safeguard European peace. The right to move troops back from the East-West German border line was guaranteed to both sides "in case the security of either part *in* Germany is threatened," said the English version; "in case the security of either part *of* Germany is threatened," said the Russian version. The difference in meaning and implication is tremendous.

The enormous translation work of the UN has been justified in part on the ground that such translations would be needed anyway for internal use in each country affected. After all, the literate populations of China and India would be interested in a verbatim account of the statements of Mr. Lodge, and the American and British populations would have to know precisely what was said by the French or Russian delegates.

As matters stand, the language of national politics, and the language of national reactions to the international scene, must necessarily be the national language. There would be little point in broadcasting or televising to an American audience, of which only one person in a thousand knows any Russian, the *original* version of an address by Zarubin or Gromyko. Hence the vast linguistic machinery of UN and UNESCO is justified in practice.

Yet one wonders whether a linguistic simplification on the level of international politics might not lead to a similar improvement on a much broader scale. Let us suppose there were an international language which would be the sole official medium at the meetings of such bodies as the UN; that all addresses, without exception, were to be couched in this language, and all official documents drawn up in this language and this language only. What would be the effect upon the people of the various countries? Might it not lead to a very active interest in the international tongue, and a very active desire to learn such a tongue on the part of all intellectual and interested persons who follow international affairs?

Even if no active measures were taken by any of the governments concerned to make such a language official in their countries, or to teach it in their schools, would there not be everywhere a concerted movement to gain possession of this new linguistic medium?

In one of the few uninspired passages of an otherwise enlightening work, a writer on language asserts that if one were to select an obscure language like Nahuatl (the indigenous tongue of the Mexican Aztecs) as the international language, no one would bother to learn it. Why not, one wonders? Languages are generally learned for a purpose. So long as Nahuatl remains an obscure language, it carries no incentive to the majority of people. Make Nahuatl the official language of the UN, and there will be a very strong incentive for a great many people.

As of today, we find not only UN and UNESCO, but the

entire field of international diplomacy and international relations, both at the official and the unofficial levels, hampered and hamstrung by the lack of a common linguistic medium. Ambassadors, consuls, and all sorts of official representatives are sent, by us and by others, to countries of whose languages they are completely or partly ignorant. These people are not chosen primarily on the basis of their linguistic aptitudes or achievements, but on the basis of their skill as negotiators, administrators, experts on law, or commerce, or military affairs, or a dozen other things. If they happen to speak the language of the country to which they are sent, so much the better; if not, they can always be given an on-the-spot six-week language course, or a staff of expert translators and interpreters on whom they can (and must) rely. This situation is said to be peculiar with us, but it really isn't so. There is the case on record where the Soviet envoy to China had to converse with Chou En-lai in English, a tongue representing a civilization they both detest, but a tongue they both happened to have learned. It is further reported, though this may be only a newspaper embellishment, that the Russian inquired why the Chinese Communists did not pick up Russian, to which the Chinese countered with the question: "Why don't our good Soviet friends learn Chinese?" "Chinese is a very difficult language," the Russian is said to have replied. "No more so than Russian is to us," was Chou's final answer.

A felicitous phrase for the state of affairs existing today in international relations by reason of language differences is "the Woolly Curtain." It was coined by a distinguished writer and journalist, Laura Z. Hobson, after she had attended, along with some seventy-five confrères, a press conference with the late President Castillo Armas in Guatemala City. The Woolly Curtain, she says in effect, blankets you completely; you can't talk save to your own countrymen and a minor part of hoteldom and officialdom; you are cut off from the small shopkeeper, the folks in the street, the kids in the park—the heart and soul of any land. Not one of the seventy-five reporters, she continues, could put pencil to paper until the interpreter began to summarize the statements of the man giving out the interview; but in the process of translation and condensation, she assures us, one loses all the clues to a man's vanity, or sincerity, or forthrightness, that one would get if there were a possibility of linking direct words with facial expressions, gestures, and mannerisms.

Of course the world's diplomatic, commercial, journalistic, even military business manages to get done without a common language. It has been so done since the beginning of time and languages. But it is inconvenient and unsatisfactory. It slows up things. It leads to confusion and misunderstanding. What is worse is that as time goes on the inconvenience of the many-language system will make itself more and more felt.

On the unofficial level, it is a matter of recent record that Americans attending the Moscow Youth Festival took it upon themselves to address large Russian audiences in the streets of the Soviet capital for the purpose of clarifying issues between the two countries. Their talks and the ensuing discussions regularly took place through interpreters. How much more clarification there might have been if the American and Russian youths had possessed a common linguistic medium is a matter of conjecture. There is little doubt, however, that full linguistic exchange between two contending parties tends to clarify the issues, and that any translation process lends itself to possible distortion, exaggeration, and misunderstanding.

An international language will not of itself prevent international conflict. It will remove areas of misunderstanding, deliberate or accidental. It will clear up muddled situations. Above all, it will aid man in his search for the truth, now so frequently distorted by factors which, though often planned, are almost as often of a fortuitous nature.

5. The immediate need: military and commercial

The Military Factor—Doing Business in a Foreign Country—Colonialism and Imperialism—Economic Penetration—A World Trade Language

One of the greatest revelations ever to strike the mass of the American people came during the Second World War. It was then, for the first time, that many of us realized that foreign languages have actual, objective reality, that there are large areas of the earth where, strange as it may seem, English is neither spoken nor understood.

To many of us, brought up with foreign languages taught by the old methodology, whereby a language was handled as an intellectual exercise, word game, and quiz topic, this was a distinct shock. Yes, we had been told that French was really spoken in France, German in Germany, Italian in Italy; but somehow we gave these propositions only passive belief, accepting them as articles of faith and little more. Considering the way they were handled in the classroom, these languages seemed more like museum pieces, cultural relics, things to be approached only through books, on a par with Greek and Latin.

To the many more of us who, in accordance with the New Education sponsored between the two wars by certain powerful pedagogical circles, had acquired no familiarity whatsoever with foreign languages, modern or antique, the revelation was even more shocking. Here we had built up for ourselves a neat little world in which everyone spoke English, possibly with a foreign accent if he was a new arrival, but English nevertheless; and suddenly these pesky foreigners rose up before us in their own lands, doggedly refusing to understand our tongue, no matter how slowly and loudly we spoke it. It was little short of outrageous.

It is to be hoped that the linguistic lessons of the war were not lost upon or forgotten by the millions of Americans who came in contact with French, Italian, German, Dutch, Polish, Czech, and Russian in one sector, with Japanese, Korean, Chinese, Malay, pidgin, and a hundred Melanesian and Polynesian languages in another. War conditions differ from peacetime tourist activities in that they do not at all points involve the services of trained interpreters, translators, and other paid foreign speakers of English. How many thousands of our men lost their lives by reason of the simple fact that they did not know a crucial foreign tongue, we will never know; we do know that millions of them were inconvenienced by the lack of a common tongue and rendered more uncomfortable than they normally would have been in that most uncomfortable of all experiences, war.

It was confidently predicted by many foreign-language experts that our war experience would lead to a tremendous upsurge of interest in languages and language study. In part these expectations were disappointed, but that is not too strange. After all, once peace is re-established and people go back to their normal occupations, it is as unreasonable to expect the continuation of wartime psychology in the matter of language as to count on an indefinite prolongation of demand for war materials.

Yet the Second World War brought in its train such widespread participation of the United States in world activities that a return to the old isolationist mentality and habits is unthinkable. The fruits of the war live on, in the far greater number of government people who are sent abroad, as well as in the expansion of foreign commercial and cultural activities of all kinds. The Hollywood director who moves to Rome to make a picture must have some contact with Italian speakers, and the oilman in Arabia cannot quite avoid Arabic.

Besides, there is the ever-present possibility (may Heaven forfend!) of a Third World War. It is all very well to say that atoms and push buttons will do the fighting, and that man's major role will be to act as a target. Mechanical means of warfare have never in the past quite done away with the need of human contingents for fighting and for occupation, and it is unlikely they will in the future.

This brings up the old question with a new twist: "As soldiers, what language or languages will best serve us for war purposes?" The records of the last war are replete with instances of people who spoke fluent French and German and were sent to the Pacific, as well as of men who took up Intensive Language courses in Japanese and were then shipped to North Africa. The blame for this is placed upon normal processes of military administrative snafu, but there is another possible explanation in man power or technical requirements. If replacements were desperately needed in the Pacific during a lull in the European fighting, and a few European-language specialists happened to be available, their qualifications as cannon fodder may have taken precedence over their linguistic attainments. Or a man skilled in both Japanese and radar may have been assigned to Europe by reason of a local shortage of radar experts.

All of which brings us down to the old proposition that it is extremely difficult to foretell precisely what language out of a possible hundred you are really going to need. Even on a single front for which you have been trained, you may come up against many languages of the enemy, of possible allies, and of possible neutrals. There is no such thing as perfect linguistic preparation for war.

Would an international language be of help to everybody concerned in a war? It undoubtedly would. The American and Spanish civil wars, in which no language differences were concerned, register many bloody, dismal episodes, but none, perhaps, quite so grim as the story of the American general caught with his staff during the Battle of the Bulge by a superior force of Germans. The hopelessly outnumbered Americans threw up their hands in token of surrender. The Germans barked out an order to them in their own tongue. "What are they saying?" whispered the general to his aide; but the latter shook his head; he, too, had picked Spanish, not German, in high school. "I think they want us to hand over our revolvers," said the general, reaching for his belt. The Germans, misinterpreting his gesture, opened fire, and most of the Americans lost their lives.

This newspaper story may have been true or not, but it points to a definite lesson. Hundreds of similar episodes happened. Many Americans, Englishmen, Frenchmen, Germans, and Japanese would be alive today if one of three conditions had been met: 1. They had studied the enemy's language; 2. The enemy had studied theirs; 3. They had had a common language in which to communicate. It is paradoxical and even cruel to say it, but a common world language, if it did not avert wars, would at least make them somewhat safer and more comfortable for their participants.

Meanwhile, we have produced language programs, of a purely local nature, for our military forces, such as the one designed to impart a smattering of French and Dutch to our NATO air forces in return for the English imparted to the French, Dutch, and Belgians. Such programs bring to light interesting facts, like the discovery that 75 per cent of the French, Dutch, and Belgian officers already knew some English, but only 25 per cent of our officers were bilingual.

What happens, though, when portions of this Europe-trained force are moved away, say to our Spanish or North

African bases, or to Formosa and the Philippines? Do we have more language courses in Spanish, Arabic, Chinese, and Tagalog? And how many of these language smatterings can we expect our men to remember?

The role of language in international trade is so obvious that we can afford to treat it briefly. Great as is the use of translators and interpreters by diplomatic and governmental agencies, these agencies are far outstripped by business houses dealing with imports and exports. Government agencies prepare dictionaries and phrasebooks for the fields that concern them; but they cannot even begin to vie with the numerous technical, legal, financial, professional, and commercial lexicons that are produced each year for the exclusive use of firms engaged in private enterprise involving two or more countries. "Help Wanted" ads in the daily press indicate to what extent there is a call for people possessing one or more foreign languages in addition to a specific skill.

All this is far from new. It has been going on since the days of the ancient Egyptian and Phoenician traders. What is new is the volume of international exchange that goes on. As this volume grows (and it is bound to grow), the need for linguistic understanding becomes greater. With the increase in the number and variety of products, with the greater complexity of the machinery and equipment that is sent out from one country to another, the need for precision and accuracy increases. Haphazard translations of business letters and written instructions for the use of machinery, casual interpretations of arrangements between importer and exporter, are no longer sufficient; in fact, they may be extremely harmful.

Our systems of interpretation and translation improve as time goes on; more and better commercial and technical dictionaries become available. Yet it is a curious fact that they always lag behind the need. The specialized vocabulary of trade and technology changes rapidly in each language, innovations appear every day, and the dictionary that was adequate ten years ago is hopelessly behind the times today.

Add to this the local differences of terminology within what passes for one language; a term used by an Englishman in a certain meaning may have an entirely different meaning to an American; the Spanish of Spain and that of Argentina, though basically the same language, may use altogether different terms for an object, product, or mechanical part. The complexity of present-day business terminology on the international level thus becomes even more apparent.

A single international language, carefully governed by a single international language academy, would prove an inestimable boon to trade among the nations. It would eliminate uncertainties along with the multiplicity of language forms and translations. The importer in Rio de Janeiro would know at once, and precisely, what the exporter in New York has to offer. There would be untold economy of time, effort, money, and man power.

Complicated and expensive sales campaigns in many languages occur not merely on the international front, but even on the national. In countries where many languages are spoken, either by the native population, as in India and Switzerland, or by large immigrant groups, as in the United States, the commercial appeal has to be made in many languages. The sales effort has to be dispersed over many radio and television channels and spread over a multilingual press. Salesmen equipped with foreign languages have to be employed. All this would become quite unnecessary if all people were endowed with a common language. The functioning of commerce, both at home and abroad, could not fail to gain.

The military and the commercial aspects of language have a common denominator in colonialism. In this and earlier centuries, the language of the colonizers, spreading usually by force of arms, became the language of trade (call it ruthless exploitation if you like) between the colonizers and the colonized. This happened with English in India, Burma, Malaya, and vast regions of Africa and Oceania; with French in North Africa and Indochina; with Dutch in what is today Indonesia; with Russian in Siberia and Turkestan; with Italian in Eritrea, Somaliland, Libya, and Ethiopia; with Spanish, Portuguese, and German in other areas of the globe.

In each instance, it was natural and normal for the colonizer to set up his own language as official in the colonized area and to have it taught to the natives in such schools as he saw fit to establish. History indicates that in a few instances the conquerors adopted the language of the conquered, but in many more the colonizing language eventually was adopted by the conquered peoples and became their own national language, displacing tongues spoken at an earlier period. Ancient Latin, of course, is the best example of this. But the Spanish of Central and South America and the Portuguese of Brazil are there to show that it could take place even in relatively modern times, where there was a disposition on the part of the conquerors to intermingle with the conquered and merge into a single race.

In other instances, where there was no such merging, history shows two possible outcomes. One is the practical extinction of the original inhabitants and languages and their replacement by the colonizers and their tongue (America and Australia are good examples of this). The other is the eventual rejection of both the colonizers (numerically a minority) and their official languages by the more numerous natives. This is in the process of happening in countries like India, Indonesia, Indochina, Ethiopia, and is likely to happen in North Africa. It can happen even where the friendliest relations persist between the former colony and its old possessors, as is the case in Pakistan with the British and in the Philippines with the U.S.A.

Linguistically, the effect of this latter process is to cut down the power and influence of the few big world-wide tongues, and to increase the number of significant languages that must be taken into account. Where one could formerly dispense with tongues like Hindustani, Malay, Vietnamese, Amharic, Arabic, Urdu, and Tagalog, because they could to some extent be replaced by the languages of colonization (English, Dutch, French, Italian), this now becomes less and less possible, as the national languages of the former colonies come to the fore and the old languages of colonization are discarded. The linguistic picture becomes more complicated rather than simpler as self-determination moves on apace.

The Russians, who in some respects have a clearer propaganda sense than we, are realistically approaching the problem by engaging in the publication of a series of fifty-seven dictionaries in Asiatic and African tongues, including Vietnamese, Malay, Thai, Burmese, Tibetan, Swahili, Zulu, and Amharic. On a much more modest scale, we, too, are preparing for reality by getting ready at Cornell a dictionary of the Indonesian language that is now replacing the Dutch formerly current in those islands, but now excluded from the schools of the Indonesian Republic.

Would an international language help under the circumstances? It would certainly tend to re-establish the broken or about-to-be-broken linguistic communications between the Englishman and the native of India, Burma, or Pakistan, between the Hollander and the Indonesian, between the Italian and the Ethiopian, between the Frenchman and the native of Vietnam or Morocco, between the American and the Filipino, at the same time extending the blessings of communication to anyone else who might happen on the scene in countries that are throwing off colonial shackles.

Economic, financial, and commercial penetration, as apart from physical conquest and colonialism, is a well-known phenomenon of modern times. It is perhaps more peculiar to the United States and the American turn of mind than to most other nations, though other countries have recently tried to imitate our methodology, with varying degrees of success.

There are at least a round dozen small Latin-American nations over which we exercise no physical dominion, but whose policies we direct almost as surely as if the Stars and Stripes waved over them. Of late, we have taken under our economic-financial-commercial wing, through Marshall Plan aid, tariff arrangements, and other devices, such old, established countries as France, Italy, western Germany, and Japan, not to mention Sa'udi Arabia and Iran.

Linguistically, there are two major devices whereby this type of penetration is effected. Either the people with whom we establish such relations learn our language, or we learn theirs. Both are effective, and the first is, of course, in full swing, with millions of Latin-Americans, western Europeans, and Orientals now in the process of learning English willingly, not to say enthusiastically. The second device is even more effective, since it usually arouses the good will, friendship, and admiration of the people we do business with. But it has the now well-known drawback. Which language or languages shall it be? Spanish or Portuguese, French or Italian, German or Japanese, Arabic or Persian? The man who wants to be a Point Four administrator, or a U.S.I.A. official, or even an ordinary private businessman, cannot learn them all, so as to be prepared for any eventuality or transfer. He can only study one or two, and hope for the best.

Would it improve the situation, now or in any foreseeable future, if there were a common trade language throughout the world? From the standpoint of the foreign peoples with whom we trade, or whom we help, or even whom we are said to exploit, the learning and use of a world tongue instead of English (or of English if it were officially recognized as a world tongue) would remove whatever stigma of inferiority they may now feel in learning and using our language while we fail to return the compliment. From our point of view, there would be the advantage that a man thoroughly grounded in the universal language would not have to fear, linguistically at least, assignment or transfer to any country whatsoever. He would have the assurance that he could carry on his work, trade, or business at a moment's notice and without further preparation, all over the world.

The same advantages, of course, would accrue to citizens of all nations, even of those we now regard as potential enemies. It would undoubtedly expedite trade matters between Soviet Russians and Chinese Reds if they had a common language both could use without losing face. If, as and when trade relations on a full scale are resumed between East and West, it would be a source of satisfaction to know that both sides could go into action at once, untrammeled by language disabilities.

Of course, trade among the nations can and will go on, as it has gone on for countless centuries, without the benefit of a common language. Interpreters, translators, people who know the two or more languages that enter into any given transaction will always be available.

But as international trade grows, the language difficulties inherent in it multiply. The two or three linguistically trained people out of a hundred who sufficed in the nineteenth century are no longer sufficient today, when business must be carried on not merely in English, French, German, and two or three more western European languages, but in scores of Oriental and African tongues. It is either a question of far bigger and better language learning than we have ever had before, with at least one out of three people learning at least one foreign language well, and a huge body of specialists in what used to be little-known tongues, or of setting up a single language that will serve the world's vastly expanded trade needs. There is no third course, if the requirements of twentieth-century world trade are to be met.

6. The immediate need: cultural and scientific

Lo, the Poor Tourist!—The Language of Guides and Guide Books—A Scholar's and Student's Language—The Language of International Scientific Congresses—The Language of Religious Propaganda—The Tongue of Literature

Basically, there is a good reason why the tourist receives all the linguistic attention he gets.

If he is a bona fide, pleasure-bound tourist, he contributes next to nothing to the commercial or economic picture of the country from which he comes; accordingly, he is viewed with favor or disfavor by his own land of origin, purely in accord with that country's financial status and its availability of currency for foreign exchange. America finds it expedient to spend dollars abroad so that foreign nations may use them to buy American-made products, and therefore America encourages Americans to travel abroad. Britain finds it hard to spare the international valuta that the tourist takes out, and therefore foreign tours are frowned upon and currency restrictions thrown in the way of the British would-be pleasure traveler abroad.

But from the standpoint of the host country, the tourist is almost invariably a gift from the gods. He brings in and spends foreign currencies, hard currencies which would be difficult to procure by trade, save at the cost of cutting imports and pushing exports to the point where it hurts. Therefore the tourist is made welcome.

Perhaps the most ostensible sign of this welcoming attitude

is the way in which the tourist is linguistically catered to. His language is spoken almost everywhere he is likely to go. Hotel clerks and managers, restaurant waiters, doormen, bellboys, taxi drivers, even government employees, customs men, and policemen seek and get instruction in the language of the tourist. Signs are posted in the tourist's language. Menus are composed in it. Guides, of course, handle it with proficiency. English headphone translations of French plays are provided in Parisian theaters. No effort is spared to make the tourist feel at home.

The tourist's response to this hospitable attitude is usually a thoroughly supine one. He accepts everything that is offered, with good or bad grace, and makes little or no attempt to reciprocate in kind. This ultimately leads not merely to a tongue-in-cheek attitude on the part of the inhabitants of host countries, but also to a feeling, as erroneous as it is widespread, that tourists are simple-minded and tongue-tied. A half-veiled contempt for the tourist with plenty of money and a shortage of brains and tongues often shines through the lip-deference that is paid to him.

All this, of course, changes as if by magic if the tourist reveals himself to be genuinely interested in the people whose country he visits and in their culture, an interest that is normally shown by an ability, or at least an effort, to speak their language. Then the natives, being civilized and responsive human beings, vie in displaying their sincere esteem toward an appreciative, though paying, guest.

What has been said applies not merely to the American tourist on a tour of Europe, but to all tourists from and to all countries. Long before Americans, by reason of economic prosperity, became the tourists *par excellence,* that distinction had pertained to the British, followed at some distance by the French and the Germans. Their experiences were quite similar.

Again we hear the usual chorus: "If you are going on a foreign tour, learn foreign languages!" Good advice, particularly if you are going to a single country. But modern times have given us, at popular prices within the reach of most, the all-inclusive tour, which visits at least half a dozen lands speaking as many tongues—England, Holland, Belgium, Germany, France, Switzerland, Italy, or Jamaica, Haiti, Cuba, Curaçao, Brazil, Argentina. Taking the well-meant and intrinsically excellent advice of the language advocates means studying at least four foreign languages in preparation for a summer tour. This is generally too much for the average tourist, so he falls back upon his hotel and the signs that say "English spoken here." At the most, he may seek the aid of Linguapix, a travel aid booklet containing pictures of what you want and to which you may point.

What he misses by this procedure is perhaps the best part of the country he visits. He sees the cafés, the restaurants, the night clubs (which are pretty much the same the world over), a museum or two, a few churches and cathedrals and ancient monuments, some scenic beauties, and many, many hotel rooms—not too much more than he could see back in the States.

But if he can go on and mingle with the natives on some sort of common ground, it's quite another story. Then he takes in the real sights, the atmosphere, the spirit of the foreign country. This he can do if he is equipped with the language. But can he be equipped with the four, five, or six languages of all the countries he visits on a whirlwind tour?

If there were a language common to him and to each of the countries he sees, the possibility of pleasant contacts, conversations, enlightenment as to local conditions and problems, absorption of the native culture would be enhanced at least tenfold. For lack of such a tongue, he must go begging for someone who speaks his language.

If the aim of travel is more serious, if the tourist is a student, a teacher, a scholar, one engaged in Fulbright-type research or purposeful observation in a given field, the chances are he knows something of the tongue of the country to which he travels. There are, however, all sorts of possible side trips and week-end excursions in a continent of many nations and languages such as Europe, and the language changes from country to country. Even where there is possession of a language or several languages, such knowledge is often imperfect, and not such as to lend itself to drawing the fullest advantage from the international contact.

Time was when few people, usually of the wealthier classes, went abroad for purposes of study. Today, with the Fulbright Act and the G. I. Bill of Rights, both of which permit study abroad on government grants, supplemented by numerous private foundations, many thousands of our students go abroad, and many thousands of foreigners come here. They are all cultured, educated people, equipped with some knowledge of languages, but there is little doubt that their problems would be enormously simplified if there existed a common language, spoken by all with the same fluency with which each speaks his native tongue.

The language problem is especially acute in international scientific and scholarly congresses and conventions, where all sorts of devices are used to overcome the difficulties presented by many languages. At some of these congresses two, three, even four and five languages are made official, with systems of interpretation, translation, and digests that remind one of a miniature UN. At others an attempt is made to use constructed languages like Esperanto or Interlingua (the latter is particularly favored for the compilation of written papers which may be read silently and at leisure). One such convention, held recently in the United States, made the unprecedented gesture of having on hand official guides and interpreters in ten languages. Another, held in Washington for cardiologists from fifty countries (including even Russia and Yugoslavia), combined written Interlingua digests with simultaneous headphone translations of oral communications into English, French, and Spanish.

But all these makeshifts simply serve to indicate the cogency of the problem, and its ever-expanding nature. The same may be said of the widely publicized UN project, carried on in Geneva with the participation of eighty-four governments, for the peacetime use of atomic energy, which has forced the UN to go to work on a new five-language atomic vocabulary, the terminology of which really has to be created in Spanish, Chinese, and many other tongues.

So long as modern science remained the prerogative of a few western nations, it was conceivable that a few western languages might suffice, with or without the aid of constructed tongues that lean heavily in the direction of these same western tongues. All this is now rapidly changing, however, with the dynamic emergence of a scientifically advanced Soviet Union. What will happen, furthermore, when more and more scientists of note appear in our midst from the lands of Asia and Africa? It is fashionable in certain quarters to claim that modern science, having had its beginnings in the western tongues, must forever continue to lean upon them, and that the future scientists of India, China, and Japan, not to mention the Slavic countries, will forever have to hold forth in English, French, and German. What if they refuse? What if their governments, having once achieved scientific and technological independence from the West, insist upon linguistic representation in scientific congresses, as some of them already do in international political gatherings? Shall we then have a scientific cleavage along language lines, with the new discoveries and inventions of the West inaccessible to the people of the East, and vice versa? The situation in the field of science, perhaps more than in all others, seems to call for a common tongue available to everybody.

Religion is a field in which the multiplicity of human tongues has always been fully recognized. Ever since the command laid upon the Apostles to go forth and preach in different tongues, missionary work has been done at the local level, with the spreader of the Gospel acquiring the language of the locality to which he was assigned. It might even be claimed that the original linguists and polyglots were the missionaries, since in many instances it is to them that we owe grammars, dictionaries, and Bible translations of many obscure tongues.

It is worthy of note, however, that these same missionaries, while recording and describing the languages with which they came in contact, also made it a point to spread the official language of their own faith or denomination, at least for liturgical purposes. Latin continued to spread in this fashion after the physical collapse of the Roman Empire, until its influence became even more pervasive than it had been in the days when pagan Rome ruled the world. On a smaller scale, the same may be said of Greek. The widespread distribution of Arabic is due in larger measure to the Koran than to the sword, and India's Sanskrit reached Tibet, China, Japan, and Indonesia through the efforts of Buddhist missionaries.

It can therefore be seen that while one of the subsidiary functions of religious propaganda has been to give recognition and dignity to local speech forms, another function, equally logical, though contrary in its effects, has been to spread a few primary tongues. It is as though each major faith, claiming universality, sought to establish it in the field of language as well as of the spirit.

Today, the spirit of linguistic nationalism makes itself felt in the realm of religion as elsewhere. National religions everywhere tend to abandon their liturgical languages and fall back upon the local vernaculars. This tendency is felt even in that most conservative of religious institutions, the Roman Catholic Church, where several spokesmen have advocated the abandonment of the Latin Mass in favor of a service in the local language. Others, however, have replied that to the extent to which linguistic universality is relinquished, the claim to spiritual universality is weakened.

What would be the impact of a universal language upon the churches? It would undoubtedly facilitate their work on a purely material plane, making accessible to them, without linguistic effort and training on their part, masses of humanity which are at present hard to reach.

That a common language would lead to greater harmony of religious thought and doctrine is extremely doubtful. Unity of language would not lead to religious unity. It would, however, serve to clarify differences and divergences, and to make each doctrine clearer to its adherents as well as to its opponents.

To quote from a recent report of the British and Foreign Bible Society: "If man is to be set free, he must have access to the truth. The barriers which cut him off from liberty are not all of his own making, and one of the most formidable is that of language. The truth imprisoned in a foreign tongue is unable to set at liberty those who are bound by ignorance and sin."

We shall touch only fleetingly upon the topic of a common written language for literary, as distinguished from scientific, commercial, or political purposes.

As matters stand today, literary works are normally produced in one of the many existing literary tongues. If they are found to have merit, they are translated and republished in other languages. This is a slow, expensive and unsatisfactory process. It is often the case that works of true literary merit go untranslated by reason of limited commercial appeal. It just as often happens that a work which is a literary gem in the original loses a great deal of its flavor in translation because the work is handled by a translator who is technically, but not literarily, competent. True literary translation is not a trade, but an art.

It is one of the most standard arguments of opponents of the international language that its establishment will lead to the loss of literary values. Actually, a world tongue would lead to an enhancement of such values. Instead of the present uncertain, hit-or-miss system, every book appearing in a national tongue would also appear in a single translation, which in economical pocket-book form would serve the entire world.

It would be far easier to create a body of truly competent literary translators into the international language than it is at present to secure suitable translators into the very numerous literary languages of the world. Also, in international language form, the work would be assured from the outset of a world hearing and response, instead of the limited national public that it has today, coupled with the uncertainty of foreign editions. The cause of good literature could not but be served thereby.

The concomitant argument that an international language, not having grown and developed out of centuries-old human experience, would be unsuited to carry literary values is raised, of course, only against constructed languages. It is understood that if a national language is selected as the world tongue, such a language will carry its own traditional literary aspects.

But even if a constructed tongue is chosen, it is incorrect to assert that such a tongue would fail to be a literary vehicle. If the constructed tongue is based on existing languages, how can it avoid absorbing the aptitudes of those languages to act as carriers of thought and concepts? And what is there to prevent it from very rapidly evolving its own grace of style and arrangement?

Let us not forget that all present-day tongues existed as tools of ordinary communication before they evolved into vehicles for literature. Latin, one of the most majestic literary devices the world has ever known or is likely to know, was the tongue of illiterate farmers and warriors before Cicero and Virgil and Horace came on the scene to endow it with grace.

A constructed tongue, evolved out of existing languages, would not be subject to the handicap of having to evolve slowly and painfully out of a material into a spiritual civilization. It would rather spring full-grown out of its parent tongues, like Minerva out of the forehead of Jupiter, and at once fall heir to the blended cultural values and literary devices of the most developed of our languages. That this is both possible and true is proved by the most thoroughly established of our present constructed languages, Esperanto, in which a considerable body of literature, both original and in translation, has already appeared.

Is it not in order at this point to cite the opinions of some of the great minds of the past concerning a problem which affected them far less than it did and does the world's masses?

Outside of philosophers and educators like Descartes and Comenius, who gave the matter their serious and direct attention, we may refer to a sprinkling of famous names, for what they may be worth.

Voltaire (1694–1778), a man not too deeply concerned with language problems, nevertheless points out that, from the time of Augustus to that of Attila and Clovis, Latin was spoken from the Euphrates to the Atlas Mountains, but in his day a man from Bergamo moving to a nearby Swiss canton from which only a mountain separates him needs an interpreter, as much as if he moved to China. "This," he concludes, "is one of the greatest scourges of life."

Herbert Spencer, in his autobiography of 1843, says: "It seems to me quite possible (probable even) that an artificial language to be universally used will be agreed upon."

Friedrich Nietzsche, in his *Menschliches, Allzumenschliches* of 1876, assumes the role of a prophet, and predicts that "in a future as far removed as one may wish, there will be a new language which will first serve as a means of business communication, later as a vehicle for intellectual relations, just as certainly as there will be some day travel by air."

Similar statements and predictions are to be found in the writings of Edward Bellamy, Octave Mirbeau ("Civilization will not have taken a great step forward . . . until there is a single language on the surface of the earth"), Abdul Baha' Ulla ("one language that may be spread universally among the people . . . in order that this universal language may eliminate misunderstandings from among mankind"), Maxim Gorky ("Mankind would realize far faster the community of its interests if it spoke a single language"), the Marquis de Condorcet, Istvan Széchenyi, Karl Kautsky ("the division of language weakens the power of mankind"), and Karl Vossler. Many more names could be added to this brief list.

7. What a world language will do for us

Ease of Travel and Communications—The Spread of Business—The Spread of Ideas—The Solution of National Internal Problems—The Problem of International Ethics—The Future Generations

A world language for the future is for a future world of peace and international cooperation, in which communications and the interchange of ideas will have their fullest development. By itself, the world language can never bring about such a world. But it can effectively aid in bringing it about, through the removal of linguistic and even, to some extent, of ideological misunderstandings, and through the creation of a healthy atmosphere wherein men regard one another as fellow human beings endowed with the capacity for intelligible human speech. If wars must go on in spite of this, they will at least be wars in which the participants will understand one another, and an offer to surrender won't be misinterpreted as a gesture of defiance. In a hypothetical war of the future in which all the military and civilians on both sides are capable of speaking the same language, there will be less suffering and dying, to the extent that the suffering and dying of the past have been due to language differences. There will be no specially endowed individuals, like the U. S. general who speaks fluent French, Spanish, Japanese, Chinese, and Korean; no special interpreters for American, British, French, Dutch, and Italian warships participating in joint maneuvers; no quickie language courses for men destined for remote areas. Neither will there be such incidents as that of American sentries and South Korean civilians killing one another because neither understood what the other wanted.

In civilian life, we shall be able to avoid such peculiar and preventable accidents as the drowning of a young Italian immigrant to Canada, who was warned of a strong undertow, was unable to understand, and went swimming in the danger area, or the almost fatal incident of the Soviet plane carrying Gromyko to London which twice overshot the London airport because the control tower directions had to be translated from English into Russian. The disasters of the *Titanic* and the *Andrea Doria* both involved heavy loss of life due to language misunderstanding between passengers and crew. Back around the turn of the century, numerous Italian workers coming to New York from the backward districts of southern Italy lost their lives because they did not understand the directions given them to turn off the gas lights in their flophouse quarters instead of blowing them out like an oil-lamp.

But without going into the comparatively rare instances of the difference between life and death made by knowledge of another tongue, the world language will mean that any immigrants, tourists, or travelers coming from one country to another will at once be able to understand and be understood by those around them, to the evident comfort and general satisfaction of all concerned.

Here is a Bulgarian ex-king in Portugal, struggling with a servant who thought he wanted to take his coat off, whereas the king was trying to put it on. Here is an American tourist who thinks anyone will understand English if you only bellow it at him, and thereby arouses ridicule for himself and his country wherever he goes. Here is another tourist on a motor tour of Europe, finding himself faced with road directions in thirty unfamiliar languages, with unpleasant and dangerous consequences. The story of the American who missed his plane in Copenhagen because the taxi driver had to stop four times along the way to ask other Danes what he was saying; the *Reader's Digest* editor in Finland who could not make the waitress understand that he wanted eggs and coffee, not smoked fish and aquavit, for breakfast; the man who knew ten languages but found himself faced with one he didn't know, and had to secure the services of an interpreter, are all familiar enough. These instances will be multiplied as time goes on, because the advances of civilization, trade, and travel will not halt to permit languages to catch up with them.

A world language will do away with the necessity for publishing a magazine in seven tongues, saying the Lord's Prayer in six for the benefit of an international body of worshipers, conducting scientific congresses in four official and ten unofficial languages, as has so often happened in the near past. It will do away with Holland's real or fancied need for tourist directional signs in five languages (Dutch, French, German,

English, Esperanto). It will make possible what is impossible today, a truly international driver's license, recently rejected on the ground that it would have to contain at least thirty languages. It will permit the transfer of thought with a single translation, instead of twenty, as has happened with so many works of literature. It will enable a single radio or television broadcast, a single motion-picture production, a single newspaper account, a single magazine article, to reach the people of the entire world.

We shall no longer need the elaborate school for UN simultaneous interpreters and foreign service translators if we have a world tongue. We shall not have to worry whether the Chinese text of a UN address in English is correct, or whether "genocide" should be translated into the literal equivalent of "destruction of racial groups" or "destruction of human groups," whether the English and Spanish "human rights" corresponds precisely to the French and Russian "rights of man" or to the Chinese "man right." We shall do away, once and for all, with the criticism voiced by students observing the proceedings of the UN Security Council that "the delegates talk too much without saying enough." There is no reason why in a world gathering what has to be said should not be said just once, in a language fully comprehensible and accessible to the entire world.

In science and technology, a world language will enable us to make the entire world output directly and immediately available to the entire world. Important discoveries and inventions will not have to wait for slow, difficult, often inexact translations, or unsatisfactory abstracts which often omit important details. The language of the atom will become clear to all who are concerned with it, and not have to be delayed until a UN corps of skilled interpreters laboriously transfers it from English to French, thence to Spanish, and ultimately to Russian and Chinese. There will be no further use for Professor Parry Moon's difficult task of standardizing scientific terminology in the major languages of the earth, or the abortive use of electronic translating machines which up to the present time have only succeeded in demonstrating the need for a skilled human translator to retranslate their jargon into something that makes sense.

With a world language, we would even have the full standardization, for international use, of geographical names which at present cause trouble not only to the makers of maps and atlases, but to those who wish to use their products. Who at present can recognize in the Finnish Yhdysvallat, the Arabic Alwellat Almotaheda, the Japanese Beikoku, the Chinese Mei Kuo what we know as the United States? Deutschland, Allemagne, Niemcy, Tyskland, Saksa, and Doitsiu all refer to the same country—Germany.

In the field of trade and business, we are faced with a five-language automobile dictionary, said to be indispensable for those who take their cars across international borders. We have foreign-language campaigns to advertise internationally used products, with international complications arising by reason of the use of a trade name like "Gillette" to refer to any automatic razor. We have large and flourishing language classes conducted for the benefit of their employees by great business enterprises with international ramifications. There are millions of job opportunities open only to those qualified for them by the possession of one or another of the world's many languages; with a single world language, these jobs would be open to all.

There is one angle of the world language question that has seldom if ever been mentioned. It is the use of the world language for the solution of internal problems in countries having large and numerous linguistic minorities, or in which many languages are at present official. In a country like Switzerland, with its official German, French and Italian (plus occasional Rumansh), there are language difficulties, because not all the inhabitants speak all the official tongues of the country with equal fluency. A Swiss conductor has to call *"Fahrkarten! Billets! Biglietti!"* as he goes through the cars; the car signs have to bear *"Nicht Rauchen! Défense de fumer! Proibito Fumare!"* For such a country, a world language might represent an ideal simplification of a complicated state of affairs.

But there are far larger and more important national units than Switzerland to which the world language would be a distinct boon in their own internal affairs—nations like India, Pakistan, the Soviet Union, Indonesia, the Philippines, regions like Africa south of the Sahara, New Guinea, the South Sea islands.

In India alone, there are over 225 languages and dialects, with 24 major tongues accounting for 96 per cent of the population. On a ten-rupee Indian banknote, nine printed languages designate the value of that piece of paper money. Hindi is "official," but the claims of Bengali, Tamil, Gujarati, Telugu, Marathi, and at least half a dozen other tongues will not be denied. English, which once served as a bridge language for the educated portion of the Indian population, is on its way out. Hindi is supposed to replace it, but the replacement gives rise to violent opposition. There have been "walkouts" on the part of members of the Indian Parliament from southern India in protest against the use of Hindi, which they cannot understand. There have been violent language riots in many parts of the country, with speakers of Bihari fighting speakers of Bengali, with Tamil, Telugu, Canarese, and Marathi speakers vying for the state of Travancore, and with Marathi and Gujarati speakers rioting over Bombay. The Indian government, powerless to solve the language problem, has been endeavoring, with little success, to divide the country into provinces that will follow language lines, but often there are no clear-cut linguistic lines, and entire regions are in dispute. Meanwhile, the Indian government radio is forced to broadcast, locally, in seventeen tongues. Is there any doubt that a world language would prove an inestimable blessing to India, since it could be used as a tongue of common intercourse by all the country's inhabitants, regardless of their original language affiliations? Would this not lead to peace and unification for the entire nation, and do away with the necessity for carving out states, like Andhra, which have no economic or political justification, but are only created to satisfy the desire of the speakers of one of the many Indian languages not to have to submit to another tongue? Since the world language would, in all probability, be neither Hindi, nor Bengali, nor Tamil, nor Oriya, the speakers of all these languages would be able to accept it and use it without any feeling of inferiority or subservience.

In East Pakistan, the struggle between the official Urdu and the local Bengali has led to bloody riots. In China, under both the Nationalist and the Communist regimes, the sixty or seventy local dialects, many of which are mutually incomprehensible, have caused trouble in the national assembly. Both these countries would be benefited by the existence of a world language, which could be used as a means of common intercourse. In Indonesia, the official Bahasa Indonesia is based on the old Malay, which has long been a trade language. But even so, not all Indonesians are acquainted with it, and some of the speakers of the seventy or more local tongues resent it. In the Philippines are sixteen major languages, and the official Tagalog is native to only a fraction of the total population. To both these countries, the appearance of a world language might represent the solution of many internal problems. The pidgin of New Guinea and the Melanesian islands, the Creole of Haiti, despite the well-intentioned encouragement of some linguists with sociological leanings, are no substitute for a true language. Would it not be better to indoctrinate the natives with a world language that they could use anywhere and for all purposes than with a form of baby-talk that is humiliating in its origins and present-day applications?

In the Union of South Africa, in addition to English and the Afrikaans of the Boers, are nine native languages of the Bantu and Hottentot-Bushman stocks, two of them, Xhosa and Zulu, with over two million speakers. In East Africa, Swahili vies with a multitude of local speech-forms. In the Sudan there are so many local languages, in addition to the Arabic of the Egyptians and the English of the former official circles, that Latin was at one time proposed as a first-class common tongue. What the advent of a world language would mean to these and similar areas of the earth can only be estimated. It would mean that all the people, regardless of their local dialect, could use it among themselves without the haunting fear that one group would thereby obtain predominance over the others; but more than that, it would offer these groups, which are at present backward, a means of communicating with the entire outside world, of quickly enriching their stock of knowledge and information, of finding themselves on a plane of at least partial equality with those who have preceded and outdistanced them in the march toward modern civilization.

Even the Soviet Union could benefit from a world tongue, because within its vast boundaries are some 150 different languages, many of them spoken by groups which in the past have bitterly resented attempts at Russification. It is likely that this opposition to Russian has waned in recent years, but the world tongue would still serve to remove all suspicion of Russian nationalism if it were to be employed as a bridge tongue between the major and minor linguistic groups.

These are some of the advantages which a world language would undoubtedly carry in its wake. They are material, immediate, practical advantages, of the bread-and-butter variety, definitely measurable in tangible terms.

The more remote spiritual advantages are there, too. What goes on today within nations speaking the same tongue and subscribing, at least in theory, to the same set of ethical principles, is not always perfect, or even praiseworthy. Yet few will deny that we have achieved, generally speaking, a higher degree of national than of international order. A world language is one of the factors, though by no means the only one, that will lead to an extension to the broader world scene of such ethical principles as are observed within individual nations. There is undoubted gain in making human beings conscious of their kinship as human beings. Community of language is one of the most powerful factors in bringing about this point of view. The need of a world language for the coming generations is second only to the need for permanent principles of peace and justice for all mankind.

A few considerations concerning those future generations are in order. People are normally anxious to leave to their children and descendants those things which they, the older generation, deem worth while—material wealth, evidence of progress, traditions, institutions. With the possible exception of the first, these heirlooms are not invariably accepted as unmixed blessings by those for whom they are intended.

It has been a commonplace, within our own lifetime, to see both time-honored traditions and institutions of all descriptions radically changed, modified, forgotten, scrapped. Each generation of mankind demands for itself the right to judge what it shall consider of value.

Even material wealth and progress fall under the taint of suspicion. Can we prove that we are happier than those who went before us, despite all our vaunted advances? Nineteenth- and twentieth-century science has brought us a longer life-span, a higher standard of living, faster and easier communication and transportation. It has also brought us greater discontent with our lot, the vastly increased problems of youth and old age, the menace of nuclear conflict and world-wide destruction.

There are few things to which we can point with pride as we say to our children: "We leave you this product of our genius, and we assure you that it can work only for your welfare and happiness." The automobile and airplane which our grandfathers did not have and which we pass on to our descendants will carry people and goods faster and more efficiently; they may also carry sudden death and nuclear destruction. Were we to devise, within our lifetime, a workable system of world government, as so many today advocate, it might put an end to international conflicts, but we would have no guarantee that it might not lead to a world dictatorship as obnoxious as some that exist today in limited areas: the difference would be that no escape could be found from such a world dictatorship to a country that represents our concept of freedom.

An international language differs from the vast majority of doubtful collective heritages passed on by one generation to another in this important respect: it can do good, but it cannot possibly do harm. It is only a useful tool, like the international postage system, or, better yet, like language itself. It infringes in no way upon national sovereignties or prerogatives. If it infringes upon the rights of the individual, it does so only to the same extent as the individual national systems of compulsory education, with their prescriptive features as to what is to be learned in the classroom. No nation, to this writer's knowledge, bars the teaching of foreign languages in its schools, but many make such study compulsory. Here it would be a question of making one "foreign" language compulsory, with all others left to the option of the students, or to the special requirements of the course of study.

Some will object to the standardization that will ensue. But standardization is the general rule today. Everywhere, from the most civilized western countries to the most backward regions of Africa, people are becoming more standardized as the material level of civilization rises. Motion pictures, the radio, television are bringing standardization to the entire world. Refrigerators and air-conditioning are in use today among the natives of West Africa and the Amazon region. For better or for worse, no one in the world today, and certainly no one in the world of fifty years hence, can escape standardization. Why not accept the good features of standardization along with the bad?

Why not pass on to our heirs one item, one tool of communication, which can serve them in all places and at all times, and which cannot in any way damage them? If the international language is viewed with suspicion as fostering an international outlook, then ought we not to be equally preoccupied with any sort of international contact, diplomatic, commercial, or cultural? Has not the world gone too far to think of turning back to the comparative (but never absolute) isolation of former centuries?

Short of a foolproof system for preventing war and ensuring perpetual peace, coupled with freedom for the individual, the adoption of an international language is the greatest gift with which we could collectively endow our children and their descendants. We need it now; but they will need it infinitely more than we do.

2

THE PROBLEM IN THE PAST: THE ATTEMPTS

8. How languages have grown

Linguistic Survey of Antiquity—The Spread of Greek and Latin—The Birth of Modern Languages—Static and Dynamic Languages—Modern Factors of Growth

The story of the international language movement in the past is inextricably bound up with the account of the natural tongues.

The Genesis episode of the Tower of Babel (confirmed by Berusu the Assyrian, who in the third century B.C. composed a Greek-language history of Babylon) offers incontrovertible evidence of two things: that in pre-Classical antiquity there was full consciousness of the language problem, and that a single language for mankind was viewed not merely as desirable, but as the natural state originally established by God. The multiplicity of tongues that plagued mankind even at the time when the account of Babel was written was rightly looked upon as a scourge, a punishment visited by an irate Deity upon the human beings who had dared challenge Its majesty.

The contemplative Semites placed the ideal single language for mankind in the past, and viewed it as something that had been lost. The more dynamic Persians placed it in the future, and looked upon it as something to be achieved. "Persia," says E. Renan in his *Vie de Jésus* (p. 18), "conceived the history of the world as a series of evolutions in preparation for the reign of Ormazd. Then men will live happily

. . . there will be only one language, one law, and one government for all men."

On a more material plane, the Babel episode and the views of the ancient Persians furnish proof, if any were needed, of the existence of many tongues, coupled with man's awareness of linguistic differences and the hardships they entailed.

Our information is too fragmentary to permit us to outline with any assurance a linguistic map of pre-Classical antiquity. We do know that our unsatisfactory accounts and historical records point to the coexistence of many diverse tongues. Beginning with Sumerian, which flourished in the valley of Mesopotamia around 4000 B.C., those records go on to Akkadian, the tongue of Assyrians and Babylonians, and to the Egyptian of the hieroglyphic inscriptions. But almost contemporary with both those major tongues are numerous references to other, obscure languages, of which only a few inscriptions appear. There are the many languages of Asia Minor—Hittite, Lydian, Lycian, Bithynian, and Phrygian; there are the Semitic tongues of Phoenicia and Palestine—Sinaitic, Ugaritic, Canaanite, Samaritan, and Ammonite, with their later descendants Punic, Aramaic, Hebrew, Melchite, and Mandaean. As the center of civilization shifted from the valleys of the Tigris-Euphrates and the Nile to the Mediterranean basin, new languages came to the fore—Minoan and Cretan, early Greek, Messapian, Etruscan, Picenan, Oscan, Iberian, Gaulish. The rise and fall of these tongues and of the civilizations of which they were vehicles would form a fascinating tale, if we knew more about them. Actually, the majority of them survive only in slender accounts of Greek and Roman writers, or in a few inscriptions carved on stone or inscribed on papyrus.

There is evidence, and plenty of it, that all these peoples of remote antiquity were familiar with the language problem. The carvings that portray the diplomatic exchanges between the Assyro-Babylonian kings who ruled Mesopotamia and the Pharaohs who wore the double crown of Upper and Lower Egypt are careful to indicate the interpreters who accompanied the ambassadors and gave meaning to their messages couched in another tongue. There is also some scanty evidence that the Akkadian of Babylonia was occasionally used as the tongue of common intercourse in those days, as Aramaic was used later for the monarchies of Assyria and Persia, from the fourth century B.C. to the seventh A.D.

In the first millennium before Christ, Hellenic culture spread the Greek language throughout the ancient world. Whether the success of Greek was due exclusively to its cultural merits, or whether it was aided by the conquests of Alexander of Macedon is a matter of conjecture. What seems certain is that the spread of Greek stemmed in large part from the fearless navigators who explored the ancient world and set up Greek-speaking colonies throughout the Mediterranean and even beyond, on the shores of the Black Sea and on the Atlantic coasts of Spain. The period between 500 and 300 B.C. might be described as one of coexistence of two mighty international languages, the Greek of the settlements that dotted the coastlines of Spain, southern Gaul, Italy, Sicily, and the East, and the Punic of the Carthaginians, whose relentless quest for tin and copper carried them to the Isles of Britain.

The rise of Rome, beginning with the third century B.C., marked the death of one of these tongues and its replacement by another. Once the naval power of Carthage was broken by Duilius at the Aegates Islands, Semitic Punic was doomed, and the star of Indo-European Latin was in the ascendant.

Greek had coexisted with Punic when Carthage ruled the waves. Now it disposed itself to coexist with the tongue of the new conquerors. The seven-century period from 300 B.C. to 400 A.D. may well be described as the Graeco-Latin era, when two languages held peaceful sway over the Classical world. It is a remarkable fact that the Romans, who did not hesitate to sweep away all traces of ancient tongues, like Punic and Etruscan, that had been the mouthpieces of great civilizations, made no move whatsoever to curtail the influence of the Greek language, which by the second century before Christ could in no way be said to be backed by material power. Not only Greece itself, but the Greek cities of southern Italy and Sicily, southern Gaul and Spain, were left undisturbed to continue their popular use of the Greek tongue, with the Latin of military and civil administration barely noticed. It is a known fact that long after the ultimate collapse of the Roman Empire, in the eighth century A.D., many ancient Greek towns of Sicily and Calabria still used Greek as their current language.

It must not be supposed that the condominium of Greek and Latin marked the death of all other tongues throughout the vast regions of the Empire. The Roman writers give us copious information about the "rustic" and "archaic" tongues spoken outside the city of Rome in the pre-Christian centuries; they inform us of the need for interpreters on the part of provincials who came into the great city from the outlying provinces of Gaul and Iberia. As late as the end of the fourth century A.D., St. Augustine tells us that in the more remote regions of the province of Africa, where the Sahara begins, there were still pockets of resistance to Latin, where people continued to speak the Punic of Carthage, while the Ulpian Code speaks specifically of the legal validity of wills composed in languages other than Latin, such as Gaulish or Iberian.

The "bilingual world" of Classical antiquity must in some respects have resembled the state of affairs in western Europe today, where large numbers of prominent people speak English, or French, or both, in addition to their native tongues. But the fact that the Empire exercised political sway over its lands, and that the official language of the Empire was Latin in the west and Greek in the east, must have led to a far deeper penetration of the two international tongues among the rank and file of the population. The emergence of the Romance languages after the Empire fell is conclusive proof that however Gaulish and Iberian and Oscan and Etruscan may have held out at the outset, by the fifth century A.D. they were definitely out of the running as popular spoken tongues.

The rise of the modern western languages is far more a matter of historical record. In Italy, France, Spain, and Portugal, where Latin had gained a firm foothold, it was Latin that gave rise to the new languages. In countries like Britain and North Africa, where new invaders arrived in overwhelming numbers, bringing new tongues with them, Latin gave way. In the northern lands of Germany and Scandinavia, which the Romans had neglected to conquer, Germanic languages emerged. The little-known movements of the Slavs and Magyars brought in other languages that submerged the Balkans; but Rumania stands forth as a center of hardy resistance, while the homeland of Greek—Thrace and Thessaly and the Peloponnesus—was never subdued by the new invaders, and continued to use the Greek of Aristotle and Plato in somewhat modernized guise.

The linguistic map of modern Europe emerges, substantially as it is today, by the year 1000. At this point of history, Anglo-Saxon controlled England, with sullen Celtic rumblings from Scotland, Wales, and Ireland; west Germanic dialects occupied the heart of northern Europe, from the Rhine to the Elbe and beyond; the Slavic languages, which had just made their bow in written form, were pressing westward and southward; the Romance lands and tongues still held their ground. Two linguistic spearheads from beyond the Urals, Finnish and Hungarian, had made their appearance, but Turkish was as yet missing from the European scene. The Byzantine Empire, lineal descendant of Constantine's Empire of the East, held sway over vast lands of

Asia Minor and the Balkans, but was rapidly being encroached upon by the Moslem power of the Caliphs and the relentless pressure of the Slavs; its universal language was a stylized, conventionalized Greek called *koine,* into which all the picturesque ancient Greek dialects had merged.

In the year 1000 A.D., one wishing to prophesy the linguistic future of Europe would have been deceived by the existing omens into making grievous blunders. French was the most widely spoken tongue of the continent, outstripping English by at least three to one. German, Italian, and Spanish all had an approximately equal number of speakers, far larger than the English-speaking population, but inferior to the French. Russian was a mysterious tongue spoken somewhere in the vicinity of Moscow; the number of its speakers cannot even be guessed at, but undoubtedly it was smaller than any of the others.

The western world was still dominated by the two Classical languages, though not quite in the same fashion as a thousand years before. Greek was still very much of a spoken popular tongue in the lands of the Byzantine Empire, as well as a tongue of scholarship. Latin, on the other hand, had become the language of churchmen, statesmen, diplomats, students, and scholars. It was practically the sole written tongue of the West and was current everywhere as a spoken language among educated persons. The peasants, who in all countries constituted the overwhelming majority of the population, but carried no weight whatsoever, used their local vernaculars, which were dialects of the big tongues that were in the process of being shaped into literary vehicles.

By the year 1500, notable changes had taken place. The Byzantine Empire had vanished, and its Greek was now almost an oral vernacular restricted to Greece and the islands; but in return, it had spread as a cultural tongue to the lands of the West, carried by refugee scholars bent on escaping the Turks. Latin found it increasingly difficult to hold its own in a new world in which the modern languages had turned literary and were even assuming diplomatic and political functions. English, French, Italian, Spanish, German, Russian had all grown apace, but not at the same rate. French still held the lead, with German, Spanish, and Italian pressing in upon it; but English and Russian had assumed greater importance, both numerically and culturally.

In another two centuries, Italian has dropped behind, while Spanish and German have caught up with French. The relative growth of English and Russian, projected into the future, indicates that these two languages will eventually step into the lead, and by the year 1900 this will have taken place. The eighteenth and nineteenth centuries establish the predominance of the easternmost and westernmost members of the European community.

The dynamic growth of English and Russian is paralleled only by Chinese in the Far East. From a speaking population of less than 150 million in the middle of the eighteenth century, when population estimates first became available, Chinese has grown to a speaking population of 600 million by the middle of the twentieth.

In the case of Chinese and Russian, accretion is mainly from within, and due to the simple factor of an expanding population. But in the case of English and, to a lesser degree, of Spanish, there is another important factor that comes into play, that of overseas migration combined with the absorption of people of other stocks and languages.

This expansionistic factor is, of course, historical. To it are due the triumph of Greek and Latin in antiquity. Had these languages been restricted to the descendants of their own original speakers, they would never have gotten very far beyond the confines of Greece and central Italy. It was because Latin attracted speakers of Gaulish and Iberian and Dacian and Punic that it became an imperial language. Spanish has drawn to itself not merely the millions of Italians,

Germans, Irishmen, and people of other nationalities who emigrated to Argentina, Chile, and Uruguay, but also the millions of South and Central American Indians who are today Spanish speakers. As for English, while the original force of expansion was supplied by the excess population of the British Isles that went off to America, Australia, and New Zealand, there are the additional hordes of immigrants of all races and colors who flocked to those outposts of the English language from the slave-belt of West Africa and from each and every country of Europe. It is languages like Latin in ancient times, English and Spanish today, which furnish living proof of the propositions that no language, at any historical period, needs to be restricted to its own original speakers, that languages, like clothes, can be put on or cast off, and that once a language is properly acquired it becomes part of the individual's native equipment. In this there is a powerful lesson for those who claim that it is difficult or impossible to implant new language views and new language habits throughout an entire world. Any language can be learned when there is a will to learn it. If it is not properly learned in one generation, it will almost assuredly be properly learned in the next. The will to learn it depends upon the motivation, the urge to seek the personal advantage and preferment that come only to the speakers of the favored language, the desire to become assimilated to the language community of which the individual wishes to form a part.

Languages are static when they have no power to grow or expand. When this happens, they vegetate for a period and eventually die out. They are dynamic when the power of expansion is conferred upon them, either by a rapidly growing population, or by the fact that speakers of other tongues wish to acquire them, or by their encroachment upon new territories, or by a combination of all these factors.

Judged by this yardstick, the four most dynamic languages of the present period are English, Chinese, Russian, and

Spanish. Other tongues, even while they are in the process of gaining more speakers than they ever had before, are being relatively weakened. French is losing many of its outposts, both colonial and cultural. Italian, German, and Japanese, as the tongues of nations defeated in a recent war, are licking their wounds and making no immediate attempt at expansion; but even prior to their military defeat, their inherent weakness was indicated by the fact that they were constantly giving up speakers, by a process of migration, to other linguistic groups. Portuguese, with Brazil, is in the same fortunate position as Spanish, but on a smaller scale, which renders its future prospects doubtful. Arabic has been the vehicle of a mighty expansionistic force in the past; the question is whether that force is spent. Hindustani, Bengali, Indonesian are far too young, as major languages on the world's stage, to have proved themselves, or their power of expansion. The surprises of history are such that none of these languages should be discounted. Yet, as matters stand today, it is difficult to escape the provisional conclusion that if Stalin's linguistic dream (see p. 111) ever comes true, the four "zonal" languages of the world will turn out to be English, Chinese, Russian, and Spanish.

If one of the four is to be selected as the international tongue, what can be the basis of the choice? Number of speakers, distribution, commercial, political and military might, cultural appeal? What arguments would induce the speakers of the unchosen three to give way? Is the only possible solution that of force of arms, as it was in the days of Rome and Carthage? Are compromises possible, and of what nature? Or is the solution to be sought elsewhere than among the world's major tongues?

9. Unconscious and partial solutions

The Classical Languages in Ancient and Medieval Times—Franco-Venetian and Lingua Franca—Malay and Hindustani—Pidgin and Creole Languages—Cocoliche and Pochismo

The historical solution of language difficulties can be rather neatly divided up and catalogued into convenient pigeonholes: a single national or supranational language imposed from above, usually by force of arms combined with the factor of prestige and personal advantage; the peaceful coexistence of two or more such languages; the compromise formula whereby two or more languages blend into one, which is then made to serve the purposes of linguistic exchange throughout a given area.

History seldom displays such solutions in their entirety and without admixture. What we more often have is a process of give-and-take in which two, possibly all three, of the processes described above take part. The governing factors in the solution also have a way of changing their historical proportions. If we take the use of Latin as an international tongue from the days of the Roman Republic to the discovery of America, we shall see that while the choice of Latin was at first dictated primarily by military might and political institutions, it gradually shifted over to cultural and religious considerations, which became paramount after the fall of the Empire. Imperial tradition and religious use were in the fore from 400 to 800 A.D., but after that time, with the emergence of modern vernaculars, we have the survival of Latin based almost exclusively on the cultural factor, until even that was lost to the modern tongues in the late Renaissance.

Coexistence of Latin and Greek also shows a different distribution through the centuries. While the languages lived side by side during the Imperial epoch, they separated after the year 400 A.D., to the point where Latin became an almost foreign tongue in the East and Greek a practically forgotten language in the West. The period of their reunion after the fall of Constantinople to the Turks was relatively brief, and altogether confined to the world of scholarship. Today both languages are cultural in the highest and most restricted sense of the word.

What is somewhat surprising in view of the long period of coexistence of Latin and Greek is the fact that there was no blending, no compromise between the two. Latin borrowed plentifully from Greek, both as to syntax and as to vocabulary, and numerous Latin elements entered the word-stock of Greek. But we have no record of a mixed Latin-Greek pidgin used for purposes of oral communication. Perhaps the overwhelmingly literary character of both tongues precluded this.

No such considerations were operative in the case of the new vernaculars, however. Since the spoken tongues of the common people were at first viewed with utter contempt, as unworthy of a written form or of any use save for material purposes, they were free to blend without restriction, and linguistic history shows us that they did, and in extensive measure.

It is an interesting fact, often noticed by those who follow the historical development of languages, that the earliest documents of several languages either do not bear distinctive dialectal traits, or show them in a surprising and illogical way. The first written document of French that has come down to us, the Oaths of Strasbourg (842 A.D.), might have been expected to indicate by its forms whether it was composed in the eastern or western or central French regions. It utterly fails to do so. Other French documents composed in the ninth and tenth centuries display curious blends and combinations of dialect features, which render their place of origin practically impossible to determine, though we know where the manuscripts were found. The very first Italian document, the Testimonial Formula of Monte Cassino (960 A.D.), supposed to have been recited by a local peasant who testifies that certain lands in dispute were known to be the property of the Abbey, bears a strange mixture of local traits from the region of Cassino with forms that can only have come from somewhere much farther north, and words which are so noncommittal from the standpoint of dialect that they may be said to foreshadow the common literary Italian that arose centuries later. In either case, it would seem reasonable to suppose that both France and Italy had developed, by the ninth and tenth centuries, some sort of universal spoken form, by no means fixed, highly fluctuating, and yet representing a blend or compromise of the various local dialects that could very often prove mutually incomprehensible.

For this supposition there is the known historical precedent of the Greek *koine,* a common, universal form of Greek representing a blend of the ancient Greek dialects, which arose in the later centuries of the Greek era and became the sole medium of both speech and writing throughout the entire Greek area, continuing in use until the fall of Constantinople. The main difference between the Greek *koine* and the national Romance languages would be that the former was a direct continuation of the Greek dialects of antiquity, while the latter would represent a continuation not so much of written Latin, which went on being used, as of the spoken Vulgar Latin of the masses. If there is any merit in this view, the Vulgar Latin, fairly unified while the Empire stood, began to break up into innumerable local forms after the invasions. But these local forms, coinciding with the spoken Romance dialects of today, tended to regroup themselves in smaller, more modest geographical units, outlined perhaps by the great natural divides, the Pyrenees and the Alps; and each of these local groups of dialects tended to evolve a common language for purposes of purely material communication, even while the needs of scholarship continued to be served by the traditional written Latin.

It has often been remarked that while the language of Dante is supposed to mark the beginning of literary Italian, a literary Italian of sorts existed long before the time of Dante, and was used by the writers of the Sicilian, Umbrian, and Bolognese schools. Dante himself speaks of a polished, refined vulgar tongue suitable for literary purposes and representing a blend or compromise of the spoken dialects of Italy. It is likely that what he had in mind already existed and was abundantly utilized by him in his Italian writings, which gave final crystallization to the *Volgare,* or common literary tongue, of Italy. Certainly the commercial exchanges that went on before the twelfth and thirteenth centuries among the great seafaring city-states of Italy—Pisa and Genoa and Venice and Amalfi—would need a common tongue. Just as certainly, this common tongue could not have been one of the local dialects, which are extremely different from one another, or the Latin reserved for the scholars and churchmen. But it could surely have accepted numerous contributions from both these sources. An actual analysis of the literary Italian tongue, from the days of Dante to the present, shows that it is precisely this sort of blend, with many words and forms coming in from the northern dialects, others from the dialects of the south, tremendous contributions from literary Latin, and a general veneer, added perhaps at the last moment, of the Tuscan Florentine that was the native speech of Dante, Petrarch, and Boccaccio.

Without going too far afield in a subject that is still hotly controversial, no one will deny the objective existence and essential role of two other compromise tongues that flourished shortly after the time of Dante. One is the Franco-Venetian in which many of the epic poems of the period appear; the other is the lingua franca of the Mediterranean, which served a much wider area in far more material fashion.

Franco-Venetian is a curious blend of northern French and the Venetian dialect of Italian. It is supposed that it was a language form devised by French *jongleurs* and minstrels who wandered into northern Italy, singing the doughty deeds of Roland and Oliver and Charlemagne. The Old French *chansons de geste* were an extremely popular literary genre in the Middle Ages, and all people, no matter what their language or nationality, liked to listen to the recital of the last stand at Roncevaux, the great treason of Ganelon, and the violent justice that was visited upon him. But when the French specialists crossed the Alps in their search for new, untapped audiences in the rich valley of the Po, they came up against the language difficulty. Italian and French stem from the same source, and there is a basic similarity in their roots and endings; but there is also enough divergence to make the two languages mutually incomprehensible. Straight translation would have resulted in too much of a distortion of what the *jongleurs* had to sing, and perhaps they were unequal to the task. But they could and did do something else; they adjusted the French words of their songs to Italian speech habits, changing a vowel here, a consonant there, an ending somewhere else, until they had finally achieved a singing tongue which, without losing the flavor of the original French, became comprehensible to the Italian audiences. Once the tongue was evolved, it became fashionable, and even original works were composed in it. There is more than a suspicion that the later Italian epics of Berni, Pulci, and Ariosto were based not upon the original French of the *Chanson de Roland,* but upon the italianized versions of the *jongleurs* who had created one of the first definitely known compromise languages on record.

The story of the lingua franca is a much different and more practical one. Here there was no question of transferring literary values, but only of making oneself understood. After the coming of the Arabs to North Africa, the Mediterranean became a welter of tongues—Italian, Greek, French, Spanish, Arabic. There was need for a language of common intercourse to serve soldiers, sailors, merchants, and galley slaves, and one was created. The name lingua franca has been interpreted to mean "free tongue," in the sense that it had common currency throughout the area, or "Frankish tongue," since it was the Moslem habit to describe all Christian infidels as Franks. The language itself, however, was far from Frankish. Using basic Italian grammar, it drew for its vocabulary upon all the Mediterranean languages, particularly Arabic, and grew more and more popular, to the point where brief literary works were composed in it. Its use lasted well into the seventeenth century, and Molière cites it abundantly in one of his plays, *Le Bourgeois Gentilhomme*. A little of it survives in present-day Maltese, which is Arabic with strong Italian admixtures.

Possibly the most extensive trade language on record is the Malay of the Straits and the islands of Indonesia, a language that began its career, if our records are to be trusted, around the thirteenth century, when the Moslem wave that had engulfed south-central Asia finally reached the islands. The languages of the Indonesian region are numerous, but they belong to the same stock, the Indonesian branch of the Malayo-Polynesian family. Among the best-known of them are Javanese, Madurese, and Balinese. Malay is a linguistic compromise among these many languages, simplified as to grammar and vocabulary, but gradually recomplicated by its use over eight centuries. It seems to have spread from the Malayan mainland to Java, Sumatra, Bali, Borneo, and the other islands of the group, then northward as far as the Philippines, where it still serves as a trade language. During the Dutch occupation, Malay was recognized as the lingua franca of the region, and its original written form based on the Arabic alphabet of the Moslem missionaries was replaced by Roman script with Dutch spelling rules. On the Malayan mainland, controlled by the British, the script assumed an English spelling, with the result that two spelling forms, English and Dutch, coexisted, reflected in place names like Bandung or Bandoeng, Surabaya or Soerabaja (the Dutch written combination *oe* is roughly equivalent in sound to English *oo* or *u*). The final enhancement of Malay came with the proclamation of the Indonesian Republic, which decreed that Malay, with British spelling, should be modified for the purpose of becoming the Bahasa Indonesia, the official Indonesian language. This language, based upon the Malay already widely spoken throughout the region, is now generally taught in the schools, and is the official tongue of a population of over eighty million. By such a process did a trade lingua franca become one of the world's thirteen leading languages.

Somewhat similar is the story of the vague tongue called Hindustani, which though split into two separate official languages, the Urdu of Pakistan and the Hindi of India, is really one. Originally one of the vernaculars of northern India, Hindustani was adopted by the Mogul invaders who renamed it Urdu, "the language of the camps," and gave it an Arabic script and a large number of Persian and Arabic words. The conquered population of northern India continued to use it in its original version, devoid of foreign loan-words and written in the ancient Devanagari characters that came down from Sanskrit. Despite cultural differences, the two spoken tongues remained substantially one, with full mutual comprehension. By the time India and Pakistan became independent, each of the two languages, Hindi and

Urdu, was the plurality, though not the over-all majority, language of its respective country. In the turmoil of languages that is the Indian peninsula, it was natural that the language that had the greatest number of speakers should become official, and that is precisely what happened. As more people in India learn Hindi, and more people in Pakistan learn Urdu, these two languages, which are basically one, will tend more and more to become predominant and crowd out the others. The reunion of India and Pakistan may yet hinge on the unification of Urdu and Hindi into one common Hindustani.

Other contact vernaculars appearing on the globe are often described as pidgins or Creoles. Typical among them are Melanesian pidgin English and Haitian Creole. Not only are they typical, but their present trend is significant. Melanesian pidgin is a blend of English vocabulary and native syntax (the latter, perhaps, originated in China) and is used throughout the islands of Melanesia. Variants of it appear in New Guinea, Australia, Tahiti, Samoa, and even on the West African coast. It is paralleled by Portuguese, French, and Spanish pidgins spoken in numerous localities. The pidgin habit seems to have originated in a linguistic misconception—that it is easier to make a native understand English, French, or Portuguese if you defer to his habits of grammar and syntax, or inflict upon him the sort of baby-talk that is so often visited upon helpless children.

Whatever the sin of origin, the pidgins of today are living realities. "You go, go, go, see one fella man by'mbye" is understood in New Guinea, while "Keep on going until you see a man" is not. Pidgin serves a useful purpose where there is a large number of native tongues. It is also of practical use for communication between the white man and the native. As schools are opened in the pidgin-speaking regions, the question comes up: "Shall we teach them in pidgin English, which they know and speak, or in straight English, which they do not know?" The question is now in the process of solution, with many linguists advocating not merely that pidgin be continued, but that it be put on the footing of an official language, dubbed Neo-Melanesian. This proposal strikes many people as incongruous, and it does mean the creation of a new language to be added to the already too numerous ones on this globe, but it also means following the course of least resistance, and, above all, recognizing local linguistic reality. If this point of view is accepted, Neo-Melanesian will follow in the footsteps of Malay, and in an undetermined number of years or centuries may become the Bahasa Melanesia of an island empire.

In Haiti a somewhat similar situation presents itself. The official tongue of Haiti is French, and many educated Haitians speak it fluently. Large masses of the lower-class population, however, employ a pidgin based on French which goes by the name of Haitian Creole, bearing roughly the same relation to standard French that Melanesian pidgin bears to English. The question that the Haitian educational authorities are now called upon to decide is whether teaching in the schools shall be based on standard French, which only a fraction of the population uses well, or on the Creole which is the common means of communication of the lower classes. If Creole is granted recognition, it will, in a number of years, turn into a standard language.

Without trying to determine at this point whether it is desirable to add to the mighty confusion of tongues already in existence, it may be mentioned that compromise languages of the same general nature as Melanesian pidgin and Creole French are far more numerous than most people think. In Africa two such tongues serve the purpose of communication in two separate areas. The Hausa of Nigeria, said to be spoken by approximately fifteen million people, is a medium of common intercourse for numerous tribes speaking mutually incomprehensible languages, while in East

Africa there is Swahili, devised by the Arabs for communication with speakers of the Bantu languages, and its speakers are approaching the ten million mark. Both these trade languages far outstrip any of the ordinary native tongues in number of speakers and general effectiveness, and both have of late begun to show literary leanings (the comedies of Molière have been translated into Swahili). It would not be surprising if in future centuries an independent Negro Africa were to call upon either or both of them to serve the same purpose that Hindustani serves in India and Malay in Indonesia.

Smaller, picturesque trade languages are in evidence elsewhere. The Taal, or Afrikaans, of South Africa, though based almost exclusively on seventeenth-century Dutch, shows tendencies toward grammatical simplification and the admission of native Zulu and Kaffir words that seem designed to make it more accessible to the native populations. In Portuguese Africa, the local mixture of native languages and Portuguese goes by the name of Benguela. On the northern coast of South America is an entire series of local compromise vernaculars, including the Nigre-Tongo or Taki-Taki (actually "Negro Tongue" and "Talkie-Talkie") of Georgetown and the Papiamento of Curaçao; the former is an English pidgin, while for the latter there is doubt as to whether the original base was Spanish or Portuguese. Farther south appears the Lingua Geral of Brazil, a mixture of Portuguese and Guaraní. In North America we have not only the general Indian talk that was used in the days of the settlers ("heap big chief," "paleface," "Great Spirit"), supposed to represent deference for the thought habits of the Indians, but also the Gullah of South Carolina, an English base mingled with West African words and expressions imported by the slaves; the extinct Chinook Jargon of the Northwest, in which English, French, and American Indian languages were intermingled; and the various immigrant dialects, now rapidly disappearing, of which one of the most characteristic is the Pochismo of the Mexican border (English words pronounced Spanish fashion, or given Spanish endings). South America also claims a hybrid of Spanish and Italian called Cocoliche, popular in Argentina, where Italian immigrants abound. Other similar mixtures are to be found along the European frontiers, but they are extremely unstable.

There is a lesson to be learned from the compromise languages described above. Languages apparently can be blended, in any proportion. The blended language can surely be made to serve the purposes of ordinary spoken communication. If it becomes sufficiently stable and enduring, it can even turn literary. Trade languages are unconscious, anonymous creations, to which seemingly many have contributed. This seems to be the only major difference between them and the constructed languages, which are normally the conscious, deliberate creation of a single individual or, at the most, a definitely identifiable group of individuals. If Malay and Hindustani can turn into major world tongues; if Swahili and Neo-Melanesian can develop literary forms; if Franco-Venetian can be devised for purely literary purposes; if Afrikaans and Haitian Creole can branch out from the languages that gave them birth and become official tongues; if, to take an extreme and still doubtful case, a trade language originating from a mixture of Italian spoken dialects can eventually develop into one of the major and most beautiful literary tongues of western civilization; are we then justified in viewing with disfavor the conscious, deliberate attempt to construct a compromise language that will bring together the major tongues of the earth, and serve the purposes of ordinary communication, diplomatic intercourse, business relations, and even literary production?

10. The growth of consciousness

Ancient and Medieval One-world Visions—The Rise of Nationalism—Printing and Literacy—Inadequacy of the National Languages—Early Proposals

Universality was implicit in the Graeco-Roman world. To its members that world constituted the universe, despite the vague awareness of a world beyond, from which came caravans laden with the treasures of India and China. But these were only tokens, symbols, of a shadowy something that had no real existence, save insofar as it contributed to the standard of living of the Classical world. The Roman Empire, once constituted, became a powerful, living reality whose *limes* was almost as much of a boundary to the ancients as the stratosphere is to us.

The Empire was one. Its sway extended over all those parts of the universe that the Graeco-Roman world cared to know. Within the Empire there was unity of command, of administration, of language, of thought. There was no question that it would endure forever, even while it was tottering and falling. Roman writers of the fifth century A.D. spoke of the Empire's everlasting qualities even as the barbarians poured over the borders. What is of greater interest is that these everlasting qualities were recognized and glorified by the barbarians themselves. They had no desire to overturn the established order of things, but only to make themselves a part of it. It has been conclusively proved by historians like

Henri Pirenne that the imperial institutions continued in the West as well as in the East until the Moslem invasions of the eighth century brought about new conditions and requirements. Those institutions were based on the concept of universality.

Even more universal than the imperial idea was the Christian idea that had joined forces with it since the days of Constantine. The world was one, the human race was one. All men were brothers, and God was their universal Father. There was one, and only one Church, however much it might be rent asunder by schisms and differences of interpretation. The darkest period of the Middle Ages, from the sixth to the eighth century, was perhaps the one when the unity of man was most keenly felt.

In this period of spiritual universality, the existence of a universal language caused no surprise. People wandered from one corner of the former Empire to another, leaving no record of language difficulties. Other languages there were, but wherever one went one encountered enough people who knew the universal Latin or the universal Greek. It is only with the coming of the Moslems and the emergence of the modern vernaculars that we begin to get once more references to the need for interpreters and translators similar to the remarks left to us by such people as Cicero in the first century B.C., at a time when the Roman state was on the verge of becoming a compact political and linguistic unit.

The Moslem invasions broke down the concept of universality, by revealing to the peoples of the West that there was indeed another world to reckon with, a world that did not worship at the same religious and linguistic shrines, a world that was separate, independent, powerful, and yet of such immediate menace that it could not be conveniently overlooked, as had been the remote worlds of India and China in an earlier era.*

* See H. Pirenne, *Mohammed and Charlemagne.*

The coming to age of the modern languages, evidenced by their ever-growing use in written and literary form, contributed in equal measure to the breakdown of the universal concept. Yet it is a curious fact that the universal, imperial idea remained. It recurs historically, again and again, in the crowning of Charlemagne, in the conflict between the Popes and the Emperors, in the writings of Dante. By the beginning of the fourteenth century, even the imperial idea is in its death-throes. Dante envisages the rebirth of a universal empire, but he uses its language, Latin, only in his minor works.

It is often stated that the rise of nationalism was responsible for the emergence of the national tongues. This view can be accepted only if we give nationalism a somewhat different interpretation from the one that is current today. Medieval loyalty was to a Church and to an earthly ruler, and the latter could be of a different nationality and language from his subjects. Charlemagne had difficulty with his Latin and even tried to substitute Germanic for Latin names of months, but no one thought less of him on that account. William the Conqueror attempted in vain to learn the language of his Anglo-Saxon subjects, but his ignorance of their language was not what they held against him. As late as the First World War, we have a reflection of the medieval state of affairs in the Hapsburg monarchy, claiming the allegiance of peoples of different languages and cultures. Switzerland, a state where language and culture do not count in the determination of national loyalties, is another throwback to the Middle Ages, however laudable its example as a harmonious grouping may seem from an ultramodern standpoint.

The concept of nationalism in connection with the rise of the national languages can be accepted only if it is linked with another historical phenomenon, that of the growing participation of the non-noble, nonclerical classes in the cultural life of the western nations. As merchants and burghers and artisans began to have a greater voice in national affairs in countries like France, England, Italy, and Germany, it was natural that the spoken tongues of this new estate should get to have greater currency and value, and the Latin of the clerics become more and more restricted. The invention of printing and the spread of literacy that it provoked simply marked the continuation of a process that had already begun centuries before.

The fifteenth century that restored to the West one of its ancient cultural tongues, Greek, also witnessed the final triumph of French, English, German, Italian, and Spanish over the Latin that had dominated the thousand-year period since the fall of the Empire. Western Europe had now assumed its modern linguistic aspect, with an array of different national tongues, both literary and official. At the end of the Middle Ages, a scholar of the type of Dante could be satisfied with possession of French and Provençal, in addition to his native Italian and his scholarly Latin. The truly cultivated man of the sixteenth and seventeenth centuries could not rest content until he knew, in addition to his native tongue, both the languages of Classical antiquity and at least two or three of the great vernaculars. It was not uncommon for him to add a smattering of Hebrew and Arabic to his Latin and Greek, and to throw in a little Dutch, or Portuguese, or Spanish with his French, Italian, English, and German.

It is not to be wondered at, under these circumstances, that many minds began to turn to the problem of a single language that would suffice for the new and numerous cultural exchanges that were being established. But what should this single language be? There was no need to suggest a return to Latin, for Latin continued in international use. But Latin no longer sufficed, as it had sufficed at an earlier date. In the thirteenth century the traveling scholar would care to communicate only with his peers, and they all knew Latin. In the seventeenth, his desire was for oral communication with all sorts of people, merchants and tradesmen and soldiers and nobles and perhaps even peasants, and they knew no Latin. The newly rediscovered Greek would not serve. The vernaculars were not merely too numerous; they were too much broken up into local dialects. Besides, there was the spirit of nationalism to be considered. Yet Comenius, a seventeenth-century educator with a wide international background, came out with a startling proposal which in many respects foreshadows the concept of zonal languages advanced by Stalin a few years ago. Being a teacher of languages, which he sought to impart by reference to objects in real life rather than by boresome repetitions of declensions, conjugations, and paradigms, Comenius was among the first of the moderns to have the modern-language sense. Let the leading languages of eastern and western Europe, he said, be used in international fashion, with Russian serving the East, and French and English the West. This, of course, was a solution which rejected the Latin tradition, as well as the tradition of universality. Today, it would be judged to be a partial, localized solution, based perhaps on the example of Latin and Greek in the later days of the Empire. Yet it was the first of its kind.

The difference between the proposal of Comenius and the one advanced by Descartes in 1629 is radical and complete. Comenius may be labeled the father of all ideas of natural languages used for zonal purposes. Descartes is the ideal founder of the constructed language, even though he did not actually create one himself.

Answering a letter written him by a Father Mersenne, who had enclosed in his missive an anonymous Latin prospectus concerning the desirability of an international language, the great French philosopher presented his own views on the subject, both of an international tongue and of language in general. Beginning with an attack on the difficulties of national grammars, which prevent people from seizing the meaning of a passage by referring to the dictionary alone, Descartes goes on to advocate the creation of a tongue whose grammar will be so simple that it can be learned without effort by anyone, by reason of its absolute regularity and absolute logic; but along with this, he proposes a word-coining system whereby there will be, among the ideas of the human mind, the same order that prevails among numbers in mathematics, so that just as there is in mathematics a logical progression from the known to the unknown, the same process may be possible with words. If this is done, he concludes, peasants will be able to determine truth in better fashion than do philosophers at present.

What Descartes advocates, though he gives no example of it, is a constructed language of the a priori ("from beforehand") or philosophical type, whose grammar will depart from known grammars to the extent that it will be regular and without exceptions, and whose word-stock will not be haphazard, but logically connected. Such a language, based on the analogy of mathematical operations, is perfectly possible, but does not coincide with the structure of any known tongue.

Descartes supplied no sample of his ideal international language, but such samples were immediately forthcoming from several of his contemporaries, Dalgarno, Urquhart, Wilkins, and Leibniz. One question apparently remains open, and that is whether these creators of constructed tongues were influenced by the letter of Descartes, or worked independently, by reason of the fact that in the seventeenth century the international language was, so to speak, in the air. The latter hypothesis might seem to be borne out by the anonymous pamphlet that had first drawn Descartes's interest to the question.

Chronologically, one of the first of these proposals to appear was contained in the *Logopandecteision* of Thomas Urquhart of Cromarty, a Scottish supporter of Charles II who was arrested by the Roundheads, freed by Cromwell, and who is said to have died in a fit of uncontrollable laughter provoked by glee at the news of the Restoration in 1660. His work, published in 1653, with the byline "An Introduction to the Universal Language," offered neither a grammar nor a vocabulary, but did describe the ideal parts of speech, genders, cases, numbers, voices, moods, and tenses, with the stipulation that there should be at least ten synonyms for each word (quite a departure from the idea of Descartes, but of some interest for subsequent developments). Each letter of each word, according to Urquhart, should have a special semantic value, so that the word would still be recognizable even though the order of the letters was changed.

More to the point was the *Ars Signorum* of George Dalgarno of Aberdeen and Oxford, published in 1661. Like Comenius, Dalgarno was a practical teacher who had made deaf-mutes his specialty and invented a special sign language for them. He offered a true logical classification of ideas, with seventeen chief classes designated by an equal number of letters of the alphabet, then Greek vowels to designate subclasses (K, for instance, to designate political occurrences; then Kε for judicial affairs, Kυ for crimes, etc.), and further classification indicated by successive consonants and vowels. Since each indication was completely arbitrary, the role assigned to the memory in this letter-game was little short of fantastic. Contrary to Urquhart, who had offered a grammar and no vocabulary, Dalgarno offered a vocabulary and no grammar.

John Wilkins, Bishop of Chester and first secretary of the Royal Society, composed in 1668 *An Essay Towards a Real Character and a Philosophical Language* which, while very similar to Dalgarno's universal classification and subclassification of concepts, goes much farther, offering a set of parts of speech and the framework of a grammar. With the letter *Z* indicating animals in general, *Za* indicates fish, and successive consonants and vowels further restrict the concept to particular classes of fish. The strain on the memory is approximately equal to that imposed by Dalgarno.

Leibniz, who straddled the seventeenth and eighteenth centuries, wanted a language that would be an instrument of reason rather than an international tool of communications. Hence his system, scattered over a large number of pamphlets issued over several years, is almost mathematical. It even offers the possibility of using numbers instead of letters, the two being perfectly interchangeable. An example of his system is the numeral 81374, which can be represented by any order of the syllables *mu bo di le fa,* since $m = 8$ and *u* puts it in the 10,000 class, $b = 1$ and *o* puts it in the 1,000 class, and so forth. Leibniz' grammar, which is not very sharply defined, involves no number or gender and only one declension and conjugation, but it applies tense to nouns and adjectives as well as to verbs, with creations like *ridiculurus,* "that which will be ridiculous."

It can be seen from these examples that the main concern of the seventeenth century was not so much with a language of international use as with a common language of thought and philosophy. Despite Descartes's fine words about peasants who would be able to think more clearly than philosophers, there was little thought of peasants, or even of merchants and travelers.

Under the circumstances, one might wonder why the minds of the seventeenth century were not satisfied with the Latin which they still held in common. The only plausible answer seems to be that to their logical minds Latin did not seem to be enough of a logical language, which indeed it was not and is not. Comenius is the only seventeenth-century scholar whose concern was really with languages for international popular use, and his choice fell on existing national languages.

The main contribution of the seventeenth century to the solution of the international language question is fundamentally that it called attention to the problem and established a principle which the interlinguists of future centuries would make use of, the principle of departing from the illogicity of the natural languages and establishing in its place a logic and order which are arbitrary, since they follow the whim of their creator.

It is perhaps premature to link these early efforts with what goes on today, yet one cannot help making comparisons. The a priori principle, so much in evidence in the earliest constructed languages, was later to clash with the a posteriori idea, whereby natural languages were taken as the foundation on which to construct. But in every constructed language, including the Esperanto and Interlingua in vogue today, there is still more than a remnant of the arbitrary logic of Descartes, Dalgarno, Urquhart, Wilkins, and Leibniz, a prescriptive element which says "all nouns shall end in *-o* and all adverbs in *-e*" or "we shall take the word for 'bird' from English and the word for 'boy' from German."

Along with this conflict between what is natural but illogical and what is logical but arbitrary, we have the beginnings of another question that vexes the interlinguists of today. Shall the international language be viewed as merely a class tool (for philosophers in the days of Descartes, for physical scientists in the days of Interlingua), or as the common possession of everyone, including those "peasants" whom Descartes took care to mention? This is perhaps more of a fundamental problem.

A priori and a posteriori systems can be mixed in any proportion. The ultimate in the former would be a purely numerical, mathematical "language" of the type that is used today in connection with computing machines. The ultimate in the latter is any ordinary national tongue or dialect. Practically everything that has been devised and offered since the days of Descartes is a blend of the two.

Perhaps a similar blend can be postulated for the other

issue. To the extent that large numbers of non-natives today speak English, French, Russian, and other world languages, all these may be described as international languages in being. If we were to select, create, or construct a language for international purposes, it might reasonably be argued that it would not at first extend to every one of the earth's two and a half billion people. Even if it were learned within the first twenty years of its existence by all who are or have the possibility of becoming literate, vast numbers would still remain untouched. To that extent, we would be creating a language for "scholars," in a very widely generalized sense of the term. Excluding dreams of immediate perfection, should we strive for maximum or minimum extension of this common means of communication, once we have devised it? Should it be a language at least potentially for all, or the common tongue of a minority of diplomats, businessmen, technicians, scholars, and travelers?

11. Attempted solutions: the national languages

Chronology—The Five Types of Solution—Unmodified National Tongues—Classical Languages—Modern Languages

Since the seventeenth-century days of Descartes, Dalgarno, and Wilkins, it is estimated that six hundred different proposals, in round numbers, have been advanced for the solution of the world's linguistic troubles. (Stojan, writing in 1929, lists 321 up to that time, and even his excellent list is not complete.) Of these, at least two hundred are intelligent enough and comprehensive enough to call for some mention or discussion.

The chronological sequence of the proposals has interesting features. Once we are past the seventeenth century and its utterly philosophical, *a priori* constructions, popular interest seems to flag. Throughout the seventeen hundreds, only four plans are found that need be mentioned, and only two of the four have features that make them worth describing. One is Delormel's *Projet d'une langue universelle* of 1795, toward the close of the century, and this is little more than a repetition of earlier ideas, with arbitrary arrangements of vowels and consonants to express ideas. The other is Faiguet's *Langue nouvelle* of 1765, appearing in the ninth volume of Diderot and d'Alembert's *Encyclopedia*. Its author, Treasurer of France, denies any intention of offering a universal language for international use, something, he says, that can be properly done only by the European learned academies, working in concert and under the auspices of their governments. He does, however, offer a plan of grammar to be applied to roots that can only be described as French, with a broad simplification of endings which includes verb endings later utilized by Esperanto. Faiguet's suggestion may be described as the first *a posteriori* constructed language—a tongue based not on pure logic or on numbers, but on elements taken from existing languages. To that extent, it marks a new era.

The international language idea continues to move slowly in the first half of the nineteenth century. Between 1800 and 1850 only four important projects appear, but one of them is Sudre's famous Solresol, based on the notes of the scale. This attracted enormous attention, was sponsored by such people as Victor Hugo, Lamartine, Humboldt, and Napoleon III, and had at one point a considerable body of speakers, with die-hard followers as late as 1900.

Between 1850 and 1880, the movement picks up momentum. A dozen new serious proposals are made, none of them with startling success. The two decades that close the nineteenth century witness the great flowering of constructed languages, including both Volapük and Esperanto, along with at least forty other serious projects of varying merit.

The period between 1900 and 1920 is dominated by Esperanto and its brood, but many other valuable suggestions appear, at the very least forty in number. It remains for the years since 1920 to multiply both popular interest and types of proposal. It is in these final thirty-eight years that we have not only a continuation of the process of building constructed languages, but also radically new offerings of the modified national language type, like Basic English and national languages with phonetic spelling; mixed language types, in which one language supplies the spoken, another the written form; and language combinations, either for zonal purposes or for the entire world, like the very recent *Monde Bilingue* movement of France, whereby all English speakers are supposed to learn French, all French speakers English, and all others one of the two favored tongues.

If this chronology means anything, it indicates that the idea of an international language got under way slowly in the course of two centuries, picked up speed at an impressive rate in the course of the nineteenth century, and is now growing at an ever-increasing pace.

It is impossible in a work of this type to discuss all or even a major fraction of the two hundred projects, more or less, which are entitled to attention. To some extent it would be idle repetition, since excellent discussions of the earlier proposals appear in existing works, particularly the one of Couturat and Léau, that of Guérard, and that of Stojan. At the same time, some of these projects hold such deep human interest and are such splendid examples of human ingenuity that some description of them must be given, even at the cost of repeating what has been said before.

The question of classification of international language

projects is of interest, along with the avowed purposes of the creators and their specific points of view. Many interlinguists offer the idea of a language that will indeed be international, but limited to a specific group, like the philosophers of Descartes or the physical scientists of today. At least as many, however, insist on a language that will be the common property of all men, or at least of as many as are in a position to avail themselves of it. In connection with the constructed tongues, some of the constructors avow that they are inspired by the principle of neutrality or all-inclusiveness, granting representation to all or most of the earth's natural languages; others just as frankly state that the only languages worthy of inclusion are those that have a long and noble tradition of civilization, or, even more specifically, those on which western civilization is based.

The classification of proposals into *a priori,* "from beforehand" (those constructed without any regard for the existing tongues), and *a posteriori,* "in retrospect" (those constructed with elements taken from the natural tongues), is a good one for what concerns man-made offerings; but it leaves out of consideration the national languages, their combinations and their minor modifications.

It is perhaps simpler, as well as more in accordance with present-day tendencies, to present the proposals in a fivefold classification, with the understanding that the boundaries are lightly fixed, and that many plans could fit into either of two classes.

First come the proposals to use a given natural language just as it stands. Select French, or English, or Spanish, or Russian, or Nahuatl, or Choctaw, make it the official international tongue throughout the world, put it into the schools on a parity with the national languages, and let it serve, just as it is, for purposes of global communication.

Next come suggestions to use two or more natural languages, either as zonal tongues to serve certain areas of the earth, which would not give us *an* international language, but a series of geographically separated international languages; or to be learned and used bilingually or trilingually by all the peoples of the earth.

Thirdly, we have national languages modified, in one fashion or another, to make them more accessible to foreign speakers, or even to their own. Here are not only the various basics, designed to work on a reduced essential vocabulary, but also the numerous proposals to revise the spelling, pronunciation, or grammar of individual natural tongues so that they may be easily acquired and used for international purposes.

Language mixtures, where two tongues are combined in various proportions, come next. The mixture is sometimes simple, as when it is suggested that one language be spoken without change, but be written with the script of another tongue; sometimes complex, as when sound-schemes, grammars, and vocabularies are fused together, after the fashion of Franco-Venetian or pidgin English.

Last and most numerous are the fully constructed tongues, which may come close to the modified national language or the mixed language, or may utterly depart from the natural tongues and thus assume a complete a priori aspect. When they are not built on exclusively a priori principles, these constructed tongues usually reveal a blend of many natural languages combined with arbitrary features of grammar and word-building.

The first of our classifications, natural, national tongues used for international purposes without modification, is the easiest to describe, but also the one that is poorest in the element of human ingenuity and richest in human naïveté.

It is simple, natural, and childlike to say: "By all means let there be a single language used by everybody; and by all means, let that language be the one I happen to know and speak." This is on a par with saying: "Let's all get together and do something; and let's do it my way."

While the proposal sounds ridiculous on the face of it, it is amazing how frequently it has been made, and how many rationalizing arguments have been advanced on its behalf. Hundreds of Englishmen and Americans have advanced the plea, "Let's use English as an international language," and then gone on to explain how English is the world's most widely spoken tongue, how it carries more industrial and commercial weight than any other, etc., etc. In like manner, many Frenchmen have argued that since their language has been in the past the tongue of culture and diplomacy, it must continue forever to fulfill that function. Italians have pointed to the sonority and ease of pronunciation of their language, Spaniards to the relative grammatical ease of theirs, Germans to the forcefulness of German, Russians to the fact that their tongue combines all the features claimed by the others.

It is perhaps an encouraging sign for the fundamental sanity of the human race that these pronouncements, numerous as they have been, have never given rise to full-fledged movements, in the same sense that there are movements for *le Monde Bilingue,* or Basic English, or Esperanto, or Interlingua. However much wishful thinking may go on, intelligent human beings seem to realize that there is a point in nationalism and egocentrism beyond which they may not go, under penalty of intellectual excommunication from the world at large.

Yet the claims of the national languages will not be denied, and in any complete and rational discussion of the problem there is no reason why they should be excluded. Points made in favor of one or another national tongue need not be scored when they are made by the tongue's own speakers; but can they be so readily overlooked when they are made by others?

At least four national tongues have repeatedly and insistently been proposed as possible international languages. Two of them, Latin and Greek, are Classical, the other two, French and English, are modern. To these have been added, in very recent times, rumblings (they cannot be otherwise described) of Russian and Chinese.

For what concerns the Classical tongues, their actual use for international purposes during antiquity, the Middle Ages, and the Renaissance merged almost imperceptibly with their avowed candidacies.

Emphasizing that all we are concerned with in the present chapter is suggestions to use natural tongues just as they stand, and not in any modified form (the latter type of proposal is far more extensive), mention may be made of the various proposals advanced between 1870 and 1880 by Gustave d'Eichthal, a French Hellenist, that Classical Greek be adopted as the universal tongue. His idea was later taken up by a group of German scholars (August Boltz, Johannes Flach, Ludwig Kuhlenbeck), who at the moment of Volapük's greatest vogue (1888–1889) wrote books in support of Greek. The very titles of these books, however, in which Greek is described as *die Gelehrtensprache der Zukunft* ("the scholars' language of the future"), reveals that what they had in mind was not so much a language for popular use as the kind of learned language the seventeenth-century people thought desirable.

A much more recent and interesting proposal concerning Greek is the one made by M. D. Christian, a teacher of modern Greek, in 1946, in a little book entitled *Greek as the International Language*. Christian first distinguishes between a universal language (the sort of thing that can be imposed only by force of arms) and a truly international language, which all can learn and use. For the latter, he offers not Classical Greek, but modern spoken Greek in its more literary form, the *katharevousa,* which does not differ markedly from Classical standards. This language, he claims, is harmonious, easy, and accessible to all who are acquainted with the countless thousands of Greek roots that appear in all modern civilized tongues. Perhaps the ancestor of this proposal was a letter addressed by Voltaire to Catherine II (the full text appeared in the Paris *Le Temps* of May 20, 1869), in which the philosopher suggested that if the Empress were to become ruler of Constantinople she could open a Greek Academy, and Greek (presumably in its modern spoken form) would then become the universal language.

For Latin, in its Classical, unmodified form, the current is much stronger. (Even Descartes, in one of his letters,* suggested that it would be easier if all agreed to learn Latin.) Considering that the language continued to be used in scholarly fashion without interruption down to the end of the last century, with numerous doctoral theses appearing in it in all countries (a few continue to appear even today); considering also that the Roman Catholic Church has an absolutely unbroken tradition of Latin used in both written and spoken form, it is not surprising that when international languages began to sprout like mushrooms in the 1880's numerous people familiar with Latin should rise up to demand: "What is all this nonsense about an international language? We have one already, and it has been going for over two thousand years!"

Paul Leroy-Beaulieu, in 1888, composed a lengthy article in which he compared Volapük with Latin and displayed strong favor for the latter. Most remarkable of all perhaps was George Henderson, who, having already contributed three different projects of the constructed variety to the literature on the subject (two were largely modifications and simplifications of Latin, while the third was a conglomeration of English and French), in 1890 launched a magazine called *Phoenix,* further described as the "International Latin Mes-

* *Oeuvres—Correspondance* (Adam & Tannery), I, p. 79.

senger," in which a brand of Latin was used that might have been displeasing to Cicero and Virgil, but would undoubtedly have passed muster with the medieval Latin scholars. The word-order was medieval or modern rather than Classical, and Henderson did not hesitate to coin such words as might be needed to describe a modern civilization (*unio postalis, naves vaporariae, ferrae viae ordines,* for instance, took care of "postal union," "steamships," and "railway lines"). In addition, he modernized place-names, using *New York,* not *Novum Eboracum.* In his advertising columns, he did not rest content with neologisms like *photographia* and *telephonus,* but went on to use *pillulae Beechamiae* for "Beecham's Pills," *Pearsius sapo* for "Pears soap," and *"Velocipedes bicyclo-foretici duodecim menstruis ratibus venduntur"* ("Bicycles sold on the twelve-month instalment plan").

Henderson's experiment was successful, to the extent that it had imitators, among which were the *Praeco Latinus* ("Latin Herald"), a Philadelphia monthly that ran from 1895 to 1902, and Aristide Leonori's *Vox Urbis* ("Voice of the Town"), published twice a month in Rome. In the latter journal especially, further attempts at bringing the Latin language up to date were made, including such expressions as *electrica lux* ("electric light"), *loricata navis* ("warship"), *fabula Milesia* ("novel"), and *diribitoria chartula* ("money order"). The vogue of international Latin grew in Europe to the point where an Italian professor, having wired a Berlin colleague for news after hearing of an accident, got this reply: *"Caput ossis femoris fractum. Spero consolidationem. Gratias multas."* ("Hip-bone broken. Hope it will heal. Many thanks.") Ten Latin-language periodicals flourished between 1889 and 1914.

When people today think of Latin as a dead language, they forget its constant use, uninterrupted since the days of the early martyrs, in the Catholic Church, where Latin is a liturgical language for the Church services, but also, and one is almost tempted to say primarily, a language in actual spoken and written use among prelates of all races, colors, nationalities, and languages on the globe. The Vatican's new Latin dictionary, brought up to date by Monsignor Antonio Bacci, includes such terms as "atom bomb" (*pyropolus,* or *globus atomica vi displodens,* literally "fireball" or "ball exploding by atomic power"), "O.K." (translated by the ancient *Amen*), "radiogram" (*nuntium per aetherias undas missum,* "message sent by air-waves"), "bomber" (*velivolus ignivomis globis verberans,* "airplane striking with fire-vomiting balls"), "matches" (*ramenti sulphurati,* "sulphured chips"), "newscast" (*radiophonica diurnorum actorum communicatio,* "radio communication of daily events"), "black market" (*annona excandefacta,* "heated-up market"), and even "Communist," which is mildly rendered by *aequandorum bonorum fautor,* "an advocate of wealth-sharing."

It might be added that the Vatican's Pontifical Annual lists the Catholic dioceses by their Latin names, so that we have Sinus Viridis, Campifons, Novarx, and Kansanopolis used for Green Bay, Springfield, Newark, and Kansas City, while the Vatican City broadcasting system gives out newscasts in Latin, along with over twenty other languages. One extremely recent episode of the use of Latin as an international language has to do with UNESCO's announcement of a Belgian film on *Aspects of Imperial Rome in the Fourth Century,* where the spoken commentary is entirely in Latin.

One interesting aspect of the Latin movement is the support it has received in scholarly circles in this country.*

The French have always been signal advocates of their own tongue for international purposes (du Bellay's *Défense et Illustration de la langue française* of the middle of the sixteenth century and H. Estienne's *Précellence du langage*

* See Oldfather, *Classical Journal,* XVI; R. Kent, *Latin as the Auxiliary Language,* Classical League, Princeton, 1922.

françois of 1579 are perhaps the earliest of many advocacies), but the French language has received numerous and even earlier tributes from other sources. One of the first is Brunetto Latini's thirteenth-century justification for having composed his *Treasure of Wisdom* in French rather than in Latin or in his native Italian: "The speech of the French is more delectable and more common to all men." No comment accompanies Marco Polo's account of his travels, dictated to Rusticiano da Pisa, but the fact is that it appears in French. The use of French at the courts of Jerusalem and Antioch during the Crusades, and at the English court until 1386, bears witness to the regard in which the language was held in the Middle Ages, while in modern times we have the astounding foreign tribute of the prize awarded by the Academy of Berlin to Rivarol in 1784 for his *Discourse on the Universality of the French Language.*

Used almost exclusively (one might fairly add unconsciously) from the seventeenth to the nineteenth century as the world language of diplomacy, French continued to supply the official text of all treaties until Versailles, in 1919. The Treaty of Portsmouth that ended the Russo-Japanese War in 1905 had Russian, Japanese, English, and French versions, but the French one alone was authoritative.

The first blow to French as a diplomatic language came perhaps in 1878, when Disraeli dared address the Congress of Berlin in his native English. The First World War marked the end of French as the sole language of diplomacy, and in 1920 French and English were placed on an equal footing for the deliberations of the World Court.

Yet the advocacy of French as a world language remains powerful. Among the very numerous nineteenth- and twentieth-century proposals on behalf of French are those advanced by a Hungarian, Baranyai; a Pole, Muttermilch; and an Italian, Rovere, who in 1900 suggested not French itself, but its kindred language Provençal. Even H. G. Wells, who in his *Anticipations,* written in 1901, sponsored the Anglo-French Condominium, suggested soon after (in the Montreal *Monde Illustré* of March 14, 1902) that we might all settle for French.

One of the very earliest hints that English might aspire to the post of international tongue came in 1767, when the philosopher David Hume wrote a letter to the historian Edward Gibbon urging him to write in English instead of French.* These words are prophetic: "Let the French triumph in the present diffusion of their tongue. Our solid and increasing establishments in America, where we need less fear the inundations of barbarians, promise a superior stability and duration to the English language."

In the nineteenth century, Bradshaw and Bell, along with Grimm, were the great proponents of English. (Strangely enough, they were joined by a Russian, Starchevsky; but since the latter advocated English in simplified spelling, he will have to be discussed later.) Today, the advocates of English are numbered by the millions in Anglo-Saxon countries, and at least by the thousands in other lands.

There is little point to repeating here the story of the wide acceptance enjoyed today by English from Scandinavia to Japan and from Italy to India. One could speak, too, of the pockets of resistance English encounters from time to time, as in Ireland and South Africa, which are endeavoring to promote exclusive use of Irish and Afrikaans, though to small avail; or in India and Ceylon, where English is rejected for official use, though retained as a compulsory second language in the schools; or in Israel, where the Knesset is preparing to abolish English as one of the three official languages of the country, leaving only Hebrew and Arabic; or in several other lands, notably in Latin America, where the inroads of English are viewed with alarm in government circles.

* See Hume in Bibliography.

Among the greatest supporters of English as an international tongue are the German Jakob von Grimm and the Dane Otto Jespersen. The former says: "In richness, good sense, and terse convenience, no other of the living languages may be put beside English," while the latter describes English as "methodical, energetic, business-like, sober, noble, rich, pleasant, expressive, interesting, masculine, the language of grown-up men, with very little childish or feminine about it."

The most recent triumph of English came at the Bandung conference, where representatives of twenty-nine Asian and African nations, speaking perhaps a hundred different tongues, without the slightest pressure on the part of the absent English-speaking nations deliberately chose English as the primary official language of the conference, forcing even the Communist Chinese representative to accept an English version of his Chinese harangue; and this despite the fact that the conference was in no uncertain way opposed to colonialism of all sorts, western as well as eastern, and cultural as well as military.

Despite our avowed intention to exclude from our presentation all advocacy of a language by its own speakers, reference must be made to the recent claims of Russian, the one language which, along with English, is today in a position to support those claims with force of arms.

The Russians have long accused the western world, and particularly the Anglo-Saxon nations, of cultural imperialism, and of a desire to impose English as an international language for the purpose of furthering the capitalistic ideology and way of life. In their oft-repeated accusations, they have spared neither persons nor logic, charging not merely English speakers, like Churchill, I. A. Richards, Bertrand Russell, T. S. Eliot, Arthur Koestler, Ezra Pound, and the present writer with conspiring to spread the gospel of international English, but linking in the great conspiracy a Dane like Jespersen and Frenchmen like André Gide and Jean-Paul Sartre.

What do the Russians advocate instead? Stalin's views about area languages were mild. Far stronger are the statements of D. Zaslavsky, expressed in the Moscow *Literary Gazette:* "The Russian language has become a world language . . . The succession of languages runs through the ages. Latin was the language of the ancient world, French of the feudal world, English of capitalism. Russian is the world language of Socialism. French is the fancy language of courtiers and English the jargon of traders. They were the tongues of the ruling classes and of snobbish intellectuals. The English language corrupted peoples in foreign lands. Russian is the first world language of internationalism. No one can call himself a scholar if he does not know Russian."

To the best of our knowledge, the Russian candidacy has not been advanced anywhere outside the Iron Curtain. But if existing national languages are to be considered in connection with the problem of a single international tongue, that candidacy will have to be taken into account. So, perhaps, will the candidacy of another tongue that is spoken by almost one fifth of the world's population—Chinese.

Other languages, too, have had their advocates, at one time or another. Gambatesa presented Italian in 1922, but an Englishman, Bramwell, had previously offered it to the British Association for the Advancement of Science in 1902. Dutch was offered in 1869, and again in 1924 by two Hollanders, Bel and Kluyver. A Dane, Thomsen, suggested Danish in 1905. Bolyai, a Hungarian, presented Magyar in 1832. A strong plea for German as a world language was entered in 1938, under Hitler, by Thierfelder. Even Malay, the "Italian of the Orient," found its advocate in Paul Carus, writing in the Chicago *Monist* in 1909.

12. Attempted solutions: language combinations

The Policy of Gradualism—Comenius' Proposal—The Anglo-French Condominium—Stalin's Area Theory—Thommeret's Language Areas

After Comenius' seventeenth-century proposal that English and French be used as common languages throughout the west of Europe and Russian in the east, we have to wait till the beginning of the twentieth century for a revival of the idea of either a language condominium or zonal languages.

For this there is perhaps a reason in the fact that both ideas are facets of a single thought, and that human beings have been so long familiar with both, operating in actual practice, that it occurred to no one to suggest that what actually was should be.

The coexistence of two or more languages, either serving together in the same area or servicing different areas, is as old as language itself. We have seen all sorts of variants of this process in operation throughout history, with the Graeco-Latin condominium of antiquity and the Middle Ages as by far the best example. In antiquity, this was best described as an actual condominium, with both languages used at once in the same regions; in the Middle Ages, they became zonal, or area languages, dividing up the territories they had once held in common.

Implicit in the scheme of condominium and zonal languages is the thought that some day the languages used in these forms will come together and produce a single, universal tongue. It is strange that this principle of gradualism should have received its most explicit formulation at the hands of one who headed the system that believes in no political or economic gradualism, but in the immediate, violent achievement of the order held to be desirable.

H. G. Wells, so widely known for his tendency to look into the future, presented in 1901 his own views as to the world's linguistic future. Languages, he held, are "aggregating" or they are not. They draw to themselves speakers of other tongues, or they fail to do so. From the place where he stood, it looked as though only three languages of modern times possessed in full the requirements that would make them "aggregating" tongues, like the Latin and Greek of old. These languages were English, French, and German, and by the year 2000 they would reduce all other languages, including Spanish, Italian, and Russian, to a secondary role. Then German, being too "ponderous," would fall behind, leaving the world to French and English. It was as simple as that. Mr. Wells apparently did not recall the historical episode of the Papal Bull dividing up the new American regions between Spain and Portugal, and the fact that France and England refused to accept it on the ground that it was not accompanied by a copy of Father Adam's will, and went right ahead discovering, occupying, and colonizing in their own right. Neither did it occur to him to project his thought farther into the future, and prophesy what would happen in a world ruled by two languages—whether they would forever continue to share their condominium, or divide up the earth between them as Latin and Greek had divided the crumbling Roman Empire. It may be of interest to note that the same kind of Anglo-French condominium was envisaged in 1903 by a Russian, Lesevich, while another Russian, Novikov, offered a trilingual condominium which would make place for German.

Since this was the period of the great vogue of Esperanto, it was natural that the bilingual system should be placed in opposition to a constructed single tongue. Since 1900 Paul Chappelier had advocated the former. In 1911 he produced a work entitled *L'Espéranto et le système bilingue,* in which he urged that all attempts to use constructed languages be dropped, and English and French be learned by everyone. *Le Français et l'anglais langues internationales* of 1915 continued this line of thought, which was supported by great French language scholars, such as Bréal and Dauzat. One of the arguments offered by Chappelier against the use of English alone was that "Negroes, who form three-fourths of the population of the Southern States, extend to the English language the horror they still feel of their former masters; they would all learn Esperanto" rather than be subjected to the horrors of English. No confirmation of all this seems ever to have issued from any representative American Negro organization.

In his *Short History of the International Language Movement,* published in 1922, Albert Guérard, who by reason of his own linguistic background might be expected to favor the condominium idea, presents in detail all the arguments that may be raised against it, including the one that a Japanese who has learned one of the two official languages, English, might have some difficulty in relaying his ideas to a Czech who has learned French. A threefold process of translation would be involved, and Woodrow Wilson is quoted to the effect that "translation is the compound fracture of an idea."

In 1951 two young French people, Jean-Marie Bressand and Denise Poulain, launched their Bilingual World movement, designed to implement the principles of Chappelier by the application of the most modern techniques of language learning. For one thing, they advocate the teaching of French and English from the kindergarten, on the purely oral level, with no formal grammar and with full combination with other childish activities, dancing, music, study, and the like. Secondly, they believe in a policy of gradualism. Let all English speakers learn French, they say, and all French speakers learn English; then, by the power of their example, the bilingual system will naturally spread to other groups, making them in effect trilingual. Among the effective devices used by the sponsors of *le Monde Bilingue* is the system of "twinning" French and English or American towns for the purpose of learning the other language. Coventry in England is teamed with Saint Etienne in France, Lambeth with Vincennes, Chatham with Valenciennes. York, Pennsylvania, is "twinned" with Arles, and Louisville, Kentucky, with Montpellier. The inhabitants of all these cities are encouraged to study not merely the language, but the folkways, customs, institutions, traditions of the town they are twinned with. Children, learning the other language in elementary or high school, correspond with pen-pals in the other town, and samples of their correspondence include not only "Chère amie" and "My dear American friend," but complete accounts of their school and home activities. "My cat, Mickey, is cute, but he is greedy," says one little Arlésienne, in simple, but good English. "My dog Jimmy is not mean. I am wishing you a Merry Christmas and I am enclosing a photograph in my letter."

The sponsors of *le Monde Bilingue* are nothing if not energetic and enterprising. Among those they have rallied to their cause, at least to the extent of offering some encouragement, are President Eisenhower, Princess Royal Mary, Lester Pearson of Canada, René Coty, Marshal Juin, former Premier Mendès-France, Edouard Herriot, André Siegfried, and André Maurois of France, and numerous political and linguistic bodies of Britain, France, the United States, and Canada.

What the movement seems to lack is support from countries where neither English nor French is the national language, but in view of the favor with which the two languages are regarded in the western world there is little doubt that some of that will be forthcoming.

Whatever may be the ultimate fate of the Bilingual World movement, there is no question that it will accomplish some good. Even if its sole practical results should be to endow a considerable proportion of English speakers with French and of French speakers with English, and to build up a firmer bond than now exists between them, it would richly repay all the time and labor expended on it.

The danger lies in the fact that it may antagonize not only the Communist lands, but also segments of the western world. Would the speakers of Spanish, Portuguese, German, and Italian resign themselves so easily to the secondary role prognosticated for them by H. G. Wells? Would they unanimously agree to become trilingual, or at the very least, bilingual? It is difficult to escape the suspicion that Anglo-French bilingualism is based upon a desperate desire on the part of French speakers and advocates of French to cut their losses to a minimum, and retain some measure of the predominant influence that French exerted over the world in past centuries.

Even for what concerns English speakers, there is some doubt that those of the United States (and they are an absolute majority) would consent to discard Spanish, for which at present they have a slight preference, as proved by school and college enrollments, and which suits their Western Hemisphere policies, to throw their unanimous support to a language that has of late lost so much in the way of political and military power, even though its cultural claims remain unimpaired. The situation is rendered all the more doubtful by the disheartening fact, revealed by a survey conducted by *le Monde Bilingue* itself, that in the United States only one out of five secondary school students studies a living foreign language, as against two out of three twenty years ago.

If we turn our attention to the other wing of the language-combination hosts, we find that its greatest contemporary exponent is no less an international figure than the late Joseph Stalin. At the close of the great Soviet linguistic controversy which put the seal of heresy on the doctrines of N. Y. Marr, Stalin, in a *Pravda* article dated August 2, 1950, made the following pronouncement, strongly reminiscent of the proposal of Comenius: "Under these conditions (after the victory of socialism on a world-wide scale, when the policy of suppression of languages will be liquidated, and national languages have the opportunity freely to enrich each other in an atmosphere of cooperation) . . . we will have to deal not with two languages, one of which will suffer defeat while the other will emerge victorious from the struggle, but with hundreds of national languages out of which, as the result of long economic, political and cultural cooperation between nations, will be sifted, at the beginning, the richest, most unified zonal languages, which will later coalesce into one general international language; this, of course, will be neither German, nor Russian, nor English, but a new language, which has imbibed the best elements of the national and zonal languages."

As can be readily seen, Stalin envisaged the zonal languages as a thing of the future, regardless of the fact that they may already be said to exist in practice. The merging of the future zonal languages into a single language for the entire world he reserves for a still more distant future.

This placid gradualism, however, is not shared by two Frenchmen, Fouché and Thommeret, who in 1951 presented their project for the actual creation of language zones, in each of which three languages would be official, two of which would be English and French for all zones. The third language would be Spanish for the western world, Russian for the Soviet Union and its European satellites, Chinese for the Far East, and Hindustani for southern Asia and Indonesia. Access to these languages would be made easier by a thorough phonetization of their system of writing (M. Fouché is one of the greatest phoneticians in the world).

This project offers trilingualism or quadrilingualism as a remedy for the world's linguistic ills. An Englishman or an American would only have to learn French and Spanish, but a Swede or Italian would have to go in for English, French, and Spanish, a Czech for English, French, and Russian, a Japanese for English, French, and Chinese. The major advantage of this system is that it may minimize the objections of large speaking groups that have hitherto been left out in the cold. Its main disadvantage is that it imposes a terrific burden of language learning upon the world's populations. Also, one may wonder whether in the long run the two languages that would have universal currency, English and French, would not tend to crowd out Russian, Chinese, and Hindustani, whose validity is limited to a single area. Lastly, what reaction may be expected from speakers of other great languages? Might not the speakers of Arabic demand a zone, on the ground that while their language does not have as many native speakers as Hindustani it is far more of a tongue of wide distribution, extent, and influence? Would the Japanese and Indonesians, with their populations rapidly approaching the one hundred million mark, resign themselves to playing second fiddle to Chinese and Hindustani? Would the speakers of German, Italian, and Portuguese not raise some objection?

13. Attempted solutions: modified national languages

Spelling Reform—The International Phonetic Alphabet—The Modified Spelling Movement—Turkish, Japanese, and Chinese in Roman Characters—English in Cyrillic Characters

There would be little reason to link spelling reform with the international language, were it not that a large proportion, perhaps a majority, of the proponents of phonetic spelling either assert or imply that English, once it were phonetically spelled, would display its other charms to such advantage that the world could no longer resist it. This attitude is in part wishful thinking, and is definitely connected with the frame of mind described elsewhere. ("How wonderful it would be if we had a language for the entire world, and how much more wonderful if that language were our own!")

Yet we must admit that there may be some grain of truth in the alleged link. There is at least no doubt whatsoever that the irrational spelling of English is the greatest element of difficulty both to foreigners and natives. Were it removed, would the rest of the world find the English language more acceptable? No reputable foreign authority, at least of the official variety, has been heard from on that score. Most allegations of this kind have been made by native speakers of English.

While the speakers of many other languages have found it

expedient to change or modify their form of writing, in no instance have they done so for any reason other than to make the written form of their language more easily accessible to their own people. Under Mustapha Kemal Atatürk, the Turks embarked upon the radical task of changing the written form of their language from the Arabic script to the Roman, a task that is now successfully completed. This was done to spread literacy, since it was far easier to make a Turkish speaker learn and use the Roman alphabet than to acquaint him with the complicated Arabic script. In the early 1920's, the Soviet government embarked upon a rather limited revision of the Russian form of the Cyrillic alphabet. This was done to eliminate confusion among various characters that had originally represented different sounds which had later fallen together, or had ceased to be pronounced. In neither of these two modern instances involving important tongues was there any statement or implication to the effect that once the Turkish or Russian language was simplified as to spelling it would become a worthier candidate for the post of world tongue.

Certain western languages, notably Norwegian and Portuguese, indulge in the practice of periodically revising their written forms, but the revisions are of a very minor nature, and involve no international overtones. Plans to change the system of writing of both Japanese and Chinese from ideographs and *kanas* to the Roman alphabet have been under way for decades, but here the transition would be of an extremely drastic nature, since it would mean the scrapping of all existing literature in both languages, and its reprinting in Roman form. Accordingly, while systems of Romanization for both languages exist, and are, in fact, constantly used to teach both languages in spoken form to foreigners, the Romanization campaign for internal consumption has not had much luck.

Little or no call for spelling reform has ever appeared in

the major western languages outside of English. This is due in part to the fact that in languages like German, Portuguese, Spanish, and Italian the divergence between speech and writing is trifling, while even in French, where the eye often "deceives" the ear, it is possible to set forth rules which may be lengthy, but are nevertheless definite, for the interpretation of writing in terms of sounds and vice versa.

English, however, is in a class by itself, with only modern Irish to rival it in the matter of divergence between writing and sound. With all the good will in the world, it is practically impossible to reduce English spelling to any sort of system, no matter how complicated. Even when such a system is drawn up, as was originally accomplished by Professor Urbain Roullier of the UN, the resulting "Phonics" methods are such as to leave a very large residue of exceptions and exceptions to the exceptions, which must be learned by heart.

Under the circumstances, it is small wonder that movements for phonetization and spelling reform have been more widespread in Britain and America than in any other land in the world. At the outset, such movements were of a purely internal and even commercial nature. It is likely that Sir Isaac Pitman, with his "Stenographic Sound-Hand," published in London in 1837, gave the original impulse by showing that English could be written not only phonetically, but far faster with his arbitrary symbols than with the ordinary alphabet (though it is only fair to remind the reader that systems of abbreviations and stenographic notation had been in use since the days of Cicero). Pitman's invention was at once commercialized, and is at the root of all our modern methods of commercial stenography. About ten years later, Alexander Ellis, using Pitman's alphabet as a basis, devised an "Ethnical Alphabet" which equated symbols with sounds, but was better suited to English than to other languages. Karl Lepsius, in 1856, devised a "Standard Alphabet" which was the forerunner of the later International Phonetic Alphabet, brought out in 1888 by the International Phonetic Association, headed by Paul Passy and Henry Sweet, a disciple of Ellis. With modifications, the International Phonetic Alphabet is used today by international scholars to represent the sounds of a multitude of languages. But since these sounds do not always coincide precisely, the symbols of IPA have multiplied to the point where only language scholars are qualified to use them properly.

Meanwhile, for use in English, the American Philological Association brought forth in 1877 a "Scientific Alphabet," revised in 1890, retitled "Standard Phonetic Alphabet," and used in the *Standard Dictionary*. In the early decades of this century we have had a further revision made in 1911 by the National Education Association and used in the *New Standard Dictionary*. The Simplified Spelling Board and the Spelling Reform Association made further revisions in 1922 and 1928, respectively. The latter organization, which continues to carry on its work at Lake Placid, New York, recently published a side-splitting little pamphlet illustrating the difficulties of English spelling in its present form. A sample runs:

If an S, an I, an O and a U
With an X at the end spell Su,
And an E and a Y and E spell I,
Pray, what is a speller to do?
Then if also an S and an I and a G
And H-E-D spell side,
There's not much left for a speller to do
But go and commit siouxeyesighed.

It may be emphasized that through the nineteenth and early twentieth centuries spelling reform had been generally presented as desirable for its own sake, and for the purpose of making English easier to its own speakers and to such foreigners as might care to learn it. True, two proposals to reform English spelling so that English might become a world language were made in the early years of this century (J. Hamilton's Cosmo-English of 1924 and F. Braendle's earlier World-English, or Veltlang, of 1910, described as "English words and English grammar, subject to the limitations of the phonetic writing of Veltlang, together with a simple phonetic world-alphabet, Seuastikon, modeled after the most primeval characters of writing ever used by the human race"). But it is really only since the Second World War that we have had spelling reform definitely yoked with English as the international tongue, and a large proportion, if not most, of the works composed since 1945 offer the link, either directly or by implication.

Can English Be a Common World Language? is the title of a pamphlet published in 1945 at Walton-on-Thames by B. C. Wrenick. "We could yield a lot to Russia in exchange for their cooperation. Someone must yield on this point, and it is generally agreed by scholars and statesmen that English is the most suitable for general use," says George Wride in *Printing by Sound with the Roman Alphabet: the Foundation of an International Language* (Los Angeles, 1946). "The best way to avoid war is to learn a common language," he continues. "My system is simple, and would make English a much more acceptable international language," says Porter Trefethen of Kent's Hill, Maine, in a letter to the writer. "American English has the best opportunity to be the worldwide language," says William Russell of Athens, Georgia, in a series of leaflets entitled *Better Spelling in a Post-War World.* Even the present writer must plead guilty to advancing at least two separate suggestions for spelling reform with "English-as-an-international-language" overtones.

But these suggestions do not come exclusively from American and British sources. As far back as 1889 a Russian, Starchevsky, published an article in a St. Petersburg review urging the use of phonetized English as an international tongue. This proposal was repeated, amazingly, in 1925, under Soviet rule, by Bogdanov in his monograph *O Proletarskoy Kul'ture*.

As for the nature of the suggested spelling reforms, they run all the way from a few and comparatively trifling simplifications in the case of words showing extreme divergence between spelling and sound (*thru* for *through, tho* for *though,* for instance) to completely new and unfamiliar sets of symbols to be used in writing, such as the late Senator Robert Owen's "Global Alphabet."

In addition to English as an international language, there is another interesting by-product of spelling reform. It is the application of whatever system is advanced not merely to English, but to numerous other languages as well. By reason of general unfamiliarity with the sounds of these languages, these extensions often lead to ludicrous results. It has been abundantly proved by the International Phonetic Alphabet and language scholars that the sound-scheme of one language can be expected to coincide only in part with the sound-scheme of another, and that even where apparent coincidence exists, it is modified by many factors which only a linguistic expert can properly recognize and make provision for. With its hundred and more characters, the IPA still remains the only suitable instrument for even the approximate recording in visual form of the sounds of many languages.

A few samples of at least the simpler systems of modified spelling suggested for English are in order. Some of them use nothing but existing Roman characters now in use, without accents or suprascripts of any description. The title of a work published in London in 1944 by Daniel Jones is itself a sample: *Dhe Fonetik Aspekt ov Speling Reform.* Mont Follick, a British MP, illustrates his method with a description of the bill he introduced in Parliament: "Ei bil tw set up ei komiti tw introdus ei rashonal speling sistem uith ei viu tw meiking Inglish ei uerld languij." The British Simplified Spelling Society offers: "In dhe sun, dhe muun, dhe skie, In dhe mountaenz wield and hie." On our side of the ocean, we have the Simplified Spelling Board's "Foerskor and sevn yeerz agoe our faadherz braut forth on dhis kontinent a nue naeshon," while William Russell of Georgia offers: "Our Faadher huu art in heven, haloed be dhie naem, dhie kingdom kum, dhie wil be dun on urth az it iz in heven." It may also be mentioned that for several years two of our leading dailies, the *Chicago Tribune* and the *Washington Times-Herald,* indulged in such simplifications as *demagog, ameba, midrif, fotografer, frate* (for "freight"), *thru, altho, donut, nite, wisht,* but latest advice is that they have both abandoned their campaign, which seems to be, in the main, an extension of some of the more advanced changes once advocated by Noah Webster.

Two somewhat more radical proposals, by reason of the unfamiliar value given to some of our existing letters, are the one advanced by the Northwest Printery of Chicago in 1944, entitled *Fonetik Crthqgrafi* ("Qur Fqdhr hu qrt in hevn, haelod bj dhai neim"); and the one proposed by Samuel Seegay, a New York teacher of printing, who in 1944 brought forth a *Phonetic System,* modified in 1946 into a *Global Alphabet,* then further modified at the suggestion of G. Bernard Shaw, who called the system good, but objected to the use of diacritics in the earlier versions. The 1952 version runs as follows: "Yiw kan lurn tiw riyd and royt widh dhis alfibet if yiw wil riymembr tiw yiwz dhu letrz az sawndz egzaktliy az dhey or pikcrd."

George Wride of Los Angeles, who advocates *1 Wrld, 1 Langwij,* makes an ingenious distinction between small letters and capitals to distinguish between various vowel-sounds (*def* for "deaf," but *lEf* for "leaf"; *rAz* for "raze" or "raise," but *raz* for "razz"; *bin* for "bin," but *bEn* for "bean"; *kostUm* for "costume," but *kustum* for "custom").

The use of suprascripts, that bane of the Anglo-American printer, is advocated by Porter Trefethen, who accuses IPA of being too complex for general use: "Thēz äkūstikȧl lėtërz är thė stȧndärd sȯwndz ȯv spōkėn lȧngwāj."

The American Phonetic League offered in a 1948 pamphlet published in New York a system of which a sample is: "Mor ðan ə bilyən dɑlərz yirli iz westid θru pur yus av alfəbɛts." The present writer's earlier tentative system, appearing in *English: A World-Wide Tongue* (New York, 1944), is exemplified by: "Aur Fā́ðyr, hū ārt in hévyn, häloud bī ðai neim, ðai kíŋdom kom, ðai uil bī don an yrθ äz it iz in hévyn."

We refrain from giving samples from the *Anglo-American Phonetic Alphabet* (Concord, Mass.), J. E. Leavitt's *Automatic Phonobet* (Cincinnati, 1933), J. R. Parsell's *An Alfabet for the World of Tomorrow* (New York, 1945) and *One Alfabet* (Kansas City, 1948), and Senator Owen's much-publicized *Global Alphabet* by reason of the numerous unfamiliar symbols which it would be difficult to reproduce.

A suggestion advanced by this writer, and published in the *New York Times Magazine* of May 24, 1953, involves the use of English with Cyrillic characters drawn not merely from the Russian, but also from the Ukrainian, Serbian, and Bulgarian alphabets, a form of linguistic compromise that might perhaps render the selection of English as an international tongue more palatable to the Slavic groups, notoriously neglected in most international language proposals.

The advantages of some sort of phonetization for native English speakers would be many and varied. Phonetic spelling would do away with the long spelling chores of our schools and make it possible for Johnny to learn how to read without going through the mental acrobatics to which he has to submit today. It would make the learning of English easier for foreigners. It would probably cut down printing costs. It would remove our written language from the status of a fossilized dinosaur, which it holds today.

The difficulties and disadvantages would also be many. There would have to be a process of relearning for the adult generations. Our existing stocks of printed matter, particularly books, would gradually have to be scrapped and reprinted. Words which are at present thoroughly accessible to foreigners in their written form, like *nation,* would become unrecognizable in phonetic spelling. Dictionaries would no longer be able to keep together words of one root whose initial syllable changes in sound but not in present-day spelling, like *nation* and *national.*

Would phonetically spelled English prove more acceptable to the rest of the world than present-day English? Advocates of spelling reform claim that it would, but other nations, and particularly other governments, have not made any pronouncement in the matter.

What appears almost certain is that if English were to be selected as the international medium, provision would have to be made for its phonetization for international use, since we could hardly expect anyone else to put up with what we accept for the sake of tradition. Whether this phonetization would then extend to the national use of the language is something that the native speakers of English would have to determine for themselves.

It is somewhat strange that other languages have not been submitted for international purposes with the lagniappe of phonetization, if we except Chappaz' *Langage Instantané* of 1900 (phonetized French; but the author also offers a system for phonetizing all languages), and the curious *Palais de 64 Fenêtres* produced by de Ria in St. Petersburg in 1788, in which phonetization for all languages is offered, but with a hint that phonetized French will become the world's choice. Can this be due to the fact that English and French are the most unphonetically written among the world's major tongues (except, of course, for languages using ideographic systems of writing, like Chinese and Japanese), and that the advocates of other languages for international use felt under no immediate compulsion to press phonetization for their protégés?

14. Attempted solutions: modified national languages (continued)

Simplified French and Italian—Simplified Greek and Latin—The Modern Shift—Basic English—Other Basics

One type of language modification, as we have seen, applies to the written language only. There is another, far more radical, which applies to the spoken tongue. Take a national language, Classical or in full spoken use, and change either its grammatical structure or its vocabulary; in either case you will have a brand-new language, clearly designed for international use. The modification may be relatively slight, or it may be drastic; it may be overt, or it may be subtle.

We have already seen that among early proposals for international languages was one conceived in 1765 by M. Faiguet, Treasurer of France, and published in volume IX of Diderot and d'Alembert's *Encyclopedia*. This was a mere grammatical sketch, avowedly meant only for the learned academies of Europe, "working in concert and under the auspices of the major powers." While the grammar is largely of the a priori type, with arbitrary verb endings and numerals, such vocabulary as is vouchsafed is borrowed from French.

Even more definitely French in its basic vocabulary is J.

Schipfer's Communicationssprache of 1839, published in Wiesbaden. The author, who conceived his idea at the age of eighty, justifies his use of the French vocabulary on the ground that "the French language is the best-known and most widespread, both as a court and a colloquial tongue of the upper middle classes, to the point of being already almost universal." The grammatical structure, however, makes concessions to other language groups; there is no article; the adjective is invariable and is compared in Latin or Germanic fashion (*gran, grandior, grandiost*); the adverb is formed by adding the English *-ly*. But infinitives end in *-er,* and forms like *fasilman, roa, cüriö,* are nothing but phonetized French. The Lord's Prayer is a clear indication of the French base of the language: "No Pera, wia ete Cielu, ta Noma sanctiferii; ta Royoma Ais arrivii; ta volonta färerii com Cielu änsi Terru. Donne Ais noa Päno quotidien; pardonne Ais noa offansos, com pardonnas Aos offanding; non permette que succombias tantationi; mä delivre Aos malu."

Serafin Bernhard's Lingua Franca Nuova of 1888 (Vienna), and his Welt-Italienisch Franca of 1891 present a barely regularized Italian, so filled with irregularities that it is hardly worth while disturbing the natural Italian language to achieve it. R. de la Grasserie's Apolema, an altogether theoretical project presented in 1892, offered Greek roots based on a regularized grammar, but faced universal rejection on the ground that Greek roots are far less widespread than Latin ones. Modern readers can judge for themselves on the basis of the following sample: "Mi ecan orexia calo, mi tsanan apo lima, me fani oti mi den fagin apo tre y emera" ("I have a good appetite, I am dying of hunger, it seems to me that I haven't eaten for three days"). Reference may also be made to two forms of modified German, Ostwald's Weltdeutsch of 1916 and Baumann's Weltpitsch (or Oiropapitschn) of 1928; and two of modified Hebrew, Lenz' Pasilingua Hebraica of 1887 and Nilson's Lasonebr of 1897.

The tongue that really achieved vogue in modified fashion, particularly in the last two decades of the last century, was Latin. For this there were two good reasons: knowledge of Latin was widespread among literate people in that era, and the roots of Latin appeared in so many of the modern western languages that they were, in a sense, already international. It was therefore not surprising that numerous modifications of Latin offered real competition to the two great constructed tongues of the period, Volapük and Esperanto.

Even before the question was taken up seriously, there had been in existence, since the early sixteenth century, a "Macaronic Latin," said to have been invented by the poet-monk Teofilo Hieronimo Folengo (1491–1544), which had great vogue among students and scholars, despite its jocular aspects. It was a simplification of scholastic Latin with the addition of popular words, mostly of Italian origin. A sample of Macaronic Latin is: "Vado per hunc boschum solus chiamando Zaninam, ut chiamat vitulum vacca smarrita suum" ("I wander alone through this wood calling Giannina, just as a lost cow calls its calf.") *

First among the reformed Latin projects was Weltsprache, advanced in 1883 by A. Volk and R. Fuchs in Berlin. The Weltsprache version of the Lord's Prayer reveals a Latin vocabulary accompanied by strong grammatical modification, which includes even the use of a declinable definite article: "Not pater, vel sas in les cöles, ton nomen sanctöt, ton regnon venät, ton voluntat söt vam in le cöl, tam in le ter. Not diniv pana da mib godie. Condona mib not culpa, vam ems condonami not debitorib. Non duca mas in tentation, sed libera mas ab le malot." Of particular interest is the use of case endings which are themselves a simplification of the case endings of Latin.

Eugen Lauda's Kosmos (Berlin, 1888) frankly avows that

* See C. Nodier, *Du langage factice appelé macaronique,* Paris, Techner, 1834.

while the grammar may be composite, the vocabulary of a true international language can only be that of Latin, the historical international language which, being extinct, cannot but be neutral. Declined definite articles (nominative *ta,* genitive *tio,* dative *te,* accusative *tan,* with plurals formed by adding *-s*), invariable nouns whose form is definitely Latin (*dominus, mensa, castra, divitiae*), adjectives which add *-ic* to the Latin root (*bonic, dulcic*), and which form the comparative and superlative by either adding the suffixes *-ir, -ist* or by prefixing *magis, maxime,* verb forms which have a quaint Indo-European flavor (*amomi, amosi, amoti,* with plurals in *-s,* for the present of "to love," and even *esomi, esosi, esoti* for "to be"), illustrate Kosmos.

George Henderson of London, one of the most prolific inventors of international languages (he offered, as we shall see, a blend of Latin and English at one point, and one of English and French at another), presented in 1890 his Latinesce, which he describes as "Latinised English," but in which there is little English that does not appear in Latin, as witnessed by: "Nostre Patre qui esse in coele, sanctificate esse tue nomine; veni tue regne; facte esse tue voluntate, ut in coele, ita in terre. Da ad nos hodie nostre quotidiane pane; et remitte ad nos nostre debites, sicut et nos remitte ad nostre debitores; induce nos non in tentatione, sed libera nos ab male." Another prolific inventor, better known for his Myrana, is J. Stempfl, who in 1894 presented, under the name of Communia, a not too modified Latin, samples of which are: "el no poteva loquere quin fleva," and "mi credi, tu esere content."

Dr. Daniele Rosa's Novlatin, presented in Turin in 1890, claims to be only for written-language purposes, and its methodological resemblance to present-day Interlingua can be gathered from the two points made by its author: "It can be read by all scholars without previous preparation, and can be written after a few pages of explanation without the need of a dictionary." How true are these claims? Judge for yourself: "Le nov latin non requirer pro le sui adoption aliq congress. Omnes poter, cum les praecedent regulas, scriber statim ist lingua, etiam, si ils voler, cum parv individual modificationes."

A very similar point of view pervades Julius Lott's Mundolingue (Vienna and Leipzig, 1888–1893). The only possible language for all people of culture must be based on Latin, which has gotten into all civilized languages, Germanic as well as Romance; all we have to do is to utilize the common knowledge and follow the spelling rather than the pronunciation. In proof whereof: "Amabil amico, Con grand satisfaction mi ha lect tei letter de le mundolingue. Le possibilita' de un universal lingue pro le civilisat nations ne esse dubitabil, nam noi ha tot elements pro un tal lingue in nostri lingues, sciences, etc." A worthy precursor of Interlingua!

But there is much additional evidence that there is nothing new under the sun. Alberto Liptay's Langue Catholique, first offered in Paris in 1892, is the work of a Chilean naval medical officer. "Don't invent, discover!" is his motto. Use Greek and Latin roots that are common to all languages and reduce the grammar to an irreducible minimum. Yet he makes one interesting grammatical innovation, slightly reminiscent of Arabic, when he extends the noun endings (none for the neuter, *-o* for the masculine, and *-a* for the feminine) to apply to the possessor of the object mentioned, so that while *cap* stands for "head" in general, *capo* refers to a man's head and *capa* to a woman's head.

E. Beerman's Novilatiin (Leipzig, 1895) comes close to Liptay's creation, though with interesting variations, and its author makes the point, repeated later by Interlingua, that the roots to be used should primarily be those which appear in six "control" languages, German, English, French, Spanish, Italian, and Russian.

Names and samples of constructed tongues based on Latin

could be multiplied. Fr. Kürschner's Lingua Komun (Ticino, 1900), presented as the "common language of science," and featuring no special endings for the various parts of speech (another Interlingua feature), is illustrated by: "Padre nose kuale tu ese in cielo, sante esa tue nómine; vena imperio tue; voluntá tue esa fate sur tera komo in cielo." Fred Isly's Linguum Islianum (Paris, 1901) comes still closer to straight Latin, as illustrated by: "Canum, dum ferabat carnum, natans per fluminum, videavit suum simulacrum in speculo lymphorum." (Phaedrus' original runs: "Canis, per flumen carnem dum ferret natans, lympharum in speculo vidit simulacrum suum," "A dog, while he carried a piece of meat as he swam in the river, saw his own reflection in the mirror of the waters.") Karl Fröhlich's Reform-Latein (Vienna, 1902) makes somewhat greater concessions to Romance structure.

The reformed Latin to end all reformed Latins, however, was the one presented by Giuseppe Peano at the Interlanguage Academy of Turin in 1903. Peano, a professor of mathematics, began his paper with straight Latin: "Lingua latina fuit internationalis in omni scientia, ab imperio romano usque ad finem saeculi XVIII. Hodie multi reputant illam nimis difficilem esse, iam in scientia, magis in commercio. Sed non tota lingua latina est necessaria; parva pars sufficit ad exprimendam quamlibet ideam." ("The Latin tongue was international in all fields of knowledge, from the Roman Empire to the end of the eighteenth century. Today many think that it is too difficult, not only in science, but even more in commerce. But the entire Latin language is not necessary; a small part suffices to express any idea.") He then went on to demonstrate that declension, formal gender, number, and conjugation could be dispensed with. As he made each point, he dropped that particular inflection from the language of his demonstration. By the time he reached the end of the paper, what had begun as Classical Latin had turned into Latino Sine Flexione ("Flexionless Latin").

"Studio theorico proba que es necessario nullo regula de grammatica, nullo suffixo de derivatione. Aut vocabulo jam es internationale, aut pote es expresso per combinatione de vocabulos internationale." ("A theoretical study proves that no grammatical rule, no derivational suffix, is necessary. Either the word is already international, or it can be expressed through a combination of international words.")

It should be added that Peano's scheme for using Classical Latin without Classical endings includes the acceptance of all elements of vocabulary arising since Classical times and used in common by the principal European languages, particularly in the field of science.

It would have seemed that after Peano's proposal (the most logical, if one is to use a Latin base with simplification of grammatical structure) there should have been no further attempts at reforming Latin. This supposition might have been borne out by the fact that since Peano's days Latin studies and the common knowledge of Latin among educated people have unfortunately been declining. This, however, is not at all the case. Here are samples of only a few of the modified Latin versions offered since Peano's time:

Beermann's Novilatiin (new 1907 version): "Us qvu na fi te, Katilina, disusar nostre patincie? Qvam longu adu fi tue furie ludificir nos?" (this will be recognized as the opening of Cicero's *First Oration against Catiline* in modern dress).

Hartl's Perfekt (1912): "Alio dramas social deb essere considerat ab illos qvi occupa se ad colonizazion" ("Other social dramas must be considered by those who busy themselves with colonization").

Martellotta's Latinulus (1919): "Leos abeo crassa capus circumdata cum longa et ticca comas de fulva colos" ("The lion has a big head surrounded by long and thick hair of tawny color").

Hély's Interpres (1908): "Nostre Pater qu ses in el celum, tu

Nomen sit sanctificat, tu regnum sit adveniens, tu voluntas sit fact in el terra sicut in el celum."

Rossello Ordines' Is (1928): "Patre nostre qui es in celes, ut tue nomine esse sanctificato, ut tue regne adven, ut tue voluntate fi in terre sicut in cel."

It remained for modern times and Anglo-Saxon ingenuity to bring forth a proposal of an entirely different type for the use of a modified language for international purposes. The modification in this case involved not the system of writing, which was left completely undisturbed, nor even the grammatical structure (save for certain limitations which could hardly be described as modifications), but rather the vocabulary.

In the 1930's, Charles Ogden of England brought forth a series of works whose purpose it was to prove that the English language could perfectly well offer all the intricacies of meaning with a vastly reduced vocabulary. This was largely indicated by the dictionary definitions of involved and abstruse terms, in which a limited number of frequently used words kept recurring. By a careful statistical analysis of such words, coupled with the elimination of certain forms, Ogden concluded that it was possible to get along perfectly well in English with as few as 850 basic words, handled in normal English fashion, save for a restriction on the use of verb forms. Typical of Basic English are combinations like "take part" for "participate" and "have hope" for "hope" used as a verb.

Public interest in Basic English received a mighty fillip during the course of the Second World War, when Churchill, commenting on the close cooperation that was made possible for the British and American forces by the fact that they spoke the same language, expressed the thought that perhaps this cooperation could be extended to other nations by the use of a common linguistic medium such as Basic English. This pronouncement led to a scurrying of reporters and magazine writers to find out what Basic English was all about, and it is fairly indicative of the general ignorance on the subject that attempts made at the time to render Churchill's own speech into Basic proved dismal failures.

Interest in the principles of Basic widened, however, and they were and are taught in various institutions either under the guise of an international tongue or under that of an aid in the teaching of English to foreigners. It appears that in the latter capacity Basic English has rendered signal services.

In the function of an international language, however, its path has been strewn with rocks and thorns. The Basic process of paraphrase and of breaking down acquired concepts into elementary definitions is difficult for both foreigners and native speakers, but particularly hard on the latter, whose English-speaking habits are firmly established. It is not everyone who can remember that he must substitute "without thought of others" for "selfish." Enthusiasm for Basic English has waned with the passing of time.

In its heyday, however, it gave rise to abortive attempts to set up Basics in other tongues, such as Spanish and French. One such attempt, conducted by Professor G. Gougenheim of the University of Strasbourg with the help of a money grant from the French National Assembly, aims at isolating the one thousand most commonly used words and the basic grammar of spoken French, with a view primarily to using "Basic French" in the North African colonies.

But these attempts seem doomed to failure from the start, by reason of the greater complexity of the Romance languages, particularly for what regards verb forms, and the fact that they do not lend themselves as easily as does English to the process of paraphrase.

The choice of languages suggested for use in modified form is interesting. Only tentative offers have been made of Greek, Italian, German, and Hebrew. Very little more appears for

French; the proposals were made, furthermore, at a period when the international prestige of French was at its zenith.

The two languages that vie for top modification honors are Latin and English, the former in the late 1800's and at the turn of the century, the latter principally in the course of the last three decades. This is in itself significant as reflecting the relative standing of the languages at different periods.

It is perhaps more significant that while suggestions for reformed Latin come chiefly from continental European lands, those for reformed English stem largely from the English-speaking world itself.

Lastly, attention may be called to the nature of the reform advocated. For Latin (as for Greek, French, and Italian) the main changes lie in the field of grammatical structure; the vocabulary is generally accepted, and the spelling and pronunciation are left to shift for themselves. In the case of English, on the other hand, the grammatical structure is left generally undisturbed, and the two major reforms suggested hinge on spelling and vocabulary.

For spelling reform in an English language designed for international purposes there appears to be good and sufficient reason. For vocabulary restriction (save as a mere learning device in imparting the initial stages of the language) the case is not at all clear. One of the chief merits of English is the abundance and internationality of its vocabulary.

15. Attempted solutions: two- and three-language blends

The First Stage in Construction—Ideological Implications—Philosophical and Methodological Disputes—Can Two Languages Be Blended?—From Lingua to Interglossa

Outside of national languages in their natural form, national languages in symbiosis or zonal combinations, and national languages in modified form, there is only one possibility, and that is for a fully constructed, thoroughly artificial language. But tongues that may be described as fully constructed nevertheless fall under quite different headings. They may be thoroughly a priori, which means that they will have no connection whatsoever with any existing language and be completely and altogether arbitrary. They may be fully a posteriori, which means that they will endeavor to imitate natural tongues, taking from them their desirable features of vocabulary and grammar, blending and combining elements from as many as a dozen or more national languages; or they may represent transitional stages, with features, usually of vocabulary, taken from natural tongues, and other features, usually of grammar, built up arbitrarily, in accordance with the inventor's concept of what is logical and desirable.

Chronologically, there is a general, though not by any means invariable, progression from the a priori to the a posteriori system, and we may henceforth find it expedient to follow the traditional order and classification: 1. fully constructed, arbitrary, a priori languages; 2. transitional systems, admitting of contributions from the natural tongues (Volapük is the best example of such a language); 3. fully a posteriori tongues, accepting contributions from all sorts of natural languages, which they strive to imitate and blend, as illustrated by Esperanto and the majority of systems offered today, like Interlingua.

The original divergence between the a priori and the a posteriori ideas may be described as philosophical. Should a language devised for international purposes be one of logic, or one of ease? Should it follow the classifications of thought, as rigorously developed by logic, or the normal vagaries of human language, which is anything but logical, but to which long centuries of speaking have accustomed the human race? One could, of course, go further, and inquire whether the ideal language should be devised for people capable of following principles of logic, who are few, or for those who employ language for practical everyday purposes, who are many.

If the second alternative is favored, as seems to be the case today, a secondary point of dispute arises, which revolves around what one might even describe as a *Weltanschauung*. Should the language composite favored by the a posteriori school be based upon all languages, or only upon the languages of western culture? Should we, in other words, favor certain languages at the expense of others? There is little doubt that most of the language builders of the past have favored this kind of solution, which continues to be favored by the language builders of today. Yet many interlinguists of yesteryear have gone out of their way to make concessions to the speech-habits of the less favored groups of Asia and Africa. As far back as 1887, Eichhorn, in his Weltsprache, showed concern for Polynesian habits of pronunciation, and reduced the number of consonants accordingly. It is a well-known fact that Monsignor Schleyer's Volapük makes practically no use of the sound of *r* because it is unfamiliar to the Chinese.

But even more important is the fact that in earlier days, when people were far less concerned than they are today with questions of racial equality, there were completely free and full-blown discussions on the subject. Consider, for example, the fact that the American Philosophical Society, which had been founded by Franklin in 1743, passed in 1888 a resolution condemning Volapük for its "non-Aryan" character and urging the formation of "an international committee emanating from the six or seven principal Aryan nations" for the purpose of devising a language to be "based on Aryan vocabulary and grammar in their simplest form." Today, this would lead to charges of racism, Hitlerism, and worse. Even in those days, the Philological Society of London, under the leadership of its president, Alexander Ellis, rejected the call of the American group on the ground that "a universal language must not exclude non-Aryan peoples, and must be independent of racial considerations."

Mention may also be made of Hamilton Holt, who at a later date openly stated that "the chief objection to Esperanto is that it is provincial—entirely ignoring Asia and the languages which are spoken by the vast majority of the human race." To this objection, the reply is made by Guérard as late as 1922 that "it is hard to imagine an *a posteriori* language fair to East and West alike, and in which the twain shall meet. If absolute, world-wide neutrality is indispensable, then we have but one resource, and that is an *a priori* language." Guérard even goes on to state that "the whole world, except one-third of Asia, is under European control"; that "the reawakened East frankly acknowledges the leadership of the West"; and that there would probably be no real objection on the part of the East to accepting a pan-Western international tongue, to which the East could make future contributions. Is all this still true today?

Even where there is agreement on an a posteriori language with a western base, interesting differences of method are in evidence. One methodology, which we shall see in operation later, consists in admitting, as synonyms, words from different national languages, which may be inserted into the text at the speaker's pleasure, and which other speakers, with a different national background, are supposed to understand, even while they may not actively use them. This, of course, involves recognition of a principle long known in pedagogical circles: that the individual has at his disposal an active vocabulary, which he uses for speaking, and a much larger passive, or recognition, vocabulary, made up of words that he would not normally use himself in speech or writing, but whose meaning he understands when he encounters them audibly or in print.

Before going on to a full enumeration and discussion of the three varieties of constructed tongues, a priori, mixed, and a posteriori, it may be well to cast a glance at a few specimens which involve the blending or combination of only two, or at the most three, natural tongues. They form a transition between the modified national language, which is one, though changed from its natural form, and the full-fledged a posteriori language, which normally involves the blending of anywhere from half a dozen to two dozen natural languages, with the addition of a few unescapable arbitrary features.

Two samples come from the pen of a single inventor, the prolific George Henderson whose Latinesce we have already seen among the modified languages. In 1888, several years before his coining of Latinesce, he proposed a language based on a Latin vocabulary, but with an English system of syntax and word-order. That this language is meant for practical business purposes seems proved by the following excerpt:

"Mesiur, me recipi-tum tuo epistola hic mane gratissime, et me propera-num mitt meo gratias u tu ob tuo accepto imperios . . . Id es-num verisimili sic, le mercs adveni-qum in Berlin circa le fini o le proximo hebdomad, quia ils es-mitt-qum per express transfer. Me mitt-num le pretio-nota cum hic epistola, non cum le mercs." ("Sir, I received your letter this morning with pleasure, and I am hastening to send my thanks to you for your welcome order . . . It is likely that the goods will arrive in Berlin about the end of next week, for they will be sent by express transfer. I am sending the invoice with this letter, not with the merchandise.")

By 1889, Henderson's views had undergone a shift. His new compromise language, which he offered under the pseudonym of P. Hoinix, now consisted of a near-perfect blend of English and French, with English again supplying most of the grammar and syntax, while French contributes most of the vocabulary (but articles, pronouns, adverbs, prepositions, and conjunctions come from English). Again the purpose is primarily commercial, as witness this sample: "Me pren the liberté to ecriv to you in Anglo-Franca . . . Me have the honneur to soumett to you's inspection the prospectus of me's objets manufactured, which me to you envoy hereinclued."

Anglo-Franca certainly presents few difficulties to the speaker of English, and it may be assumed that the French speaker who learns some two hundred English words will find the language equally simple. One sometimes wonders whether the Anglo-French linguistic condominium envisaged by the founders of *le Monde Bilingue* might not in due course of time develop into an Anglo-French pidgin of this type.

J. Puchner of Linz proposed in 1897 a Nuove-Roman which he described as based on the Romance languages, and particularly on Spanish, "the most excellent of the Romance languages." Perusal of Nuove-Roman, however, would seem to lead to the conclusion that Italian has at least as much of a share as Spanish (consider *io* for "I," *noi* and *voi* for "we" and "you," *mio, tuo, suo, nostro, vostro, loro* for the possessive series, *amo, ami, ama* for the present singular of "to love," *andar via* for "to go away," *uom, buon, nuov, albero, note, forza* for "man," "good," "new," "tree," "night," "strength," all forms which coincide with Italian rather than with Spanish).

Among two-language combinations, there is record of a Latin Esperanto, presented by C. Vanghetti in 1913, and described as "Latin vocabulary with Esperanto endings." Its primary interest lies in the fact that it is a blend not of two natural languages, but of a natural with a constructed tongue.

Attempts to blend the Slavic tongues into a Pan-Slavic go back to 1666, when Križanić offered his combination of Russian and Serbo-Croatian. Sapelj in 1790, Herkel in 1826, Budilovich in 1891 (Obshcheslavyansky Yazyk), Konečný in 1912 (Slavina), Kolkop in 1913 (Slovanština), all tried their hands at a universal language for the Slavs, which might perhaps also serve the world. Slovan is a recent addition to this family.

There is unconfirmed mention of a New Chino-Japanese which blends the two great Far Eastern languages.

Molee's Tutonish of 1902, recast into an Altutonish in 1912, is a blend of Germanic languages for international use. It is described in the author's own words as "Ein union spiek, makn up ov deuch, english, skandinavish and hollandi, for to agenfererein [unite once more] al tutonish folka into ein spiek mitin feivti jiera [within fifty years]."

For Cheshikhin's Nepo of 1907 (slightly modified in 1915 under the new name of Neposlava), which attempts to strike a balance among Latin-Romance, Germanic, and Slavic elements, see page 170. His 1915 version, however, gets rid of the Slavic elements (see Appendix A).

There is one constructed tongue, devised in very recent

times, which is of particular interest by reason both of its underlying philosophy and its methodology. This is Interglossa, advanced in 1943 by Lancelot Hogben, who will be remembered as the author of *Mathematics for the Million* and the editor of *The Loom of Language*. Hogben advocates a language completely devoid of flexions and endings, with a syntax and word-order taken directly from Chinese, but a vocabulary that is altogether Graeco-Latin, as befits a tongue meant for scientific interchanges. One might even say that it is the Greek roots that predominate (*hydro,* not *aqua,* for "water"; *chron,* not *tempus,* for "time"). A sentence like "I went there in order to do it" would read in Interglossa "Mi pre kine topo tendo un acte re," which literally runs "I past motion place purpose a do thing"; "Mi no nun acte re" has the literal meaning "I not now do thing" ("I am not doing it"). The Lord's Prayer ("U Petitio de Christi") has the following form in Interglossa: "Na Parenta in Urani: Na dicte volo; tu Nomino gene revero; Plus tu Crati habe accido; plus u Demo acte harmono tu Tendo epi Geo homo in Urani. Na dicte petitio: Tu date plu di Pani a Na; plus Tu acte pardo plu malo Acte de Na; metro Na acte pardo Mu; Su acte malo de Na. Peti Tu non acte dirigo Na a plu malo Offero; Hetero, Tu date libero Na apo Malo. Causo Tu tene u Crati plus u Dyno plus un eu Famo pan Tem. Amen." A literal rendering is not easy without some knowledge of Chinese syntax, but it would run somewhat like this: "We Parent in Heaven; We say want; you Name become revere; more you Rule have happen; more the People do harmony you Intention on Earth like in Heaven. We say request: You give more day Bread to We; more You do forgiveness more bad do of We; measure We do forgiveness Them; Their do bad of We. Ask You not do direct We to more bad Offer; Else, You give free We from Bad. Cause You have the Rule more the Power more a well Fame all Time. Amen."

This is hardly an easy language to learn for anyone who has

been brought up in a western tongue, but it does attempt to make allowances for the speech habits of that one sixth of the world's population that speaks isolating languages of the Chinese type. Its similarity to pidgin, which is also based on Oriental speech habits, is obvious.

The criticism was made at the time when Interglossa was first presented that the Chinese speaker who might be flattered by syntactical similarities would nevertheless be stumped by the Graeco-Latin vocabulary, while the westerner, who might be expected to recognize the vocabulary (though even that is somewhat doubtful) would be frustrated by the highly unfamiliar syntax. The ultimate result would be that in trying to please everybody, no one would be pleased. This, of course, is the old stock argument of those who base their constructed tongues on a mixture of western languages: "Of what avail to try to please the Zulus by giving them six or ten words in the international tongue, which is all their numbers or importance would entitle them to? Let us rather try to make things easy for the majority of civilized people, who are in one fashion or another acquainted with western tongues."

Whether this philosophy of "to them that have shall be given" can continue to hold in a world in which the balance of power seems to be shifting is a difficult question to answer. Perhaps the ideal constructed language ought to be deliberately designed so as to please and flatter nobody, and make concessions to no one's existing language habits.

This, at any rate, seems to have been the point of view of the original language builders, the a priori people who refused to give even a glance at extant languages, but preferred to make their appeal to man's logical mind.

But before leaving for good the field of language blends, a word must be said concerning a very recent proposal made by the Reverend Theodore E. Leidenfrost of the Lutheran

Mission in Monrovia, Liberia, and published by Floyd Hardin in his *International Language Review.*

Dr. Leidenfrost suggests that linguistic specialists go to work and construct a Universal Grammar (and, presumably, vocabulary) on the basis of a blend of ten "representative" languages, for which he makes the following tentative suggestion: Iraqi Arabic, Mandarin Chinese, English, Hindustani, Hungarian, Indonesian, the Kpelle of Liberia, Russian, Spanish, and Swahili.

This ten-language blend would give representation to Indo-European in its most widespread and diverging varieties (English, Hindustani, Russian, Spanish), to Semitic (Arabic), to Sino-Tibetan (Chinese), to Ural-Altaic (Hungarian), to Malayo-Polynesian (Indonesian), and to the two chief branches of African Negro languages, the Sudanese-Guinean, represented by Kpelle, and the Bantu, represented by Swahili. If we were to replace Kpelle with Hausa (a much more widespread language of the Sudanese-Guinean group), and add Japanese, and either Tamil or Telugu, representing the big Dravidian language group of southern India, the ideal blended language envisaged by Dr. Leidenfrost would give representation to well over 90 per cent of the world's populations, literate and illiterate, backward and advanced.

There would be no possible doubt concerning the "neutrality" of such a tongue. Whether it would meet with favor, or incur the sort of criticism that has attended Interglossa, raised to the *n*th power, is an altogether different matter. The great merit of such a project, if it were carried out, would be to give us the sort of "Universal Grammar" that has been the dream of linguists and philosophers from the days of Duns Scotus and Scaliger to those of Whorf.

16. Attempted solutions: a priori languages

Polygraphists and Philosophers—A Musical Language—Return of the Philosophers—The Language of Numbers—Complete Neutrality Equals Complete Arbitrariness

The a priori language is one which has no connection with pre-existing tongues, but rather endeavors to link language with logical thought. Commercial codes used for economy in sending telegraphic messages are good examples, while on a more limited scale one may refer to musical notation, or to astronomical, chemical, or other symbols. As applied to an international tongue, the great advantage of the a priori system lies in its complete neutrality, since it favors or resembles none of the known languages.

The idea of polygraphy, or the "universal sign," or the "real characters," whereby ideas might be reduced to a system of writing comprehensible to people of different speeches, is a very ancient one. Chinese ideographic writing is nothing but a polygraphic system. It permits all who are acquainted with it to read the *ideas* betokened by the written symbols, going on to pronounce them as they please, which is exactly what the speakers of the different Chinese dialects do. In their origin, Egyptian hieroglyphic and Sumerian-Akkadian cuneiform characters seem to have had the same symbolic, ideographic nature, replaced only later, and in part, by phonetic values, which restricted them to the representation of a single, specific spoken tongue.

For a language with a phonetic alphabet, like Greek, to go back to a system of ideograms is, in a sense, a retrogression. Yet the advantages of international comprehension sometimes outweigh the advantages of the link between speech and writing. Two Greek speakers, Diodorus the Sicilian and Galen, are reported to have thought of systems of symbols which would remove all uncertainty from human communication. A similar idea, based perhaps on the western discovery of Chinese ideographs, is said to have occurred to Francis Bacon.*

Unconfirmed reports of a priori languages are connected with the names of St. Hildegarde, in the twelfth century,† and of Mohyieddin the Sheik in the eleventh century of the Hegira (roughly our own seventeenth century; Balaibalan is the name of his alleged invention).‡

Raymund Lull, a thirteenth-century Catalan philosopher, is claimed to have been a forerunner, in his Ars Generalis of 1280, of the international language movement,§ but the editions of his works that have come down to us from later centuries would seem to indicate that polygraphy was his main concern.¶

Other polygraphists (L. Alberti, Trithemius, G. B. Porta) flourished in the fifteenth and sixteenth centuries.

The transition from polygraphy to the international language idea occurs when the constructed set of symbols is suggested for spoken as well as written use, and here there is no denying the primacy of Descartes.

In the seventeenth century, the latter's initial pronouncement was followed by a rash of offerings, all based on the a priori principle, some of which have already been described. In addition to Dalgarno, Urquhart, and Wilkins, mention

* See Stojan in Bibliography. See his p. 31.
† See Schmelzeis in Bibliography.
‡ See Bergmann in Bibliography.
§ See Peri in Bibliography.
¶ See Stojan in Bibliography. See his p. 34.

may be made of Francis Lodwick (1647) and Cave Beck, who in 1657 offered an ingenious system based on combinations of letters and numbers to be used in writing, while the numbers were replaced by sounds in actual speech. "Honor thy father and thy mother" would appear in Beck's written system as "leb2314 p2477 pf2477," which would be read *"lebtoreonfo peetofosensen piftofosensen"* (each numeral stands for a spoken syllable). It is perhaps obvious why this system, or the one illustrated by Leibniz' *mubodilefa* or *bodifalemu* for the figure 81374 did not take hold. The strain imposed on the memory is tremendous.

The most successful tongue of the a priori type came in 1817, and was the creation of the Frenchman Jean-François Sudre. It was called Langue Musicale Universelle, or Solresol, and was based on the international names of the musical notes, all words being formed out of combinations of the syllables *do, re, mi, fa, sol, la, si.* Statistically, these combinations would yield 7 words of one syllable, 49 of two, 336 of three, 2,268 of four, 9,072 of five, which was as far as Sudre cared to go. Shifts of accent from one syllable to another would then yield the possibility of changing the function of a word from noun to verb or adjective or adverb. Sudre further pointed out that his syllables could be abbreviated to their initial consonant for purposes of speedwriting, using *s* for *si* and *so* for *sol;* that the language could be sung or played or hummed instead of spoken; that it could be written as music; that knocks, or even colors, could be substituted for the syllables for communication at a distance, as by flags; that it could be used by deaf-mutes, who would tap their message. Sudre's vocabulary was, naturally enough, completely arbitrary, although a principle of classification according to thought appeared, with *do* standing for man, moral or physical, *dodo* indicating a subclass, *dododo* a subclass of the subclass; but the logical classification obviously breaks down as the composition of the word becomes more complex. Of the seven original monosyllables, *do* stands for "not," *si* for "yes" (a concession to some of the Romance languages, perhaps?), *re* for "and," *mi* for "or," *sol* for "if." But *dore* is "I," *domi* is "you," *redo* is "my," *doredo* is "time," and *doresol* is "month." Some attempt is made to show opposites by reversing the order of syllables: *domisol* for "God," *solmido* for "Satan"; *sollasi* for "go up," *silasol* for "go down." A phrase like "I don't love" is "dore do milasi." The grammar of Solresol, as one might expect, is quite complicated. The plan, first conceived in 1817, was presented to the Academy of Fine Arts in 1827, and gained wide acceptance, being sponsored by such figures as Victor Hugo, Lamartine, Humboldt, and Napoleon III. Sudre died in 1862, but his language continued to find followers, such as Gajewski, who published a book about it as late as 1902. Even on the eve of the First World War, despite the Volapük and Esperanto that had appeared in the intervening years, devotees of Solresol continued to air their views.

Shortly before Sudre's attempt, in 1795 Citizen Delormel had offered the French National Convention a system designed to bring all human beings together through the use of a tongue which, "without suppressing or replacing others," would favor none of the existing languages. Possibly even more than its seventeenth-century predecessors, Delormel's language worked on a logical basis, with an arbitrary arrangement of vowels and consonants designed to express various ideas (*ava,* "grammar"; *ave,* "letter"; *avi,* "syllable"; *avo,* "accent"; *avau,* "word"). History records nothing beyond the presentation.

A. Grosselin's system of 1836, with its 1,500 roots and 100 derivational affixes, capable of forming 150,000 words; E. Vidal's Langue Universelle et Analytique of 1844, in which *B* stands for animals, *bu* for quadrupeds, *be* for fish, *ba* for insects; C. Letellier's device of 1852, in which *ā* is animal, *āb* is a mammal, *ābo* is a carnivore, *āboj* is a feline, and *āboje* is "cat"; all indicate the same mental process. The same may be said of Sotos Ochando's project of 1855, designed to be an international scientific language, written rather than spoken (*aba,* simple bodies or elements; *ababa,* "oxygen"; *ababe,* "hydrogen"; *ababi,* "nitrogen"; *ababo,* "sulfur"; *ababu,* "selenium"). Frederick Dyer's Lingualumina, or "language of light," conceived in 1875, but published in 1889, attempts to rival triumphant Volapük and Esperanto, but at a period when a priori languages were definitely on the defensive.

Maldant's Chabé Abane (or Langue Naturelle) of 1886, and Larsson's Luftlandana of 1893 ran into the same difficulty. A sample of the former is: "Peme ad J(e)nev om peme ad Konstans ib as ob ai agig peme ad Süis" ("The Lake of Geneva and the Lake of Constance are the two largest lakes in Switzerland"). A sample of Luftlandana runs: "Ri napa luft byser hinsko. Napa ri spru freiste naj bar jorahb" ("We have invented a new language. We have seven moments of rest daily.").

Another attempt was the one made by Carl Dietrich in his Völkerverkehrssprache of 1902, presented on the ground that the language of international communications should be not a compilation, but a logical, homogeneous, and independent organism, for people are divided by words, but united by thought and common sense.

The twentieth century has comparatively little to offer in the way of a priori languages. This is perhaps due to the fact that it is a practical, utilitarian, not a speculative or philosophical epoch, and that logical thought no longer holds the prestige it once had.

Yet the a priori idea continues to crop up in curious ways. We have, for instance, a purely numerical language, conceived by a Berlin architect, and presented in 1921 under the name of Timerio, after its creator, Tiemer. Basing himself upon numerical "languages" of limited application, like

Dewey's decimal classification of books for libraries, Herr Tiemer offers such combinations as 1–80–17 for "I love you." Peano, inventor of Latino Sine Flexione, had already presented a scheme for use in mathematical treatises, in which conventional signs of international application replace the majority of words. Gibson's Code, devised by a Coast Artillery officer, uses numbers, with the proviso that nouns must start with 1, 2, or 3, verbs with 4, adjectives with 5, adverbs with 6, pronouns with 7, conjunctions with 8, prepositions with 9. With verbs, -10, -20 and -30 are used as "suffixes" to denote present, past, and future. "The boy eats the red apple" comes out as "5–111–409–10–5–516–2013." But such schemes, needless to say, could at the most replace only the written language, and would have no application in speech; to this extent, they are continuators of the systems devised by the medieval and Renaissance polygraphists rather than true constructed languages. Also, they require the syntax or word-arrangement of a specific language; Gibson's 5 for "the" would be unnecessary and perhaps incomprehensible to a Russian speaker, since Russian uses no articles. In final analysis, they become numerical codes for specific spoken tongues.

Mannus Talundberg's Perio of 1904 is described as a language built on logic, while Ro, offered by the Reverend E. P. Foster in 1912 to boost his native city of Marietta, Ohio, is based on a classification of ideas. Since Ro displays considerable ingenuity, and is one of the few American contributions to the constructed language field, it may be worth while to exemplify it. On the root of *ta-,* which covers expressions of time, Foster forms *tab,* "moment"; *tac,* "minute"; *tad,* "hour," *taf,* "day"; *taj,* "night"; *tak,* "week"; *tal,* "month"; *taq,* "year." If to the *ta-* root you add the suffix *-ma-* for "season," you can then form *tamab,* "spring"; *tamac,* "summer"; *tamad,* "fall"; *tamaf,* "winter." The Ro numerals, from 1 to 10, run: *zab, zac, zad, zaf, zag, zal, zam, zaq, zar, zax,* which gives at least one of them a strange, but purely chance resemblance to what is supposed to be an ancient Etruscan numeral, as it appears on a pair of dice. The beginning of the Lord's Prayer in Ro runs as follows: "Abze radap av el in suda, ace rokab eco sugem; ace rajda ec kep; ace va eco uz in suda asi in buba."

Italian offerings include Gigli's Lingua Filosofica Universale pei Dotti of 1818, Gaetano Ferrari's Monoglottica of 1877, Cesare Meriggi's Blaia Zimondal of 1884, and philosophical considerations going back to P. Francesco Soave's *Reflections on the Institution of a Universal Language* of 1774 and G. Bellavitis' *Thoughts on a Universal Tongue* of 1862. Mention may also be made of Rethy's Lingua Universalis Communi Omnium Nationum Usui Accommodata of 1821, and Edmonds' Universal Alphabet, Grammar and Language of 1856. Tgransar's Sehlerai, seemingly composed around 1800 but published in 1921, also appears to belong to this classification ("Rum shai yran bes lerai vom, shaiz il le sam lerai iun sim, mim serai vam shaiz il le som," "In the world shall be preferred one scientific tongue to many tongues with one science").

Two languages of the a priori type call for special attention by reason of the fact that they show a beginning of the trend toward the other, a posteriori class of constructed tongues, despite the fact that they appeared at a time when the latter type was already in full swing. Dr. Nicolas, a retired French naval medical officer, had already been a Volapük official when he devised his Spokil in 1900. But his dissatisfaction with Schleyer's product led him to create a tongue built on the arbitrary principles of the seventeenth century, but with roots that are at least faintly reminiscent of the words of the western vocabularies (*gn,* for instance, conveys the general idea of "fire," and is reminiscent of *ignis; dr,* the root for "water," forms part of *hydro;* in like manner, *pn* stands for "air," *fr* for "fruit," *skr* for "write"). The result is that we have *pne* for "breathe," *pna* for sigh," *pni* for "breath," *pno* for "puff," with sentences like "meona vai le tsael di le veol," "man is the king of nature." The beginning of the Lord's Prayer in Spokil runs :"Mael nio kui vai o les zeal, aepseno lezai tio mita; veze lezai tio tsaeleda; feleno lezai tio bela, uti o zeal itu o geol."

More recently, we have Beatty's Qosmiani of 1927, of which the following samples are offered: "Ha sedirt or el sediluli" ("She would sit on the little chair"); "Qwoq fiip te?" ("How do you do?"); "Ho fiaf hi" ("He shall do it"); "Quq sensip te al dolori?" ("Where do you feel a pain?"); "Esip hi distel?" ("Is it far?"). The Qosmiani version of the Lord's Prayer, given in Appendix A of this book, clearly reveals the transitional nature of the language.

Leaning still more in the a posteriori direction is Ferdinand Hilbe's Zahlensprache, or "Numerical Tongue," of 1901, which features generally international roots, but with completely arbitrary endings, and the possibility of replacing each individual word with a number. Here we have declension by prefixes and suffixes, which may be attached to the noun or to the article, so that while *la pane* means "the bread," "of the bread" may be either *la epane* or *ela pane.* Endings in *-d* for adjectives, in *-k* for adverbs (*boned,* "kind"; *bonek,* "kindly") give the tongue a faintly exotic flavor, and the reader faced with *eserek* for "day before yesterday evening" or *larifikarer* for "to gild" has a vague feeling that he is dealing with Magyar or ancient Umbrian.

It could perhaps be said that Spokil, Zahlensprache, and Qosmiani constitute a transition to a transition, since they are intermediate in nature between the fully arbitrary a priori tongue and the group of languages, headed by Volapük, which form the true bridge between the two great classes of constructed languages.

Polygraphy, an international language of signs for written understanding, was mentioned at the beginning of this chapter. It reappears at the end, as one might expect. In

1913, Cheshikhin, in his *Ideografiya i Neosinografiya,* suggested Chinese ideographs as an ideal written tongue for international purposes. In 1924, this idea was readvanced by F. R. Gilbert, and still later by others. To date, nothing has come of it.

The very latest language of the a priori type offered for international use seems to be an American offering, Russell's Suma (the 1000-Word Universal Language) of 1957. The language has roots that are claimed to be altogether arbitrary and not linked to any known tongue, thus giving assurance of perfect neutrality. Its phonetic structure, with words that are for the most part of the two-syllable, consonant-vowel-consonant-vowel type, is reminiscent of Malay or Japanese, and assures ease of pronunciation. In the vocabulary, the principle of association is used to the full (*kato,* "boy"; *kito,* "girl"; *poma,* "good"; *pema,* "bad").

The grammatical structure and the orthography are extremely simple, with no articles, no plurals, no declension or conjugation, and no capital letters. It is reminiscent of Esperanto that in general nouns end in *-o,* verbs in *-i,* adjectives and adverbs in *-a,* but there are exceptions, due, in the words of the author, "to practical necessity in order to avoid ambiguity when speaking or in transmission of the voice by mechanical or electrical devices."

Suma has only one real prefix, *nea-* ("non-," "un-," "dis-"), and one real suffix, *-sima* ("-like" "-ive," "-ish"), other affixes assuming the status of independent words: *vuni,* "agree"; *nea vuni,* "disagree"; *nea vuni puto,* "disagreement" ("not agree deed"); *moti,* "begin"; *moti sima,* "first," "in the beginning"; *moti pute,* "beginner" ("begin doer"); *kosa,* "large"; *kosa puti,* "enlarge" ("large do"); *bisi kolo,* "hotel" ("sleep house"); *toki kolo,* "restaurant" ("eat house"). The Suma numerals from 1 to 10 are *baba, dia, fua, goa, kea, lai, mimi, nui, poi, rei.*

Here is the beginning of the First Book of Genesis in Suma

with a literal interlinear translation, illustrating the functioning of the system:

talo moti sima baki boto e beto e beto te peka e
God first-wise make sky and earth and earth be empty and

ena gide e ena doba. e talo poti, sui doba te
without shape and without light. and God say, let light be

mora; e doba te mora. e talo oki sute tu te poma sute
here; and light be here. and God see that this be good that

doba te mora. e talo vesi temo ale lato e lito. tu te
light be here. and God divide day to day and night. this be

temo 1.
day one.

Suma is definite proof that Descartes's a priori ideal is not dead.

17. Attempted solutions: mixed systems

A Linguist Speaks—The Heyday of Volapük—Bopal and Dil—Balta and Orba—The Blue Language

One of the most revered names in the field of linguistics is that of Jakob von Grimm, whose profound studies on the Teutonic and Indo-European languages formed the foundation of the comparative and historical pursuit of languages. In 1860, when the ideal for the international tongue was still Sudre's Solresol, Grimm offered a brief program embodying his concept of the main requirements for a satisfactory world language. Such a language, he held, should be rigidly logical, with a word for every concept and a concept for every word, and with absolute simplicity of grammatical structure and word derivation, yet with a rich vocabulary and a free, elastic word-order. Grimm was enough of a Romantic to urge that the future world tongue be harmonious in sound, and suited to poetic declamation and singing; for this, he pointed to Italian as approaching perfection, by reason of its syllabic structure generally consisting of a consonant followed by a vowel. He also advocated a thoroughly phonetic spelling.

So far, there is nothing in Grimm's program that is in conflict with the a priori methodology. The real innovation comes in his description of the vocabulary. Grimm rejects the arbitrary principle, and suggests that the words of the new tongue be based on Latin roots. Why? Because Latin is a dead, and therefore "neutral" language; because it is closely related to all the languages of the Indo-European family; because it is familiar to the learned element of all nations.

Here begins the real transition from the arbitrary language of logic to the conglomeration of many tongues that marks the a posteriori system. Once the principle is established of taking as a vocabulary base the roots of one or many existing tongues, the path is cleared for the mongrel mixture that will represent "the greatest ease to the greatest number."

Grimm's pronouncement also opened the way for the first successful constructed tongue, if success is to be measured by thoroughly popular support rather than by the endorsement of a few highly placed individuals. This tongue was Volapük, the creation of Monsignor Johann Martin Schleyer, a German prelate whose vast acquaintance with languages (tradition has it that he knew, in one fashion or another, eighty-three) led him, during a sleepless night in 1879, to evolve a system, largely based on Grimm's principles, which was finally embodied in a work published in 1885, *Grammatik der Universalsprache für alle Erdbewohner,* a title which is in itself a program, since it heralds Schleyer's tongue as being meant for all the inhabitants of the earth, not for an intellectual elite. In its creator's mind, Volapük was intended for general spoken use, and it was his earnest hope that it would contribute to world understanding and world peace. "Menade bal, püki bal," "For one mankind, one speech," was Schleyer's motto.

Volapük spread like wildfire, not merely among intellectuals, but among all classes of people, to the point where at a Volapük congress held in Paris in 1889 not merely the delegates, but even the waiters and porters spoke Volapük. Societies for the propagation of Volapük appeared all over the earth, not only in the cities of Europe, but in Mexico, China, the United States, Australia, and South Africa. In a single year (1888), 182 books on the study of the language appeared, composed in twenty-five different tongues. There were at one time no fewer than twenty-five journals devoted to Volapük, of which seven were entirely composed in the new "World-Speak."

Yet by 1890 the vogue of Volapük had come to a standstill. By 1911, when its inventor died, Volapük had sunk to the point where its speakers numbered barely one third those of the new international tongue, Esperanto.

Many reasons have been advanced for the decline of Volapük, among them the stubbornness of its creator in rejecting any and all suggestions for modifications that seemed desirable, coupled with the insistence on the part of many of his followers that such modifications be made. In part, criticism is laid upon the rather cumbersome grammatical system devised by Schleyer, and his propensity for lengthy word compounds rivaling those of his native German (*klonalitakipafablüdacifalöpasekretan,* cited as a sample, is probably a joke).

Schleyer's underlying principle in vocabulary was to adopt as its base the popular English tongue, "because it is the most widespread of all civilized languages, save for its spelling." At the same time, he was deeply preoccupied with the language habits of other language groups, to the point where the majority of his words reject *r* because the Chinese cannot pronounce it (he admits, however, middle vowels like *ö* and *ü* which do not appear in many important languages). It is a fact that his words are largely taken from English, but in many cases they are distorted beyond all recognition by English speakers (Who would, for instance, recognize "World-Speak" in the name *Volapük,* or "I don't want the book, but a book" in "no vilob eli buki, sod uni buki"?). Schleyer's nouns are endowed with the four cases of German, nominative, genitive, dative, and accusative ("house": *dom, doma, dome, domi;* to form the plural of each singular case-form, add *-s*). Adjectives end in *-ik* (*gudik,* "good"); adverbs in *-iko* (*gudiko,* "well"). Numerals are quite as arbitrary as in any a priori language; those from one to nine run: *bal, tel, kil, fol, lul, mäl, vel, jöl, zül; bals* is 10, *balsebal* is 11, *tum* is 100; but, strangely enough, *mil* is 1000. In the verb system, we have generally English roots combined with arbitrary endings (*löfob,* "I love," *löfol,* "thou lovest," *löfom,* "he loves"; add *-s* to get the plural forms). Then a system of prefixes and suffixes, quite as complicated as anything appearing in Latin or Greek, serves to form an endless series of tenses, moods and voices (*älöfob-la,* "I would love"; *ilöfobs-la,* "we would have loved"). It is even claimed that a Volapük verb, like that of some American Indian languages, could take 505,400 different forms, a sample of which is *ulöfofs-öz,* "Ladies, I charge you to have loved by a certain time."

The Volapük version of the Lord's Prayer runs as follows: "O Fat obas, kel binol in süls, paisaludomöz nem ola! Kömomöd monargän ola! Jenomöz vil olik, as in sül, i su tal! Bodi obsik vädeliki givolös obes adelo! E pardolös obes debis obsik, äs id obs aipardobs debeles obas. E no obis nindukolös in tentadi; sod aidalivolös obis de bad. Jenosöd!"

The language which in 1888 was taught in Italian technical schools and spoken in French department stores was, a few years later, quite dead. It proved, however, that the world, or at least a considerable segment of it, was ripe for the idea, and that a fully constructed tongue could be lifted out of the domain of scholars and philosophers and turned into a spoken, popular language acceptable to all classes of the population. Had it not been for dissensions and bickerings born of normal human failings, it is possible that the world's language difficulties might have been solved over half a century ago, and that Volapük might today be the common language of mankind.

But the dissensions were there. The Volapük Academy broke up in confusion, and the Biblical story of the Tower of Babel was repeated in its entirety, even to the point where each modern son of Noah went off in a different direction with his own descendants, each group speaking its own tongue, incomprehensible to all the rest.

The descendants of Volapük were many and varied. Sebastian Verheggen's Nal Bino of 1886 had, if anything, fewer merits and more drawbacks than Schleyer's creation, but it is to Verheggen's credit that he first described, in clear, unequivocal language, the essential role that the world's governments ought to play in the matter of a world tongue. Pointing to the example of the success that had attended the creation of a world postal and telegraphic union, whereby international communications are made possible, Verheggen suggested that a similar union be created by the governments for the purpose of selecting a single world language. This all-important proposal fell upon deaf ears.

Charles Menet's Langue Universelle of 1886 was a minor modification of Volapük, distinguished only by its one-syllable roots, to which Volapük itself was partial. Other systems of the Volapük family are perhaps more interesting by reason of their poetic, exotic names than for their actual content. St. de Max's Bopal (1887); Georg Bauer's Spelin (1886); Fieweger's Dil (1893); E. Dormoy's Balta (1893); José Guardiola's Orba (1893) all share the characteristics of Volapük, over which they mark no noticeable improvement, save perhaps for the fact that Balta eliminates noun declensions. As a single example of them all, here is Spelin's version of the Lord's Prayer: "Pat isel, ka bi ni sieloes! Nom el zi bi santed! Klol el zi komi! Vol el zi bi faked, kefe ni siel, efe su sium! Givi ide bod isel desel is. Fegivi doboes isel, kefe tet is fegivis tu yadoboes isel; et nen duki is ni tantoe, boet libi is de mal."

For various reasons, mention may be made of three more constructed languages of the "mixed" family. Wilhelm von Arnim's Veltparl of 1896 introduces the novel idea of applying declension not to the noun, but to the article that precedes it, so that we have *el dog* ("the dog"); *ela dog* ("of the dog"); *ele dog* ("to the dog"); *eli dog* ("the dog," object). Plurality, however, is indicated in the noun; all the above forms are made plural by changing *dog* to *dogy.* In vocabulary, Veltparl distinguishes itself from its sister mixed languages, to the extent that it offers some measure of proportional representation to nonwestern tongues; "garden" and "fire," for example, are *kert* and *tys,* taken from Hungarian; "apple" is the Hindustani *seb;* "eight" is the Vietnamese *tam.* It is of interest to note that the comment of Couturat and Léau, made in the year 1903, to this attempt to give broader internationality to the international language runs: "Such fantasies show absolute indifference in connection with internationality."

Marchand's Dilpok of 1898, one of the last tongues of the mixed family to appear, already betrays its leanings toward the Anglo-Romance combination by such samples as "Mi ese glad" ("I am glad") and "al nom de Got" ("in the name of God"). Leon Bollack's Langue Bleue, or "Blue Language," of 1899, on the other hand, frankly avows its leanings toward people of western civilization, particularly of Germanic and Latin stock. The language has no literary pretensions, and is destined solely for commercial and everyday purposes, with conciseness, precision, clarity, and rigidity as guiding principles. Yet this sample is more poetic than commercial: "Markesin beled, vae logu beled mortigo ma fri lov" ("Lovely marquise, your beautiful eyes make me die of love"). More seriously, the Lord's Prayer runs as follows: "Nea Per, ev ra seri in silu, vea nom ech santigui; vea regn ech komi; vea vil ech makui ib gev so in sil; ev givo dach nea pan taged ana, it ev solvi nae fansu ana so ne solvo ache re unfanso na; it ev nu lefti na to temt, bo ev bevri na om mal." (We have transcribed by *ch* a special letter in the Langue Bleue alphabet which has the sound of *ch* in *church*.)

Bollack's "Blue Language" marks, to all intents and purposes, the end of the mixed system, which in the early decades of the twentieth century was more and more encroached upon by Esperanto and its brood. Yet four more languages of this type are recorded for the early years of this century: A. Hoessrich's Tal (1903); and three products of the year 1906, Max Walde's Weltsprache Pankel, described by its author as "the easiest and shortest language for international communications," F. Greenwood's Ulla, and Spitzer's Parla. A sample of the last is "Mao natura-lekse e-troveti et konoseti, mao se stimuli homa ten suito medita." The Lord's Prayer in Ulla begins: "Vus Patra hoo este n ciela, sankted este dus noma, dus rexdoma vene, dus desira esta färed n terra als tu este n ciela," which would seem to place it practically in an a posteriori classification. For Pankel, however, we have this version, which displays a strong tendency toward a monosyllabic and telescoped structure: "Sai Fat in sky, y sanu so nam; so land komu; so viy apsu up glob l sky."

That the mixed ideal is not 100 per cent dead, even in these days of Anglo-Romance predominance, is proved perhaps by the very recent Mongling devised by Kenneth Littlewood of Leeds, England, a tongue consisting exclusively of one-syllable words, Chinese fashion, with English roots and a "Chinese" syntax which smacks strongly of a priori influences: "Ling et top pi-ken ad ploi il klar top bon" is Mongling for "The language that is easiest to know and use is clearly the best."

18. Attempted solutions: earlier a posteriori systems

The Multilanguage Combination—The First Attempts—Pantos and Pasilingua—The Tongue of Dr. Hopeful—The Spawn of Esperanto

The a posteriori language is by definition one constructed on the analogy of existing tongues. This does not mean, however, that it may not have arbitrary features, particularly in the matter of grammar. All existing natural tongues display irregularities of one sort or another, which complicate the language for the learner and make language study a chore. The elimination of irregularities is a predominant feature of practically all constructed tongues. Aside from that, they may or may not borrow grammatical structure from the languages on which they draw. One might, for example, ape the grammar of Spanish, at the same time regularizing it, to this extent: 1. All nouns shall be masculine or feminine (this rule actually exists in Spanish); 2. All masculine nouns shall end in *-o,* all feminine nouns in *-a* (a great many Spanish nouns behave just like this, but there are other classes of nouns which do not, and have to be separately learned); 3. The plural of all nouns shall be formed by adding *-s* to the singular (this rule, or a mild modification of it, is almost, but not quite, universal in Spanish). Now we have a language which, so far as nouns are concerned, is modeled on Spanish, yet displays absolute regularity, which Spanish does not. If to this selection of grammatical rules we add a vocabulary drawn from Spanish (*muro* for "wall," *casa* for "house," etc.), we have a perfect a posteriori language.

We have seen a few constructed languages of this type, like Latino Sine Flexione. But the average a posteriori language goes much farther than a mere modified natural tongue. It is, generally speaking, a blend or combination of many tongues, both as to grammar and as to vocabulary. One might even say that the great question facing the constructed tongue is how many and which natural languages it shall admit into its composition, thus paralleling the problem of world organizations like the UN, which has to decide how many and which nations to admit.

While a posteriori languages of the composite type constitute the majority of constructed language offerings, it is an interesting fact that they got started rather late. We have seen national languages used internationally since the beginning of civilization; a priori languages offered in profusion as far back as the seventeenth century; modified national languages since Faiguet's 1765 attempt. The full-fledged combination a posteriori language is a nineteenth-century product, and in the twentieth century it has acquired almost uncontested predominance among those who give conscious thought to the problem.

First among the combination languages, uniting the elements of nine different national tongues, is Lucien de Rudelle's Pantos-dîmou-glossa ("All People's Language") of 1858. Greek, Latin, English, German, Russian, French, Spanish, Italian, and Portuguese elements all go into its composition. The grammar makes provision for five cases, three natural genders, two numbers, and a full roster of verb-tenses and moods. In nouns, the final vowels *-e, -a* and *-o* mark masculine, feminine, and neuter (*el eke,* "the stallion"; *al eka,* "the mare"; *ol eko,* "the horse" in general). Nouns are pluralized by adding *-ci,* articles and adjectives by adding *-i* (*eli grandezi ekeci,* "the big horses"). "Potere-no konsolardzam Kalipsoa dol eksito did Ylise" is Pantos-dîmou-glossa for "Calypso could not console herself for Ulysses' departure."

Pirro's Universalsprache of 1868, while more modest in its conglomeration (he admits only French, German, English, Italian, and Spanish), has invariable nouns which, however, add *-in* to form the feminine, German fashion (*son,* "son"; *sonin,* "daughter"; this principle was later adopted by Esperanto, where *knabo* is "boy" and *knabino,* "girl"). Even in the plural, nouns are unchanging, the article alone showing number (*el kaval, li kaval,* "the horse," "the horses"). A sample of Pirro's language is self-explanatory: "Men senior, I sende evos un gramatik e un verb-bibel de un nuov glot nomed universal glot. In futur I scriptrai evos semper in dit glot. I pregate evos responden ad me in dit self glot."

E. Courtonne's Langue Internationale Néo-Latine of 1885 combines English and the Romance languages, but its word-formation is strongly reminiscent of German (*pax-mar-mall-vap-nav-compna,* "Pacific Mail Steamship Company"; *mifrat-fijuxa,* "my-brother-son-wife," or, more clearly, "my niece by marriage").

The principle adopted by Paul Steiner in his Pasilingua of 1885 was to take everything from the natural languages, thus imitating the processes by which lingua franca, Chinook Jargon, and pidgin English had been created. His constituent languages are for the most part English, German, French, and Latin. One interesting principle is that for international roots, such as *nation,* the pronunciation shall follow the spelling rather than the reverse. Steiner's nouns have natural gender, with the ending *-o* for males, *-e* for females, *-a* for concrete things, *-u* for abstract ideas (*to homino, te femine, ta cita, ta modestiu:* "the man," "the woman," "the city," "modesty"). A four-case declensional system works at your own pleasure, by suffixes or prepositions (*to kingo, ton kingon,* "the king," subject and object; but "of the king" may be *tode kingode* or *de to kingo;* "to the king" may be *toby kingoby* or *by to kingo;* and even the accusative *ton kingon* may be replaced by *an to kingo*). Adjectives are compared Latin or English fashion: *bono, boniro, bonisto,* "good," "better," "best." Pronouns, prepositions and conjunctions all show a strong Latin influence (*mio, tüo; illo, isto, ipso; quo, que, qua; et, aut, sed, ergo, quando, ubi, ut*). Verbs display four "conjugations," but unlike those of Latin or French, these serve a highly practical purpose: *grander* is "to be big"; *grandir* is "to become big"; *grandar* is "to make big"; *grandor* "to be made big." A principle of vocabulary that was largely criticized at the time as indicating inability to make up his mind on the author's part, but which in the light of recent developments may yet supply an answer to our most vexing problems, is that of having synonyms from the two main branches used, Germanic and Latin-Romance. "Good" may in Pasilingua be *bono* or *guto,* at your pleasure; "God" is *Deo* or *Gotto;* "language" is *lingua* or *spracha;* "small" is *petito* or *littlo;* "often" is *saepe* or *oftis.* The implication is that each speaker will use the word that is closer to his language habits, but be able to recognize the other word. An extension of this principle may yet solve the great problem of proportional representation for the major world language groups. The Lord's Prayer in Pasilingua runs: "Patro miso, quo er in coela, nama tüa sanctore, kingdoma tüa kommire, tüa willu fairore sur erda ut in coela. Donnare misbi misan brodan taglian; pardonnare missas dettas uti mis pardonnars misosbi debitorosbi. . . . " It is a little surprising that this highly intelligent and thoroughly liberal system met with no widespread approval at the time of its presentation.

Eichhorn's Weltsprache of 1887 introduced a new principle, whereby each part of speech would be identifiable by its form, with nouns showing two syllables, adjectives three, pronouns one (with the additional proviso that they must begin with a consonant and end in a vowel), while verbs are endowed with a one-syllable root beginning and ending with a consonant, and prepositions must begin and end in a vowel. *Wiro* is "man" and *wira* is "woman"; *nikrile* is "black"; *sdo* is "this one" and *klo* is "that one." *Dok-* is the root of "to teach," and to this, arbitrary endings, often reminiscent of Japanese, are added (*mo dokiosho,* "I would have taught"; *du dokisen,* "to have taught"). Little interest seems to have attended Eichhorn's project.

But the time had now come for what is probably the most famous and successful of all constructed languages, Louis Lazarus Zamenhof's Esperanto. Born in Bialystok, then a town of Russian Poland, Zamenhof had been struck at an early age by the difficulties caused by language differences in his immediate surroundings. German, Russian, Polish, Yiddish, Lithuanian, all vied for supremacy in nineteenth-century Bialystok, and there was much hard feeling caused by racial, religious, and linguistic factors. Zamenhof's idea of an international language, based on absolute regularity and ease of grammar and suffixation plus a Romano-Germanic vocabulary, had been incubating since 1878, but it did not come to light until 1887, and then under a pseudonym, that of "Doktoro Esperanto," "Doctor Hopeful," and it was not until 1896 that the language took hold in western Europe.

The spread of Esperanto not as a theoretical exercise, but as a popular spoken tongue in the decades that followed was such as to warrant a fairly complete description of the language here. The alphabet makes provision for sounds which are invariably represented by a single symbol, and the accent in words of more than one syllable is always on the penult;

this, coupled with a simple syllabic arrangement, makes Esperanto a harmonious tongue, easy to speak, read, and spell. One drawback that has often been criticized is the use of suprascript signs (*ĉ, ĝ, ĥ, ĵ, ŝ, ŭ,* to indicate the sounds of English *ch, j, kh, s* in *pleasure, sh,* and *w,* respectively); these symbols, it is charged, complicate matters for printers in countries speaking languages, such as English, which use no suprascripts.

The Esperanto definite article is *la,* invariable like English "the." All nouns, without exception, end in *-o;* all adjectives in *-a;* all adverbs in *-e;* all infinitives in *-i.* Nouns and adjectives are made plural by the addition of *-j,* pronounced like English *y;* an accusative form is provided by adding *-n,* in both singular and plural: *la bona patro* and *la bonan patron* mean "the good father," the first as subject, the second as object; "the good fathers" is translated by *la bonaj patroj* and *la bonajn patrojn.* A verb, which ends in *-i* in the infinitive, shifts to *-as* in the present, *-is* in the past, *-os* in the future, *-us* in the conditional, *-u* in the imperative (*ami,* "to love"; *mi amas,* "I love"; *vi amis,* "you loved"; *li amos,* "he will love"; *ŝi amus,* "she would love"; *amu,* "love!"). Provision is made for word-formation by simple rules; a noun denoting a male, for instance, is turned into the corresponding feminine by the insertion of the suffix *-in-* (*patro,* "father"; *patrino,* "mother").

The vocabulary is a near-perfect blend of Germanic (including both German and English) and Latin-Romance, with plenty of international Greek, and very little in the way of other language groups. The Lord's Prayer in Esperanto runs as follows: "Patro nia, kiu estas en la ĉielo, sankta estu via nomo; venu regeco via; estu volo via, kiel en la ĉielo, tiel ankaŭ sur la tero. Panon nian ĉiutagan donu al ni hodiaŭ; kaj pardonu al ni ŝuldojn niajn, kiel ni ankaŭ pardonas al niaj ŝuldantoj; kaj ne konduku nin en tenton, sed liberigu nin de la malbono."

For one brought up in the western tradition, the appeal of Esperanto is hard to resist; yet Esperanto's first victories were won in nonwestern lands, notably in Russia, where it was at first welcomed in official circles, but later banned because of an article published by Tolstoy which aroused suspicion, in Tsarist circles, that Esperanto was a "subversive" movement. Even in its early years, Esperanto gave evidence of being a language well suited for the translation of literary works, as well as for the production of what one might call a "native" literature. When it finally reached France, in 1896, it met with a hearty welcome. Louis de Beaufront, who had been working for a dozen years at a language project of his own, called Adjuvanto, made the singular gesture of scrapping his own plan to become an ardent propagandist for Esperanto.

In the course of its somewhat checkered career, Esperanto has received not only the honors of an actual speaking population, but also a considerable measure of official recognition. It may be used internationally in telegrams, along with Latin. In 1921 it received the endorsement of the British Association for the Advancement of Science, over all dead and modern competitors. Its adoption as an international auxiliary language was seriously discussed at the old League of Nations in Geneva, and is periodically brought up at all sorts of international gatherings, including those of UNESCO. Enthusiastic Esperantists claim that the speakers of Esperanto number several million, and point to their flourishing and numerous clubs and periodicals scattered all over the world, from Japan to Brazil and from Norway to South Africa. In Gallup polls conducted in minor European countries, Esperanto turns out to be the second choice for an international tongue, with English as the first choice.

But, as is customary in human affairs, criticism of Esperanto began to arise not so much from without as from within. Zamenhof was charged on the one hand with not having been sufficiently "international" or "neutral" in his choice of a vocabulary, on the other with having granted admission to too many Germanic roots that have no true internationality (*tago* for "day" and *monato* for "month," for instance). Yet Esperanto also shows the beginnings of a system that may prove to be the solution of its own troubles, that of adopting roots from different sources to distinguish between meanings of what is, even in natural languages, the same word: *piedo,* for instance, is "foot" as a part of the body, but *futo* is "foot" as a measure.

At all events, Esperanto congresses frequently broke up in confusion, with schismatic movements arising from them. Among the best-known of these "Protestant" sects is Ido, an abbreviation of Esperantido, or "derived from Esperanto" (the *-id-* suffix means "descended from"). The differences between orthodox Esperanto and its many schismatic descendants may be described as trifling, but it is useless to deny that they weaken the movement for an international language by dispersing the energies of the interlinguists.

19. Attempted solutions: recent projects

The Esperanto-Ido Group—The Anglo-Latin Group—Representation for Slavic—An International Esperanto—Interlingua and Cosmoglotta

Esperanto and its descendants are characterized by a more or less arbitrary grammar, which is nevertheless reminiscent of the more general features of the western languages, and a vocabulary which is "neutral" or "international" to the extent that it takes its major elements from Latin, Greek, Romance, and Germanic.

Esperanto, however, opened up new vistas in language construction, even to its opponents. Some of them insisted that if various vocabularies could be blended, there was no reason why the same treatment should not be applied also to grammar, and all arbitrary, a priori features be completely excluded. This point of view is largely embodied in the most recent of constructed tongues to show signs of success, Interlingua.

In between, we have a welter of languages, many of them merely repetitious of what had already been accomplished, others displaying ingenious innovations. The same American Philosophical Society that in 1889 called for a congress of Aryan nations and drew upon itself the charge of racial discrimination from British sources also advocated a language for science and trade that would be completely phonetic as to spelling, close to Spanish or Italian as to pronunciation, close to English as to grammar, and would combine in its vocabulary the major elements of English, German, Latin-Romance, and Russian.

In 1893, Fred Mill came out with his Anti-Volapük or Mezzofanti-Sprache (Mezzofanti was a cardinal who had been one of the greatest linguists on record). This language ingeniously combines international connecting words, taken largely from Latin-Romance, with nouns, verbs, etc., of the speaker's own language, with the proviso, presumably, that each speaker will learn enough of the other speakers' nouns and verbs to be able at least to understand them. Thus an English speaker, a French speaker, an Italian, a Spaniard, and a Russian would utter the same sentence in the following five ways:

Io	no	know	u	es	tu	brother,	ma	io	think	ke	le	es	in	le	street.
"	"	savoir	"	"	"	frère,	"	"	croire	"	"	"	"	"	rue.
"	"	sapere	"	"	"	fratello,	"	"	credere	"	"	"	"	"	strada.
"	"	saber	"	"	"	hermano,	"	"	creer	"	"	"	"	"	calle.
"	"	znat'	"	"	"	brat,	"	"	dumat'	"	"	"	"	"	ulitsa.

The comparative principle employed by Interlingua today makes its first bow in Eugen Heintzeler's Universala of 1893, where German, Latin, English, French, Italian, Spanish, and Portuguese forms are laid side by side, and the form common to the majority of them is abstracted and put to use. In practice, this seemingly democratic majority rule means that the Latin-Romance tongues, being in the majority, will invariably win out. Even the addition of Russian to the picture does not change the situation. If English, German, and/or Russian happen to coincide with the majority, well and good; if not, so much the worse for English, German, and Russian. In a table containing *Abfall, desertio, desertion, désertion, diserzione, deserción* and *deserção,* it stands to reason that the isolated German form will go up in smoke, and *deserción* will be the will of the majority.

The principle of maximum internationality was claimed even by earlier followers of Volapük, like Woldemar Rosenberger who in 1902 produced Idiom Neutral. The Lord's Prayer in Idiom Neutral runs as follows: "Nostr patr kel es in sieli! Ke votr nom es sanktifiked; ke votr regnia veni; ke votr volu es fasied, kuale in siel, tale et su ter. Dona sidiurne a noi nostr pan omnidiurnik; e pardona a noi nostr debiti, kuale et noi pardon a nostr debtatori; e no induka noi in tentasion, ma librifika noi da it mal." A reformed version of Idiom Neutral, brought out in 1907, shows change, but no noticeable improvement.

Beyond this point, a description of the systems advanced in the course of the first half of the twentieth century would prove wearisome, by reason of their similarity of principle and structure. A partial list of the more important projects could be drawn up to include the following (a more complete listing will be found in the Bibliography and Index):

Hummler's Mundelingua of 1904 (*Ego hava ame,* "I love"; *Ero e va ame,* "he loved").

Molenaar's Universal of 1906 ("Patr nostr, qui es en ziel, ton nom ese sanktifizet, ton regn vene, ton voluntat ese fazet in ter kom in ziel").

Trischen's Mondlingvo of 1906 ("la patro, del patro, lan patro, las patros, dels patros, vivibes bone, al revidonti").

de Saussure's Lingwo Internaciona of 1907 ("Li estas hodie en koleroza humoro," "He is today in an angry mood"; "Vidwino havis du filinoin," "A widow had two daughters").

Seidel's Ile of 1909 ("Internatsional lingue musta korrespondan a du konditsiones: le musta essan kapabl di vast ekspansione e fassil lernebl").

Colas' (or Esperema's) Adjuvilo of 1910 ("Un ex meas amikos, qua habitan en Paris kun sua familio, havan multas infantos; quin filios e tri filiinos").

Ferranti's Simplo of 1911 ("Internatione lingo; contributo al studios dil internatione lingo pem simpligite foneticegrafice sistemo").

Kovalyov's Mezhdunarodny Nauchny Yazyk of 1911 (*li menzil fo patr,* "the father's house"; *zoal,* "animal"; *fagir,* "to eat"; *tawr,* "ox"; *halizir,* "salt"; *adelf,* "brother").

Nesmeyanov's Viva of 1913 ("Patr no ki es en ska, santanu to im, komu to regn, makru to vil ut en ska it on ge").

Lott's Mundelingua of 1917 (described as "une langue internationale anglo-latine").

Michaux' Romanal of 1917 ("Nos consideran sicut evidenti isti verites que omni homos estan creati pro vivar equali").

de Wahl's Occidental of 1922 ("It es un erra creder que li multita de systemas ha impedit li solution del problema").

de Saussure's Antido of 1924 ("Kita ti ciy bela knabino venis domew, shia patrino insultis shu, pro kio shi rukvenis tiente tarde dey la fonto"; "When that beautiful girl came home, her mother insulted her, because she had come back so late from the spring").

Talmey's Arulo (or Gloro) of 1924 ("La okulo vidis agri

devastita e sur oli la militof mult viktimi mutilita, oksidita"; "The eye saw fields laid waste, and on them war's numerous victims, mutilated and slain").

Lavagnini's Monario of 1925 ("El surio splenda in cielo et illumina el terre," "The sun shines in the sky and illuminates the earth"; "Filio el jardineri ha un roze," "The gardener's son has a rose"; "Avio vola in cielo, piwo nata en mar," "The bird flies in the sky, the fish swims in the sea"; "Gutto aqui kava el lapide," "A drop of water hollows out the stone").

Weisbart's Medial of 1925 ("Un Englo, un Franco ed un Deuto havit le taske pintir kamele. Le Englo voyajit ad Afrike for studiir le kamele in tisui doimie, le Franco gidit al zoologi jarden, ed le Deuto pintit on kamelo ex le profunde de sui psyke").

Milner's Cosman of 1927 ("Esperanto ut i lingue con crueli misfones e defectes nullim can conquer el munde").

Jespersen's Novial of 1928 ("Nusen Patro kel es in siele, mey vun nome bli sanktifika, mey vun regno veni, mey vun volio eventa sur tere kom in siele").

Wood's Interlingu of 1929 ("Til nu nul interlingu aev gan sukses, tamen an interlingu be nedic," "Till now no interlanguage has had success, yet an interlanguage is needed").

The most recent attempt to reach us is Heimer's Mondial of 1957, a poetic sample of which is:

Parla sempre de amor,	Speak always of love,
dica me que tu amara	tell me that you will love
me con tute tui ardor	me with all your ardor
tanque tu i yo vivara.	as long as you and I will live.
Non lontano e le dia	Not distant is the day
u nu sera via, via.	when we shall be away, away.

It may be added that the offerings come from many, not to say most, lands: France, Austria, Germany, Britain, the U.S.,

Poland, Italy, Russia, Czechoslovakia, Switzerland, Latvia, Brazil, Spain, Denmark, Sweden, Estonia, Holland, New Zealand, the Balearic Islands; one comes even from India, which offers *The Elements of Om;* another, from Vietnam, is entitled *Frater.*

One might even say a special word concerning the fancifulness of the names of these constructed tongues. Side by side with wearisome repetitions of the theme of Esperanto (Esperanta, Esperantida, Esperantido, Esperido, Espido, Espo, Esperema, Ispirantu, Spiranta, Aspiranto) and similar combinations (Adjuvanto, Antido, Anglido), we find such imaginative names as Adamitik, Ariadna, Corintic, Hom-Idyomo, Liana, Luftlandana, Orba, Panskrit, Sermo, Ulla. There are very short names like Ao, Eo, Esk, Ile, Is, Tal, Lips Kith, and very long ones like Carpophorophilus, Astegonagraphianek, Noematopasigraphielalie. There are names that sound like advertising slogans: Perfekt, Simplo, Serve, Viva, Unita, Clarison, Federal, Expreso, Geoglot, Homapar, and others that are all but unpronounceable: Dey Daynd, Lanopiküro, Mezvoio, Oiropapitschn, Patoiglob, Quji, Sehlerai, Tersboca.

The list is very far from complete. This, however, may be said of the overwhelming majority of systems devised in the last decade of the nineteenth and throughout the first half of the twentieth century: they are all inspired by the spirit of "the greatest ease to the greatest number," even if that "greatest number" means, in effect, only speakers of western tongues. The claim is often advanced by the creators of Interlingua that their tongue is such that it can be at least read (if not written and spoken) with ease by any western speaker. But the same claim may be advanced legitimately by practically any constructed tongue on our list. The real question, in the year of Our Lord 1958, is what happens when the speaker of a nonwestern tongue who has not had the blessings of western linguistic indoctrination comes up against a language of this type. The man who has some knowledge of

English, German, Latin, one or more Romance tongues, and international Greek roots does not really need an international language for purposes of scientific reading; conversely, while it may be true that he can read Cosmoglotta or Interlingua without previous preparation, the same holds true of Italian, Spanish, or Portuguese.

One interesting attempt to apply the principle of greater internationality appears in W. Cheshikhin's Nepo of 1910, in which the beginning of the Lord's Prayer runs: "Vatero nia, kotoryja estas in la njeboo, heiliga estu nomo via; kommenu regneo via; estu volonteo via, jakoe in la njeboo, ebene soe na la erdeo." Here pure Germanic, undefiled by Latin-Roman influences, supplies *vatero, heiliga, kommenu, ebene soe,* and *erdeo,* while Slavic appears in *kotoryja, njeboo, na* and *jakoe.* But the vast Afro-Asian world is still left completely out of the running, while it is undeniable that the Teutonic-Slavic admixture makes things harder for the Romance and even the English speaker.

Reverting for a moment to the more common type of twentieth-century constructed tongue, here is a sample of Cosmoglotta or Interlingue (not to be confused with the American Interlingua), a tongue that flourishes in European circles: "Li 2 may noi havet li plesura del visita de Dr. F. Schmolinsky, ex Germania, con su marita. Du semanes antey nor excellent propagandist, sr. Lienhard de Zürich, passat che nos pos un viage a München. Ex li raportes de nor visitatores noi aprendet con joya que hay un renascentie interlinguistic in Germania. Noi posse expectar tre bon resultates in ti land por li proxim tempor." For a western speaker of fair education, no translation is needed.

Neither do we need a translation for the American Interlingua version of the Lord's Prayer: "Nostre Patre qui es in le celos, que tu nomine sia sanctificate; que tu regno veni; que tu voluntate sia facite como in celo assi etiam in terra. Da nos hodie nostre pan quotidian, e pardona a nos nostre debitas como nos pardona a nostre debitores; e non duce nos in tentation, sed libera nos de malo; quia tue es le regno, e le potentia, e le gloria in sempiterno. Amen."

A special word concerning Interlingua and its creators is in order. Almost twenty years ago, a group of linguists, heavily subsidized by a very wealthy lady, undertook to construct an international language on a truly "scientific" basis. The "scientific" method consisted of carefully comparing both vocabulary and grammatical forms offered by English, Latin, French, Spanish, Italian, Portuguese, German, and Russian, and isolating and adopting those features and forms which the majority of these languages held in common. The result could have been predicted from the outset: since Latin-Romance holds a five-to-three majority over any possible combination of Germanic and Slavic, what comes out is a pan-Romance tongue, accessible to Germanic and Slavic speakers to the extent that the Germanic and Slavic tongues have adopted Latin-Romance elements. To make assurance doubly sure, where the Latin and Romance vocabularies did not coincide, and there was consequently no clear-cut majority for any given form, the constructors simply adopted the Latin word (as indicated in the Lord's Prayer by *etiam,* "also," *hodie,* "today," *quia,* "for").

But the major proponent of Interlingua, Dr. Alexander Gode, presents a defense and justification of his system which is well worth considering. His international language, he claims, is meant primarily for use in written form at scientific congresses (indeed, it has already been so used, and with seeming success); the language of science and technology, he goes on to add, is purely and simply a conglomeration of western tongues, and particularly of Latin and Greek international roots, with next to no participation by Slavic, Oriental, or even the popular element of Germanic languages. The Russian, Japanese, Indian, or African scientist who wishes to attend a scientific gathering must perforce have learned the essential western scientific vocabulary in order to have taken even the first steps in his profession; therefore, the adoption of a western international language works no hardship on him whatsoever.

A further point that he strikingly illustrates is this: we can grant proportional representation to the major Oriental tongues (Chinese, Japanese, Persian, Malay, Arabic, and Hindustani), but these tongues are mutually incomprehensible. Without special study, the speaker of Hindustani will be just as much at a loss before a Chinese as before a Latin word. Hence, by insisting on broadening our international base, we run a decided risk of making our language comprehensible to no one, westerners or Orientals.

By way of demonstration, he offers the following passage, first in Interlingua as it is, next in Interlingua as it would be if proportional representation were granted to the Asian group:

"Le sol dice: 'Io me appella sol. Io es multo brillante. Io me leva al est, e quando io me leva, il es die. Io reguarda per tu fenestra con mi oculo brillante como le auro, e io te dice quando il es tempore a levar te. E io te dice: "Pigro, leva te. Io non brilla a fin que tu resta al lecto a dormir, sed que tu te leva e labora, que tu lege e que tu te promena." ' " (This should be readily understood by any speaker of a western language, including English. But just in case, the translation goes: "The sun says: 'My name is sun. I am very brilliant. I rise in the east, and when I rise, it is day. I look through your window with my eye as bright as gold, and I tell you when it is time to get up. And I say to you: "Lazy one, get up. I don't shine so that you may stay in bed sleeping, but that you may get up and work, that you read and go walking." ' ")

Note now the transition to an intercontinental version:

"Mata-hari yu: 'Wo-ti nama mata-hari. Wo taihen brillante. Wo leva wo a est, dan toki wo leva wo, ada hari. Wo miru per ni-ti fenestra sama wo-ti mata brillante como kin, dan wo yu ni toki ada tempo a levar ni. Dan wo yu ni: "Sust, leva ni. Wo non brilla sam-rap ni tomaru a toko a nemuru, sed wo brilla sam-rap ni leva ni, dan que ni suru kam, ni yomu, dan ni aruku." ' "

The first point is that no westerner will even begin to understand this without very special study. The second, and perhaps even more important point is that the Malay speaker, who supplied *mata-hari* and *sam-rap,* will not understand the Chinese *wo-ti, ni,* and *yu,* or the Japanese *taihen* and *nemuru;* nor will his words be understood by the speakers of the latter languages.

Summary of Part 2

It must be stressed that our survey, lengthy though it may appear, is far from complete, particularly with respect to constructed languages. Man is an ingenious creature; to what person who has devoted serious attention to the subject has it not occurred that he (or even she) could devise a better mousetrap than the ones already devised, or at the very least suggest some improvement, however slight, upon the one he favored? How many constructed international languages, bereft of any support outside of their constructor, have not died a-borning? Examples could be multiplied, like that of the letter received from South America by a Jesuit friend of the writer, composed in a language which baffled its recipient, but which I believe I interpreted correctly as an attempt to combine Spanish and English into a new constructed tongue for international use.

The historical background of the international language, however, displays much more than attempts to build artificial tongues, and the people of today, if they feel called upon to solve the problem, ought not to overlook the other possibilities: the adoption of a national language, great or small, just as it stands or modified as to spelling, grammar, or vocabulary; the possibility of combining two or more existing languages into a mixed language that will partake of the characteristics of both or all; the selection of two or more national languages, designed to live in a state of peaceful coexistence and to serve either specific areas or the entire world. If a constructed tongue is preferred merely for reasons of "neutrality," then it seems obvious that the choice should fall on an a priori language, having no connection with any known tongue, but rather serving as a brand-new vehicle of human thought. If existing languages form the base of the selected tongue, what languages shall they be? The tongues of western civilization, or the tongues of the entire world, or at least of the major language groups? To what extent should arbitrary, a priori principles enter the grammatical structure of such a tongue? Or should the grammar, as well as the vocabulary, be a blend? Should any attention be paid to the principle of proportional representation, or to the interesting thesis, so gruffly discarded by the interlinguists of the past, that for certain words an entire series of synonyms be used, offering each language group its own spoken choice, with the proviso that there will be recognition of the other words of the synonym series? Would it be possible, for example, to adopt the general structure of Esperanto, but with the word for "man" represented indifferently by *viro, homo, manno, ĉeloveko, ĵeno, mardo, otoko, orango,* and *ragilo,* to satisfy the speakers of Latin, Romance, Germanic, Slavic, Chinese, Hindustani, Japanese, Indonesian, and Arabic, respectively? Could we expect that in due course of time such an eight- or nine-word series of synonyms would develop semantic differences leading to different uses and shades of meaning, as happened with Latin *vir* and *homo,* Greek *aner* and *anthropos,* German *Mann* and *Mensch,* Russian *chelovek* and *muzhchina*?

The eventual choice will in large part be determined by our final concept of the function of an international language. Is it to be merely an aid for international communications of a limited type, such as inquiring about the way to your hotel or asking for a pound of sausage, or is it to become a true language, capable of supplanting the national tongues in every field, including even literature and poetry? Is it to be a language for scientific congresses, appearing largely in written form, or a spoken tongue for general use? Is it to be handled as a cultural tool, like high-school Latin, or as a language of everyday communications, used on the radio, in television, and in spoken films? In short, do we want a language for limited or widespread use?

The discussion of this all-important question has been postponed and soft-pedaled long enough. It has to be brought out into the open, because our ultimate choice will largely hinge upon it.

The other all-important issue in connection with the international language is the method by which it is to be achieved. The language for the world has far too long been at the mercy of movements of the fad or hobby type, with circles and clubs and periodicals and congresses reminiscent of philatelic societies in their approach and of political organizations in their relentless insistence that each one of them possesses the sole perfect solution of the world's language problems. A new outlook and a new method of approach are essential if any lasting results are to be gained.

3

THE PROBLEM IN THE FUTURE: THE SOLUTION

20. A partial or a complete solution?

A World Language for Whom?—Restricted or General?—Read and Written, or Spoken and Understood?—A Language for Science—A World Language for All

As we advance into the second half of the twentieth century, we find that the movement for a world language is keener, more aggressive than it has ever been, with widespread recognition of the need for a prompt and satisfactory solution. But we also find that at no time in the past has it been so lacking in unity of purpose and method. It is not merely that there are many clashing ideas and projects, marked by varying degrees of intransigence, with natural, combined, modified, and constructed languages all being actively sponsored by their respective advocates. The rift goes deeper than the choice of one tongue from among the many. There are involved two conflicting philosophies, two adverse ideologies, as was the case from the very beginning.

In the days of Descartes the controversy revolved around the question whether the international language should be restricted to the philosophers and scholars, or extended to the peasants. Today, the physical scientists largely replace the philosophers and scholars of the seventeenth century, while Descartes's peasants are represented by the masses of human beings who are neither illiterate nor overly educated and specialized—tourists and business people, artisans and migrants, manual and agricultural workers, soldiers and sailors and airmen, as well as professors and teachers and students and diplomats and missionaries, who might be expected to follow the old philosophical and scholarly tradition. The big question, though it is constantly soft-pedaled, is whether the international language shall be for all of them, or for a minority of intellectuals. Do we wish, in the matter of language, to apply the democratic standards and procedures that have so much vogue in modern politics, sociology, and education, or do we wish to revert to a policy of education only for an elite?

Before hastening to answer on an emotional basis, it may be well to examine the arguments that are advanced by the restrictionists. The advocates of Interlingua are an excellent illustration of this school of thought. Their language, constructed on scientific principles, is frankly discriminatory, both in its structure and in its aims. Structurally, it considers only the languages of western civilization to be of importance, and discards without mercy all elements, both of grammar and vocabulary, that do not stem from occidental culture. This might at first glance seem to be connected with unpleasant traits of racialism or, to put the best face on the matter, upon assumptions of cultural superiority. But that is not the underlying spirit of Interlingua, which aims to be of service to all mankind. Rather it is predicated upon the firm belief that the age which we have recently entered is one dominated by the physical sciences; that these sciences, having originated in the West, and more specifically in Europe and North America, have perforce taken as the basis of their terminology the words and roots of the western languages, particularly Greek and Latin. All this, of course, is undeniable. From these premises, the sponsors of Interlingua go on to assert that there is no possibility of a change in the status quo within the foreseeable future. The terminology of modern technology is incurably western, and western it must forever remain. Any student of this technology whose native language happens to be something other than the tongues of the

West must simply learn the terminology as it stands, even if he wishes to apply it to his own language.

Let us couch this proposition in the words of Interlingua's leading proponent, Dr. Alexander Gode: "Have I told you about my idea that Interlingua should be exploited as a standard for the forms under which technical terminologies are to be developed in minor and 'underprivileged' languages? It would be disastrous for the terminology of nuclear physics, for instance, to be evolved in Burmese and Arabic and what have you after the principles of loan translation rather than in accordance with occidental standards." Dr. Gode goes on to point out that if you write for a group of specialists (doctors, electrical engineers, biochemists, molecular spectroscopists, etc.), you can reach perhaps 55 per cent of them in English, 2 or 3 per cent in Russian, 1 per cent in Japanese, but over 95 per cent (at least in the field of medicine) in Interlingua.

To these considerations one might object that in the world of the future the amount of participation and contribution to scientific progress that will be made by any given segment of the human race is very much a matter of conjecture, and that if Arabic-speaking scientists are able to contribute both to science and to its nomenclature in the twenty-first century as they did during the Middle Ages, they should not be prevented or restricted from so doing.

But something more fundamental is involved. Is the language for the world to be merely a language for scientists and scientific interchange? Are all the nonscientists of the world, who are a vast majority, to receive no consideration of their needs and wants? Descartes spoke of peasants, who in his day were overwhelmingly illiterate and attached to the soil. The descendants of those peasants today are largely literate, and many of them have occasions for international contacts of one kind or another, even if it is merely to serve as forces of occupation in a foreign land.

It can be argued that the scientists are those who need the international language the most. It can also be argued that they are the ones who need it least. The philosophers and scholars of Descartes's day were all acquainted with many languages. If the worse came to the worst, they could communicate in Latin. The scientists of today, particularly in countries outside the United States, have all received an education which includes foreign languages, both Classical and modern. In a pinch, they, too, can communicate with one another in English, or French, or German, and if what is claimed about their common western scientific terminology holds true, then they will have little trouble filling in the gaps. The need of the nonscientist, of the soldier stationed in a strange land, of the migrant worker who must travel from place to place in search of a livelihood, even of the tourist who travels for pleasure or for education, seems far greater.

One of the arguments most frequently used on behalf of a world language is that it will allay antipathies and prejudices. In the case of scientists and of the more educated segment of the population generally, these antipathies and prejudices have already largely ceased to exist. It is the less cultured portions of the populations of all lands that must be reached with the spirit of international good will. It has always been recognized that the educated of all lands find it easy to get along with one another, whether they meet in diplomatic conclaves or at scientific gatherings. They may, even by deliberate intent, inflame and precipitate race riots and nationalistic outbursts, but they seldom take direct part in such disgraceful demonstrations, for they personally tend to shrink from violence. If the more brutish, less educated portions of the world populations can in some way be given the understanding that those who do not speak their language are nevertheless human beings like themselves, we may hope to cut down some of the more malignant manifestations of man's intolerance toward his own kind.

The world language should be a language for the world. It should be the sort of thing that is not restricted to any nation or group of nations, or to any social, cultural, or professional group. It should not be a device for the reading of scientific or learned papers, read and understood with difficulty by a polyglot audience, but rather a common tongue, used with absolute ease and fluency by everybody, spoken and written with the same ease with which the bulk of the population of any civilized land today speaks and writes its own language. It should emphatically not be a classroom exercise, of the type so often witnessed in our high schools and colleges. It should not be a little secret language, spoken and written by a few adepts for the bewilderment of outsiders, but a tool of expression as freely accessible to all as is English in the United States, or Russian in the Soviet Union. Only in that fashion can the international language perform its proper function, which is to supply an absolutely free means of communication and interchange of ideas among all of the world's people, whatever their station in life.

Can such a language be achieved? There is no doubt whatsoever that it can. Can it be achieved by handling it in the fashion in which Volapük was handled at an earlier date, and Basic English, Esperanto, and Interlingua are handled today? No, because in that fashion it will forever remain the property and prerogative of a few enthusiasts, to the exclusion of at least 99 per cent of the world's peoples. Can it be achieved by handling it as foreign languages are handled in our American high schools and colleges, or even as they are handled in the linguistically more enlightened countries of Europe? No, because that is superlatively the hard way to go about learning languages, and only a chosen few can profit by it.

To make the international language a reality, we must

apply the two lessons painfully learned through centuries of experience: 1. Any and all languages can be learned with equal ease if one starts early enough and keeps up one's practice; 2. There is no substitute for compulsion from above in the matter of what is to be learned.

21. Two great delusions: logic and ease

Descartes and His Followers—The Search for Logic—The Search for Ease—Overlooking the True Nature of Language—Basic Ease of All Languages to Their Own Speakers—Bilingualism and Multilingualism

The great preoccupation of the a priori school was, as we have seen, with creating a language that would follow the "logical" classification of thought and ideas. This proved to be a will-of-the-wisp on two separate scores. In the first place, all sorts of classifications of ideas are possible, and what is a logical pigeonhole for an idea or the word that represents it to one man need not be at all the proper pigeonhole to another. Historical misnomers appear by the score to inform us that what seemed a proper classification and description at one time turned out later to be erroneous (three cases in point are "Indian" for a native of America; "atom," which means "indivisible," for what later on turned out to be fissionable; "oxygen," or "that which gives rise to acids," when it is actually hydrogen that enters into the composition of all acids).

The seventeenth century, and other centuries before it, thought they had achieved perfect knowledge of the universe, with the consequent possibility of perfect analysis and classification of thoughts and concepts. It remained for the twentieth, with its ever-broadening relativistic discoveries, to find out that man's information about his universe is still woefully imperfect.

Aside from this sin of origin, however, the a priori school made the bad error of trying to treat as a logical entity that which is by its very nature illogical. Language is based on the acceptance of symbols, and symbols, being unreal, cannot be logical.

There was, however, another factor that led to the general discrediting of the a priori methodology. A logical language, even if it could be achieved, would present enormous difficulty and an unbearable strain on the memory and faculty of association of the average individual. Hence, people turned with a sigh of relief from systems that had no connection whatsoever with the processes they had learned to associate with speech to the systems which displayed some sort of associative link with the known spoken tongues.

This, in turn, led to another frantic search, the search for the greatest ease to the greatest number. "That language is best which is easiest for the majority" became the slogan, even before Jespersen made it official.

It is this process of seeking ease that colors most of our thinking about the international language today. Esperantists extol their very simple grammar, which presents so few complications that anyone can learn it in half an hour. Interlinguists bestow glowing words upon their international vocabulary, which anyone (that is, anyone brought up with English or a Romance language) can recognize at a glance. When the natural tongues are mentioned as possibilities, it is pointed out that one is easier because it has simple sounds, another because it has few exceptions to its grammatical rules, a third because its vocabulary is already international. Conversely, certain languages are discarded because they are "difficult," in sounds, grammar, or vocabulary.

Difficult for whom? For foreigners who have to learn them, obviously. There is no case on record where a language in its spoken form has been considered difficult by its own speakers. To the native speaker, who has learned it from childhood, by the natural, spontaneous process of imitation and repetition, every language in the world is easy. No proof is needed of the fact that Chinese and Russian children of six speak and understand Chinese and Russian as readily as the American child of the same age speaks and understands English.

Beyond the child stage, once speaking and understanding reflexes are fully formed, the story is altogether different, for then language learning becomes a conscious, not a reflex process; the intellective faculties rather than the ability to mimic and memorize come into play; and all sorts of associations are built up, so that a new language is judged to be easy or difficult to the extent that it coincides or fails to coincide with previously set language habits. To the two-year-old American child, learning spoken Chinese would be as simple as learning spoken English; but the same child at twelve will find Chinese extremely difficult, and will far prefer a language like German and French, to which he can tie his acquired English by reason of similarities in sounds, word-order, or vocabulary.

This has been known all along, but in a confused, hazy sort of way. It has long been fashionable for the children of the European privileged classes to be brought up by foreign governesses who would speak to them only in the foreign tongue, and it invariably turned out that children brought up in this fashion would speak, easily, fluently, naturally, without a trace of accent, three, four, or five different languages.

But it was also believed that something similar could be achieved by putting an older child in a high-school class and giving him intensive instruction in the grammar, vocabulary, and literature of the foreign language. In a few rare cases this worked. In the majority of cases, what came out was a person who would possess grammatical information, reading ability, sometimes even the ability to write in the foreign language, but whose handling of the spoken tongue left a good deal to be desired.

In recent times, a discovery as obvious as that of Columbus's egg was made. If you want children to learn a foreign tongue so that they will speak and understand it like natives, start them off young—the younger the better. Our more progressive educational circles are now working on this theory, putting foreign languages into the kindergartens and elementary schools, where they properly belong if what is wanted is a conversational knowledge of the language. The results are bound to be satisfactory.

The principle involved is that all languages are easy to those who learn them from childhood. This principle, however, applies only to the spoken language, not to its written counterpart. In writing, languages have intrinsic ease and intrinsic difficulty, based on the relation which the written form bears to the spoken. Where the written form of the language is thoroughly phonetic (that is to say, where the actual sounds of the language are accurately isolated, and each one is given an individual written symbol to represent it) it is easy to learn to read and write. Where the spelling does not accurately reflect the sound, as in English, or where there is no connection whatsoever between written symbols and spoken sounds, as in Chinese (the Chinese characters are like our $-sign, not like our written word "dollar"; they represent ideas, not sounds), it is difficult to learn to read and write even when one speaks and understands the language fluently.

This being the case, the international language does not have to be particularly "easy" for anyone, nor does it have to be linked with familiar languages. Learned in spoken form at the proper, or child, stage, it will be found by the child-learners to be just as easy (or just as difficult, for that matter) as any of the languages they are actually in the process of learning at their mothers' knees. The only element of ease we should be preoccupied with is that of making the written form of the language completely phonetic, with a set of individual symbols each one of which will correspond to one of the sounds of the spoken language, and to that sound only.

Under the circumstances, the business of making the international language one of the greatest ease to the greatest number becomes sheer nonsense. Any language, natural or constructed, will be learned equally well by child learners. If its spelling is thoroughly phonetic, it will be learned with speed, accuracy, and ease in written form when the time comes to teach the child to read and write.

Dr. Wilder Penfield, Director of the Montreal Neurological Institute, calls language learning "the human brain's first miracle." He claims that by conditioned reflexes, and with no effort, a child can learn two or three languages. He also warns that after the ten-to-fourteen-year-old period "the brain becomes senescent so far as language-learning is concerned."

The experiment of discovering what is the linguistic saturation point of the individual has never been tried. How many different languages, all started from early childhood, can be absorbed, learned, repeated and understood, and to what degree can control over them be retained in later life?

The maximum number of such languages that have come to my own notice is three, though I have it on hearsay that four, five, and even six are quite possible. Let me again stress that what I mean is languages spoken with absolute native-speaker accent and fluency, not languages handled with a foreign accent, however slight, and with hesitation over words and forms, however fleeting. Polyglots (people who can speak, understand, read, and write, in some fashion or other, anything from two to a dozen languages) are fairly numerous; but our discussion is not concerned with them.

On the other hand, people who handle two or more languages with absolute ease and accuracy, subject only to the disabilities that would be inherent in native speakers, are somewhat rarer. Almost invariably investigation discloses that they started speaking the two or more languages they handle like natives, not in high school or college, not in a Berlitz or Intensive Language class, but in very early childhood.

Very recently I had occasion to observe a little girl of four, whose father is American and whose mother is French. Subject to the limitations of a four-year-old child, both her French and her English were impeccable. The miracle of the situation (and it is an unexplained miracle, in this and all similar cases) is that her French was not in any way influenced by the fact that her father's French, though fluent, was not of the 100 per cent native-speaker variety; neither was her English in any way influenced by her mother's heavy French accent.

In another instance, a French colleague of mine and his French wife, both of them speaking English grammatically, but with an unmistakable French accent, have brought up a family of four children, whose French and English are both as perfect as it is possible for native languages to be perfect. Here the miraculous sixth sense of the growing child must have warned them that while they should slavishly imitate their parents' French, they should at the same time avoid imitating their English, giving preference instead to the English of their teachers and schoolmates.

J. P. McEvoy, Roving Editor of *Reader's Digest,* who is himself an accomplished linguist and student of languages, is responsible for the most comprehensive and successful experiment in this field that has yet come to my direct notice. Spending part of his time in Paris, part in Havana, and part in the United States, he undertook to have his two daughters trained by native governesses and companions in French, Spanish, and English. Pat and Peggy handle French like Parisiennes, Spanish like better-class Cuban *señoritas,* and English like cultured New Yorkers, without the slightest trace of hesitation, confusion, or mutual interference. To date, they are my best living proof that not merely two, but at least three languages can be imparted to the young child with absolute success. They also constitute utter refutation of the theory, frequently advanced in certain pedagogical circles, that bilingualism or multilingualism interferes with a child's psychological or intellectual development, for they are psychologically normal and, intellectually, at least on a par with other young ladies their age. They are now, in their teen-age, acquiring Russian, and I think I can confidently predict that their Russian, however well and thoroughly they learn it, will never quite equal their English, French, and Spanish.

How many languages could be successfully imparted before ten is still in doubt. The point I am interested in making is that at least two languages can be acquired with equal ease and fluency in the first decade of any individual's life, and that point has been demonstrated beyond the shadow of a doubt. If one of these languages were the national tongue of each country, and the other an international tongue designated to serve the purposes of linguistic exchange throughout the world, there could be absolutely no doubt that the second tongue would be spoken and understood as thoroughly as the first.

22. The problem of the present generation

No Ease for the Adult Learner—His Two Alternatives—Phonetization of the International Language—Correcting Basic Errors—The New vs. *the Old Generation*

All that has been said in the previous chapter is fine for the children, for those who are being born as we write, or who are about to be born. Their problem of world communications will be easily and painlessly solved. But what of the present generation, of those who have achieved adulthood and are beyond the reach of formal education?

This is the true crux of the situation, the shoal on which all past attempts to achieve a world language have been wrecked. In each century, from the seventeenth to the present, the adults of each generation have behaved as if the problem concerned themselves, and themselves alone. They have utterly refused to view it in the light of future world history.

Each time the magic word "ease" has been mentioned, it has been invested with a highly emotional semantic charge. To each speaker who uttered it, to each listener who heard it, to each reader who read it, "ease" has meant "what is easy to me, and to me alone."

Not one, but two facets of subjectivity have been uppermost. On the narrower plane, each world-language planner has thought of the international language in terms of something that would be easy to learn, easy to assimilate, by himself, and at his existing, adult level. To a grownup raised in an English or Romance tradition, with an English or Romance language at his disposal, something based on Latin, Greek, English, and the Romance languages is relatively easy, since it falls in with his pre-established language concepts, with the language he speaks and those he is likely to have acquired in the course of his education. Anything else is correspondingly difficult.

But apart from that, the adult is accustomed, sad though it may be to have to confess it, to going about the business of learning languages in the hard way. From the time he entered high school and began to take up, as one of his school chores, the study of French, Spanish, Latin, German, or whatever else he might choose, he became accustomed to viewing language learning as an exercise in mastering grammatical rules, in memorizing a vocabulary, in translating from the language he already knew into the language he was trying to acquire. This, needless to say, colors all of his thinking about languages and the learning of languages. It is difficult for him to view the international language as anything but the same school chore, the same weary process of deliberate study and drill.

Yet the success of the international language demands that it be imparted, from earliest childhood, by perfectly natural methods, by hearing and speaking and repeating—in short, by precisely the same process by which one learns one's own native tongue. On the whole, this can be successfully done only by children.

The adult, who views the international language as something primarily designed for himself, shrinks from the simplicity of this solution which is designed to work with absolute certainty for the world's future generations, but threatens to leave him out in the cold. The old, familiar, petulant query "But what about me?" rings from every side whenever such a solution is mentioned. Selfishly, the adult seeks a solution which will work easily for himself, a language that will be easy to learn by the old traditional language-learning methods, and that will coincide as largely as possible with his own set language habits. He therefore seeks a simplified grammar, forgetting that all grammars are simple to those who acquire their functioning from childhood; and an international vocabulary, forgetting that in a world in which there are so many languages of so many different types, no vocabulary can be internationally familiar to all.

In this breathless quest for ease, simplicity, and internationality, the generations succeed one another, and nothing is accomplished. The international language is always a mirage, just beyond arm's reach.

"That is easy which is familiar." But what is familiar to one is not necessarily familiar to another. It is amazing to what degree this type of utterly subjective thinking prevails, even in scholarly linguistic circles. A great name in the field of the development of the Romance languages, for instance, states that it is inconceivable that illiterate Roman soldiers and Gaulish peasants, in the days of the Roman Empire, could have spoken Latin, with its case-endings and verb-endings. My learned colleague thinks that because he had difficulty in learning the Latin declensions and conjugations when he first entered high school, the soldiers and peasants of the early Christian era encountered the same difficulties. He forgets that in the present-day world there are populations that were until recently largely illiterate, like those of Russia and Lithuania, yet which speak languages having case-endings and verb-endings just as complex (to us of the west) as those of Latin. The point is that the illiterate Romans and Gauls did not learn these inflectional forms as paradigms out of a grammar; they learned them in set contexts at their mothers' knees, and thereafter used them automatically in the same contexts. An illiterate Russian peasant (if any are left in these days of enlightenment) will correct the foreigner using a wrong case-form, though he will be utterly unable to tell him the grammatical reason why, or, for that matter, tell him the name of the case that should be used. But he will tell him "This is the way to say it, because this is the way we have always said it."

If the international language ever gets to be properly viewed as something primarily designed for the future generations, what will be the role of the existing adults?

Shorn of their selfish desire to have things in the way to which they are accustomed, they will be faced with a double choice. They can either learn the international language in the only way in which they, as adults, can learn it—the old, traditional way of grammar, vocabulary, and translation, aided, however, by the most modern methodology that we now have at our disposal, a methodology that stresses the spoken and conversational aspect of language; or they can live out their lives in blissful monolingual unconcern, since the existing languages will continue in full national use throughout the world for years, and even centuries, far beyond the normal life expectancy of any individual living today.

If they select the first alternative, they can attend up-to-date adult classes where the international language will be taught, in precisely the same fashion that adults attend classes in French, or German, or Russian, or any foreign language. They will not learn the new language as easily, or as painlessly, as their own children who will be acquiring it in kindergarten or elementary school, but they will learn it as well as they could learn any tongue at the adult stage.

If they choose to ignore the international tongue, no one need object. It will be some decades before the international language begins to make serious inroads upon the national tongues, and in the course of those decades many of the current generation will retire or die. But as the people unequipped with the world tongue gradually disappear from the world's scene, their place will be taken by their own children, who will speak, fluently, easily, and naturally, not only their own native tongue, but a tongue common to the entire world as well.

Does this mean that we are to be totally unconcerned with the problem of ease in connection with the international tongue?

As we have seen, while there is no intrinsic ease or difficulty in spoken languages, there is definite inherent ease in the correspondence of the written with the spoken tongue. This means that whatever tongue is chosen, natural or constructed, it must be phonetically spelled. Constructed tongues generally are. Natural, national tongues generally are not. This in turn means that if the choice falls upon a national language, like English or French, that language must be ruthlessly phonetized for international purposes.

In other respects, the question of ease does not exist. Rather, there is a question of general preference. If the representatives of the majority of the world's peoples betoken a preference for one language, or type of language, there is no reason why this preference should not dictate the ultimate choice. Perfection has never been a characteristic of language, and it is useless to seek it. Natural languages, such as English or Russian, are far from perfect, yet they serve their purpose.

The quest for perfection and ease is the foe, not the auxiliary, of the international language. It is the thing that has caused wide rifts in the ranks of those who have given serious attention to the problem, and has broken them up into conflicting schools, each working at cross-purposes with the rest. What the world needs is not a perfect, or an easy, world language. It is simply *a* world language.

23. Present and future status of the main contenders

English vs. *Russian—Is Chinese a Possibility?—The Resurgence of French and German—The Claims of Spanish and Italian—What of the Smaller Languages?—Status of the Classical and Constructed Tongues—Does Consciousness Exist?*

The world emphatically does not need additional candidates for the post of international language. With 2,796 natural tongues, and 600 or more constructed languages, all the elements for an immediate choice are at hand.

Zonal languages of the Stalin variety are merely a recognition of the status quo, and offer no true solution. Combinations of zonal languages, as envisaged by Thommeret, present the same unsatisfactory feature, plus the difficulty inherent in learning three or four different tongues. The "Bilingual World" made up of English and French (or of any two languages, for that matter) might be an excellent thing for the speakers of those languages, but for anyone else it would impose a double burden of language learning, and resolve itself into a trilingual situation. Simplicity and efficiency demand that no one be required to master more than one tongue in addition to his own.

This means that if things are to be done speedily and well, the world's choice will have to fall upon a single language, natural or constructed, which will serve the purposes of international exchanges and run side by side with each national language in each country. What shall that language be?

It is useless to deny that despite the vast number of natural languages at our disposal, only a handful will be seriously considered by the world's peoples. Yet the "dark horse" possibility is there, as at a political convention. Despite the large number of constructed tongues that have been and are being proposed, only two or three enjoy sufficient popularity to be known, at least by name, beyond the circle of their immediate proponents.

Leading the field, by reason of their political, military and economic preponderance, are English and Russian. Chinese, as the tongue of the greatest mass of people on earth, must be considered. French, the former language of diplomacy and international culture; German, numerically and in other important respects the leading language of the European continent; Spanish, the tongue of great areas of the New World; Italian, the language of music and art—all have their claims. We should not, of course, forget such great Oriental tongues as Japanese, Hindustani, Indonesian, and Arabic, but the factor of world-wide distribution is against them. In the case of all these languages, particularly the two world leaders, English and Russian, the adverse factor of international jealousies and the charge of cultural imperialism must be taken into account, and this opens the way for the consideration of "dark horses," small, obscure tongues, unaffiliated with major language groups, and against which no charge of cultural imperialism can conceivably be raised.

Among the constructed tongues, there are at the present moment only two that can advance the claim of having achieved some measure of success and general acceptance. They are Esperanto, with its variants and offshoots, such as Ido, and Interlingua.

In an international linguistic congress, there is little doubt that the first vote of the representatives of English-speaking countries would go to English. How many non-English-speaking representatives would join them is a matter of conjecture. English has displayed a mighty power of penetration into practically all lands, but even while it continues to expand in numerous areas, there are signs of recession elsewhere, and not only behind the Iron Curtain. Mexico and other Latin-American countries object to too many English-language billboards. French newspapers protest at the invasion of English terms like "standing," "pep," *teuf* (for "tough"), *trilleur* (for "thriller"), "living room," "week-end," "knockout," *skoot* (for "scout"). Russia, which forces the replacement of English-language courses with Russian in the satellite states, barely accepts "O.K." The Philippines, South Africa and Israel are in the process of abolishing English as an official tongue.

Most distressing, from the standpoint of English as an international tongue, is the news that comes from Asia. While the Bandung conference did use English as its main language, Ceylon drops English as an official language in favor of Singhalese and Tamil, Pakistan replaces it with Urdu and Bengali, India not only drops English road-names, but replaces English with Hindi in the secondary schools, and this despite the fact that Nehru advocates the continuation of the English-language tradition for practical uses. At the same time, the number of newspapers published in India in English falls behind those published in Hindi.

Nevertheless, English continues to be the first choice in the high schools and universities of practically all countries of the western world. It is perhaps an exaggeration to say, as does a Yugoslav newspaper, that 600 million people can be reached with English, but the figure is probably not too far off.

Russian is definitely a language on the make. Restricted not too many years ago to little more than half the population of the Soviet Union, it is now expanding in all directions, among the satellite countries and in the East. But Russian encounters hostility and rejection at the borders of the Communist world. It has gained relatively few students in the west, and practically no one outside the Soviet domain would care to sponsor it as an international tongue.

French, which has recently lost considerable ground, is still a formidable contender. Relying on the weight of tradition and cultural prestige, it can also point to its bridge function between east and west, since neither the adherents of English nor those of Russian would regard it with the same uncompromising aversion with which they view each other's languages. While French does not possess the mass of speakers that other languages can boast of, it is nevertheless native to nearly 70 million people and is handled fluently by additional millions who enjoy the distinction of being the most cultured, and therefore most effective elements of their respective countries. It has of late become fashionable for supporters of French to hitch their wagon to the rising star of English, and advocate some sort of Anglo-French bilingualism. This probably weakens rather than strengthens their position, since in any such combine English would be the dominant partner, while the Communist world, which might be persuaded to accept French alone, would resent the Anglo-French condominium as much as it would resent straight English.

The standing of other great tongues is definitely influenced by their respective drawbacks. Spanish is primarily a Western Hemisphere language (as is Portuguese), while the great cultural traditions of German and Italian are at the present moment obscured by the lack of political, military, and economic power of the major nations that speak them. The great Asiatic languages, Chinese, Japanese, Arabic, Hindustani, Indonesian, are removed from the scene of major world activity, at least for the moment, hampered by widespread illiteracy, save for Japanese, and divided by dialectal differences among their speakers, again with the same exception.

Dark-horse candidates among the minor languages are as numerous as the languages themselves, but the embarrassment of the choice among them would be truly impressive. A good many among them are subject to the same charge of partiality toward a major language group that besets the great languages. Scandinavian tongues or Dutch would be accused of leaning too heavily in the direction of the great Germanic tongues, English and German. The minor Slavic tongues would favor Russian. Minor Asian languages, to which no one has given a serious thought, might tend to fall within the Chinese, or Indian, or Indonesian, or Arabic orbit. Tongues like Finnish, Turkish, or Hungarian, representing a minor language family concerning whose imperialistic tendencies no one is worried, might well be a possibility. There are also American Indian, African Negro, and South Sea languages to be thought of, but the task of equipping any one of these to become a tongue of common intercourse for the civilized world would be staggering, though not insurmountable.

Among the constructed tongues there are many and excellent possibilities, as we have seen. But it is undeniable that as of the present moment only two, Esperanto (or a modified version of Esperanto) and Interlingua, are in the running, so far as popular favor and acceptance are concerned.

A few scattered facts about Esperanto were brought out at the latest Esperanto Congress, held in Oslo, which attracted 1,600 delegates from 32 countries. The number of Esperanto speakers throughout the world today comes close to half a million (though something like eight million are said to have some acquaintance with the language), and Esperanto is taught in no fewer than 625 schools located all over the globe. Esperanto has been used as the language of the invading "enemy" force at American Army maneuvers. There are more than 50 monthly broadcasts in Esperanto from European countries alone. Over 7,500 books, translated and original, are available in the language, with over 100 periodicals.

Stamps in Esperanto have been issued by four countries, and the language is acceptable, along with Latin, for international telegrams. In the United States and Britain, Esperanto has been tested in the schools as an introduction to the study of foreign languages, and the experiment has successfully demonstrated that Esperanto-trained youngsters did better in the languages they took up later than did the ones who had not had the training. So far as popular favor is concerned, a Gallup poll conducted in smaller European countries like the Netherlands and Norway showed that Esperanto was second only to English as the people's choice for an international language.

Interlingua, a much later arrival on the scene, seems favored by scientific and technological groups, which appear to find the language particularly suitable for the printing of formal papers circulated among their members. A striking demonstration was given recently in Washington at the meeting of the second World Congress of Cardiology, where 2,200 delegates from 50 nations agreed that they had little or no trouble understanding the common artificial language, at least in printed form.

Among constructed languages, as among natural languages, there are numerous dark-horse candidates, each with its own small body of followers. It is not inconceivable that at a world linguistic congress designed to select one language, natural or constructed, from among the many to serve as the international tongue of the future, a delegate might resurrect Schleyer's Volapük, Sudre's Solresol, Peano's Latino Sine Flexione, or even the forgotten a priori creation of Bishop Wilkins or Cave Beck.

The time for deliberation, planning, study, and creation is past. The need is immediate. What the present-day world needs is not a process of greater refining of existing systems, but the selection of one of the many already in existence. We have planned for four centuries. It is now high time to go into action.

The world's peoples, as has been fully proved by Gallup and other polls, want a language that they may all hold in common. They want it in order that they may get better acquainted with one another, because they sense that despite all the artificial factors dividing them, they are all fundamentally akin. They want it in order that their living problems may be simplified, that one of the major roadblocks to their efficient cooperative activity may be removed. But above all, they want it for their children, who will live in the world of tomorrow, a world in which there will be no distances and no barriers to material communication, in which people of different races, nationalities, and backgrounds will be forced to rub elbows as they never have before, and will need to exchange thoughts quickly, easily, and directly.

Why delay the process further? Why wait for further improvements on what fundamentally cannot be improved—language?

24. Inefficacy of "movements"

The Volapük Movement—The Esperanto Movement—The Basic English Movement—The Interlingua Movement—Popular Appeal, or Government Support?

As we observe the growth and decline of the various movements on behalf of a particular solution for the problem of the international language, we are struck by the enthusiasm and missionary zeal of each movement's supporters no less than by the general indifference displayed by governments and their official organs, even when these governments and organs act in concert, as was the case with the old League of Nations and as is the case with the United Nations today.

These two factors, together, add up to certain failure. The very nature of the international language calls for universality. It must be accepted not by some, but by all. So long as we have dozens of diverse movements, all working in opposition to one another, there will be utter confusion in the ranks of international language advocates and sympathizers. A language for the world, yes. But which of the many proposals unfolded before the eyes of the world's masses shall these same masses strive for? English, Russian, French, Chinese, or any of a hundred other natural languages? Or shall it be a bilingual world, or a series of zonal languages? Or a constructed language, and if so, which one of the many? Esperanto, Ido, Interlingua, Novial, Romanal, or something else?

There is little point to going too deeply into the motives that inspire the smug complacency and indifference of governments and their organs so long as this situation persists. It may be, as some cynics claim, that governments are interested in keeping their peoples divided by the language barrier, because the antipathies fostered by linguistic differences help to fasten the hold of each national government upon its people. But it is more likely that the indifference of the statesmen is the product of inertia coupled with uncertainty. After all, government officials are only human beings. It is only natural for them to be as bewildered as are the rest of us before the conflicting claims of so many different languages and systems.

The interlinguists of the past have erred in putting the cart before the horse. They have invariably advocated the adoption of one particular language or system long before endeavoring to convince the world at large that *an* international language, *any* international language, is needed and must be adopted. Each of them has sinned in presenting his own particular solution as the only possible solution, failing which everything connected with the international language must perforce fail.

Starting with Solresol and Volapük, the two early movements to gain a measure of popular support, we see this mentality at work. Sudre and Schleyer both thought they had evolved not merely *a* solution, but the only possible, practical and conceivable one. Today, most advocates of Interlingua, Esperanto, Basic English, Bilingual World, straight English, straight French, straight Russian, are almost equally obdurate in refusing to recognize any merit in any system other than their own. In the case of the natural languages, this might be attributed to the good old spirit of nationalism, French, English, Russian, or of a dozen other varieties, manifesting itself along linguistic lines. But we also have an Esperanto and Interlingua nationalism that says "Outside this language, there is no salvation."

Oddly enough, some interlinguists, recognizing the danger of excessive intolerance, fall into the opposite error. They turn themselves into debating societies which go on forever arguing the merits of minor points in the constructed tongues; whether it is better to form the plural with *-j,* Esperanto fashion, or with *-s,* as do many other systems; whether a certain root should be drawn from Latin, or Greek, or Germanic; whether it is better to have an infinitive end in *-i,* or in *-r,* or in *-re;* whether we cannot continue to work upon and improve Esperanto or Interlingua, thereby making the language of our choice a more perfect instrument; or, for that matter, whether we cannot take a natural language like English, and by limiting its vocabulary, or by getting rid of a few irregular plurals and past participles, turn it into a thoroughly regular tongue that everyone will accept.

There would be undoubted merit in such discussions, if they did not tend to go on forever, creating, as they go along, new languages, new solutions, new possibilities, further to confound and confuse those who seek a practical and, above all, an immediate solution.

If the inventors of the automobile or the airplane had doggedly insisted on making all sorts of minor improvements on their blueprints instead of going into production as soon as they had achieved a workable model, it is probable that we should still be awaiting automotive or air transportation. A good many of our 2,796 natural tongues and our 600 or so constructed languages are workable models.

Of course, the language that is selected for world use will not stand still. It will grow, expand, and change, as all languages do, once it is put into effect. But we need not allow avowed and minor imperfections to keep us from putting it into immediate operation.

If a national language is selected, we need have no undue fears by reason of its complexities. National languages are normally fairly well mastered by their own speakers. Two important points, brought out by Couturat and Léau as far back as 1903, bear repetition: a language spelled as it is pronounced has a very good chance of being understood by all who learn it (therefore, if a national language is chosen, it must be phonetized as to spelling); if the foreigners generally make themselves understood better than they understand, it is the fault of the native speakers, not of the foreigners (this means that the language selected must be spoken clearly and distinctly, not mumbled and mutilated by its original native speakers; it also means that a standard form of the language must be adopted, to the exclusion of the picturesque dialectal variants that plague every living tongue).

If a constructed tongue is adopted, these drawbacks need not be feared. Fully constructed tongues are normally born fully phonetized, with precise instructions for the use of both sounds and symbols. The fact that their grammars ordinarily display absolute regularity minimizes the possibility of dialectalization.

On the other hand, consideration of a constructed language brings another danger in its wake. This is the tendency to go on changing and reforming it, in the manner in which Esperanto was changed by the Idoists and other reformers. The international language, as Guérard rightly points out, must have permanence, or people won't waste time on it.

At the present moment, the chances of success of *an* international language are excellent, since at no time in history have people been more aware of its need and possible benefits. At the same time, specific movements are languishing. It takes far more than the few million adherents of Esperanto, or the undetermined number of believers in Ido, Basic English, Interlingua, or any other of the existing constructed or modified tongues to enable us to speak of a successful international tongue. It takes more than a few enthusiasts in each twinned city to bring about the Anglo-French condominium. The peoples of the earth are many—over two and a half billion in round numbers. To reach them by the methods by which current interlanguage movements have reached their few million adherents would take not centuries, but millenniums.

There is one, and only one way in which they, or at least a considerable portion of them, can be reached and affected within the foreseeable future, and that is by direct, compulsive government action—the same kind of action that has proved so successful within the last century in extending the benefits of literacy to world populations which at the dawn of the nineteenth century were still fully 80 per cent illiterate.

The peoples of the earth are already convinced of the desirability of a world tongue. It is the governments that need to be convinced. Once that is achieved, the rest, though fairly complex, is relatively easy.

Believers in the freedom of the individual and restraint

upon government activity may be somewhat shocked at the implication of direct, coercive government action in achieving the international language. They may be reminded, however, that such action in this connection does not affect the social or economic structure of any given country, and does not, in fact, materially differ from the prescriptions issued by each State Board of Regents in this country, or by the national Ministry of Education in most foreign lands, as to what shall be included in the ordinary school curriculum.

We could go further and say that there is no educational system on earth, to our knowledge, that objects to the inclusion of instruction and training in the use of the national language in the schools, and that most educational systems make definite provision for instruction in additional languages. If, instead of the compulsory study of one or more foreign tongues, we had the compulsory study of a single supranational tongue, with the study of other foreign tongues left optional with the students, the impact upon the world's educational systems could hardly be described as destructive to the freedom of the individual; not, at least, to any greater degree than compulsory instruction in the national language, mathematics, science, history, and geography is today.

Universal governmental acceptance of the principle of a world language is admittedly difficult to secure. Yet, from a purely mechanical standpoint, it should be no more difficult than was the acceptance of the world postal and telegraphic union which permits us to communicate with people beyond our borders. No infringement of national sovereignty is involved. The mere fact that the peoples of the world will have a language in common does not at all mean that they need have the same form of government or the same social or economic structure. Yet if the possession of a common tongue succeeds in allaying fears and antipathies and in bringing about a greater degree of international cooperation, as was claimed by Churchill in the famous speech in which he suggested the use of Basic English as a world tongue, no one should be frightened by that prospect.

There is, of course, a machinery that will have to be created and put into operation for the selection of a world language once the world's governments are in agreement that one should be selected. There is an even more complex machinery that will have to be evolved for the imparting of that language once the choice is made. Neither of these problems is insurmountable.

Before we study the nature and operation of these twin pieces of political and educational mechanism, it may be well to cast a glance at the possible alternatives if they are not created.

25. The only two possible solutions: war or accord

Historical Solution of the Problem—Languages and Individuals—The Esthetic Choice—The Practical Choice—The Hour for Decision

Historically, the solution of the language problem has been more often a violent than a peaceful one. Languages can easily coexist for centuries under the same sovereignty, but normally only on condition that one language predominate, officially or unofficially.

In the ancient world, we find, at various epochs, the predominance of Sumerian, Akkadian, Egyptian, Old Persian, Greek, and Latin. None of the empires that spoke these languages was monolingual, to be sure. Yet the records of antiquity are filled with the names of forgotten tongues that were forced to give way and disappear before the inroads of the predominant language. In the case of Latin alone, with whose history we are best acquainted, we find that not only the ancient languages of Italy (Etruscan, Oscan, Umbrian, Sicel, Messapian, Venetic, Liguric, and scores of others) eventually vanished, with their speakers turning into speakers of Latin, but also the Iberian of Spain, the Gaulish of France, the Dacian of what is today Rumania, and the Punic of North Africa.

A language depends for its existence upon a speaking population, and if the latter turns elsewhere for its linguistic medium, the language shrivels up and vanishes. It is a question of speaker's choice, and the choice of the speakers is only occasionally determined by esthetic and cultural factors. Far more often, it is a matter of social and economic prestige and political and military might.

Latin was at the outset the rough tongue of a group that was at first nomadic, later agricultural, and had nothing in particular to recommend it as the world choice in preference to older and more cultivated languages, such as the Etruscan and the Greek from which Latin so widely borrowed, or the Punic of the Carthaginians which Latin rejected almost in its entirety. Yet in due course of time Latin became one of the most polished, expressive, and majestic tongues the world has ever known. But most of this development took place after, not before, the period of expansion of Rome as a world power.

Castilian imposed itself in medieval Spain, Francien in medieval France, by reason of political and military, not cultural predominance. The choice of Anglo-Saxon English over Norman French in medieval England was, more than anything else, a tribute to the numerical superiority of the Anglo-Saxon element in the English population. The French of the Normans was esthetically a far superior tongue, and proved it by producing a flourishing Anglo-Norman literature at a period when English could only offer the *Ormolum* and the

Ancres Riwle. On purely esthetic grounds, French, not English, should have become the language of England.

At the present time, it would take considerable hardihood to claim that the recent vast expansion of English and Russian is based primarily on cultural or esthetic factors. The economic power of penetration of the one language, the military preponderance of the other, the political force of both, are the main factors leading to their expansion and to the consequent restriction of the other great languages of European culture, French and German and Italian.

If a peaceful solution of the language problem is not reached, it is more than likely that a solution will come anyway, as the outcome of the clash (which need not be military) between the two great political systems and social ideologies of the twentieth century, collectivistic Communism and capitalistic Democracy. If no third force develops, and the expansion of the two continues, the language that is the symbolic standard-bearer of the one or the other will emerge victorious along with the political ideology it represents.

There will emphatically be no question of ease or logic, of literary or cultural values in a choice that is left to historical chance. English, with its drawbacks of spelling and grammatical looseness; Russian, with its disadvantages of grammatical complexity; both languages, with their difficulties of pronunciation to those who do not speak them as natives, will stand a far better chance of becoming the world tongue than any of the more graceful, refined, euphonic languages that have vied with them in the past, or any of the phonetic, logically constructed artificial tongues that man's fertile brain has evolved.

The choice will be a practical one, as it was a practical one for the speakers of Etruscan, Iberian, and Gaulish who turned into speakers of Latin. The tongue that carries prestige and is valid under all circumstances will emerge as the world tongue.

This solution may be viewed with alarm for what concerns its political and social implications. Linguistically, it need not arouse any deep concern. English and Russian are each thoroughly qualified to play the role of world tongue, if it is the verdict of history that the mantle once held by Latin is to fall on either of them.

The question is rather whether we should seek a solution based not on the old historical determinism of power politics, but on the free, intelligent choice of all men. Granted that this is a startling innovation in a world that has always been run by force, it might perhaps be more in line with the democratic tendencies to which so much lip-service has been paid in recent times by both sides.

Outside of an element of power that ultimately resolves itself into the brute force of arms, is there any valid reason why a choice should not be offered to the many peoples of the world (and they form the overwhelming majority of the world's inhabitants) who subscribe to neither English nor Russian, in the matter of what language shall be used for purposes of world communications?

It is quite possible that if such a democratic method is employed in the field of language it may serve as an inspiration for the application of similar methods in the solution of other international problems, with definite advantages for the cause of peace.

On the other hand, there is no good reason why the establishment of an international tongue should be linked to political factors, save in the most general way. One of the errors made by interlinguists in the past has been precisely that of linking the choice of an international tongue with the establishment of world peace, which has had the effect of arousing suspicion among those who do not favor foreign entanglements, the United Nations, or the theory of world government.

An international language will emphatically not be tantamount to a world government. It will not, all by itself, lead to world peace and the abolition of international conflicts. All that it will do will be to make world communications easier, like the international postal union, to which no one in his right senses objects today. If, as a by-product, it serves to allay international tensions among governments and individuals, that is all to the good. But as matters stand today, the international language is to be viewed purely as a tool for international communications, not as an instrument of international policy.

26. The machinery of a peaceful solution

UN and UNESCO—The Linguistic Commission—Membership—Procedure—Outcome—The Judgment of Solomon

As far back as 1894, Hugo Schuchardt, one of Europe's foremost philologists, who had opposed Volapük since its first appearance and predicted its eventual downfall at the time of its greatest triumphs, made this interesting statement: "If all the governments of Europe had introduced it as a compulsory subject in the public schools, its future would have been assured in spite of all superior projects."

In 1922, Albert Guérard said: "Without official recognition, the fate of the best system is precarious; with it, any scheme that is not totally unworkable would do well enough."

These two pronouncements from two of the greatest minds that have ever devoted their attention to the international language problem sum up the situation.

Even the support of revered learned bodies is not enough.

In 1901 no less a group than the International Association of Academies warmly endorsed the adoption of an international language. This body included, among others, the academies and scientific societies of Amsterdam, Berlin, Brussels, Budapest, Christiania, Copenhagen, Göttingen, Leipzig, St. Petersburg, Stockholm, Vienna, and Washington, as well as the Royal Society of London, the three great academies of Paris, and the Accademia dei Lincei of Rome. In a lengthy resolution presented by the secretary of the Paris Academy of Sciences, which was unanimously approved, it was pointed out that the progress of science demanded the unification and coordination of scientific production through the medium of a single world language. This plea fell upon deaf ears, so far as the dozen or more governments of the countries represented at the Congress were concerned.

The Congress of International Associations, meeting in Brussels in 1920, endorsed Esperanto as the world auxiliary language, with the recommendation that all improvements deemed necessary be deferred "until the moment when the language has been officially adopted by the governments." This moment never came.

It is true that at the first Assembly of the ill-starred League of Nations, in 1921, a motion favoring Esperanto was made and carried. But this motion simply stated that the League "follows with interest the experiments of official teaching of the international language Esperanto in the public schools of some members of the League, hopes to see that teaching made more general in the whole world, so that the children of all countries may know at least two languages, their mother-tongue and an easy means of international communication, and asks the Secretary-General to prepare for the next Assembly a report on the results reached in this respect." This emphatically was not enough.

As recently as 1955, a general meeting of UNESCO held at Montevideo discussed, quite inconclusively, the endorsement of Esperanto as a universal auxiliary language. Subsequently, the writer enjoyed the privilege of an hour-long interview with Dr. Luther Evans, Director General of UNESCO, at which the question of UNESCO's official and even unofficial attitude toward the question of an international language was fully discussed. The gist of this interview is to the effect that the organization holds a completely neutral attitude toward the various projects now afloat; that no scientific study of the problem has yet been made (!); that the problem ought indeed to be investigated; that a scientific study should be made. That is as far as UNESCO cares to go at the present time.*

In return, for what it may be worth in relation to the problem, there is a full description of the achievements of UNESCO in the matter of spreading literacy in backward countries. This activity is in itself highly praiseworthy. It is only fair to point out, however, that the methodology followed leads to the multiplication of existing languages and the consequent linguistic confusion that prevails in the world. This methodology calls for instruction in local language forms rather than in the big language supposed to be prevalent in the area under consideration (Haitian Creole, for instance, is imparted to the children and illiterates of Haiti in preference to French, and pidgin English is similarly used in Melanesia in prefer-

* Chapter 6 of UNESCO's *Scientific and Technical Translating and Other Aspects of the Language Problem,* published in 1957, is entitled "The Possible Use of Languages Internationally Understood." This is a 35-page discussion of the international language problem, treated, however, as a matter exclusively connected with scientific and technical translating, and not at all from the aspect of a common language for the world's masses.

It is perhaps natural that the four possibilities discussed at greatest length are English, Basic English, Esperanto, and Interlingua. Of the sixty draft critics (of various nationalities) who voiced an opinion as to which language or system held out the greatest hopes, 35 favored English, 2 favored Basic English, 6 voted for Esperanto, 7 for Interlingua, and 6 were in favor of a mixture of languages of the Monde Bilingue type, but with Spanish, German, Russian, and Chinese included.

Many valuable suggestions are voiced in the course of this chapter, but they deal with the problem of scientific translation rather than with the international language as such.

ence to English). To the extent that this system continues to be followed, it will lead to the fractioning and dialectalization of national tongues by placing an official imprint upon substandard forms that might be expected, in a period of swifter and better communications and education than the world has ever known, to disappear by a process of merging into the standard languages.

There is little more to be said concerning official governmental attitudes. The general policy of UN, UNESCO, and the individual governments is one of hands off. Individual movements, or the movement toward any solution whatsoever of the problem, are left to private initiative, where it is safe to assume that they will get nowhere, as they have gotten nowhere in the past.

If there were a will on the part of the governments to solve, once and for all, this thorny problem that has so long agitated the world, the machinery of accord would not be too difficult to create and set in motion.

The first step would be a general accord among the governments for the setting up of a linguistic commission to select the language that is to serve the world, and an advance pledge on the part of those same governments to abide by the decision of the commission, and to implement it by putting the language chosen into all grades of their educational systems, from the lowest to the highest, with the added provision that instruction could, at the discretion of the country's educational authorities, begin at the lowest, or kindergarten level, and be gradually extended upward, year by year, so as not to cause too great a dislocation of programs.

The linguistic commission would consist of duly qualified delegates selected by the government of each country. The basis of representation for each national delegation would be a matter for discussion. The large nations, whether they be western democracies or the teeming countries of Asia, like

China and India, might favor representation by population. Other considerations might suggest representation by adult literate population only, or representation based on a weighted index in which population, literacy, and industrial and scientific productivity would all play a part. Nations with small populations and high indexes of literacy and productivity, like Sweden, might favor the weighted index. It might be claimed that basing the representation, and therefore to some extent the choice, upon present-day factors is unfair to nations that might in the future achieve either a higher birth-rate or a higher standard of literacy and productivity. In the final analysis, the method of apportioning representation would not make too much difference. No one nation, or group of nations speaking the same tongue would under any circumstances be able to exert direct control over more than one fifth of the total vote. Nations that in the course of the balloting find themselves in danger of being overwhelmed by a single aggressive delegation would be able to form the same kind of coalition that appears in our national conventions under the form of a stop-somebody alliance. The ultimate choice could never represent the will of a minority, but only the compromise of various conflicting tendencies.

The choice of the delegates allotted to each nation would rest with the government of that nation, by whatever methods it pleases. This does not differ materially from what goes on today in the UN Assembly, and ought not to shock the advocates of the democratic process. If we are to reject the assumption that the governments represent, if not the consensus of the people governed, at least the effective power to make those people move, then there is no point to any kind of international gathering, for linguistic or any other purposes.

The delegates would presumably represent each nation's best available linguistic talent. We must, of course, be prepared for the eventuality that certain delegations will arrive with full and precise instructions as to how to cast their votes, while others will consist of individuals who will in the main be guided by their own linguistic conscience. This, too, is a situation with which we are acquainted and know how to cope. The voting procedure will be such that even fully instructed delegations will be powerless to affect any but the preliminary results.

The delegations should know in advance that it is their mission not to create a new language, but only to pass judgment on those that are already available. This will exclude any creative efforts and time-consuming discussions.

The voting procedure will be simple. At the outset, any member of any delegation may propose the candidacy of any language, natural or constructed, already in existence. Nominating speeches will be held to a maximum of ten minutes, in the course of which the delegate may propound the advantages of the language or system he advocates. In actual practice, this will not mean the presentation of some three thousand languages, but of only a small fraction of that number; for one thing, no delegate will be allowed to sponsor more than one language; secondly, the vast majority of minor languages and projects will not find anyone to sponsor them. It may safely be prophesied that no more than a couple of hundred languages and systems will be nominated.

Once the nominations are closed, a brief period of discussion, half an hour at the most, will be allotted for each language that has become a candidate, with ten minutes for the supporters and twenty for the opponents (along with the nominating speech, this will mean twenty minutes for and twenty against each candidate).

This preliminary process may be expected to consume at least a month of the congress' time. It will be time well spent, since both delegates and the world's peoples at large will be able to familiarize themselves with the issues. Some of our national nominating conventions have lasted almost as long.

Once the discussion period is over, the voting will begin. Here the procedure will be purely automatic. On the initial ballot, any delegate may vote for any of the two hundred or so candidates he wishes. When the results of the first ballot are known, that half of the total number of language-candidates that have received the smallest number of votes automatically drop out of the running, and only the leading 50 per cent remain in the field.

Additional runoffs are compulsory even in the very unlikely eventuality that on the first ballot one language should receive an absolute majority of all votes cast. This provision works against numerically large delegations and permits the coalescing of minor forces.

The runoff ballots continue to the end, with half the candidates automatically eliminated on each ballot, and the delegates obliged to redistribute their votes on the surviving languages. If at the outset two hundred languages are in the field, they become one hundred, then fifty, twenty-five, twelve, six, three, two. The eighth or ninth ballot should tell the story, and it will probably be a vastly different one from what the first ballot foreshadows, as the delegates are obliged to recede from their favorite sons and take their choice of what is left.

The language selected in the final ballot has automatically been accepted in advance by the governments of the world. If it is a national language, it is understood that it will be rigidly phonetized as to spelling for international purposes, though the nation or nations speaking it may continue to use the old form of writing for purely national use. If it is a constructed language, it will be examined for perfect phonetization, and whatever changes are needed will be made on the spot.

Now comes a five-year period of teacher training, before the international language is placed in the schools of the world, on a basis of absolute parity with the national tongues.

This period of preparation is necessary. Teachers who are to impart the international language primarily in the kindergartens and lower grades must know it and speak it perfectly, and must be perfect as teachers. This period may also serve the purposes of perfecting and improving upon the chosen tongue, if it is felt that such improvement is needed. Going to work upon a language that is already chosen and established, smoothing out its rough edges, polishing and refining it, is altogether different from what has gone on in the past at congresses of interlinguists, who did not feel bound to respect the languages they had under consideration and who normally solved divergences by creating still another language.

At the end of five years, the international language goes into operation in at least the kindergartens of all countries, though it may, at the discretion of the country's educational authorities, be also introduced into the elementary and high-school grades and the colleges and universities. Half of the kindergarten instruction is imparted, by normal, natural speaking processes, in the international tongue, the other half in the national language. This system continues to be applied as the kindergarten generation passes on into the lower grades, upper grades, high schools, colleges, and universities. School instruction is supplemented by radio, television, and motion-picture programs. The kindergarten generation of, say, 1964, when the program first goes into operation, becomes adult by 1984. By the end of the century, it constitutes a majority of the world population. Long before the middle of the twenty-first century, the world language is indeed universal, and the person unable to speak, understand, read, and write it far more rare than the illiterate is today.

The method we have outlined is radical and drastic. But it is the only effective one. It calls for an end to planning and a beginning of direct action. It places the responsibility for the international language squarely where it belongs—on the shoulders of the world's governments.

It calls for an end to wishful thinking and acceptance of a process which is democratic in the broadest sense of the word, since all nations and peoples, without exception, will participate in the choice.

It calls for courage on the part of the governments, which must realize that the attainment of a world-wide means of communication requires some action on their part rather than the indifference or supine neutrality they have so far assumed.

It calls for a realization on the part of the world's peoples that the existence of a single language that will be valid for all sorts of international exchanges is far superior to the study of one or more foreign tongues which are of limited currency, no matter how widespread they may be.

It calls for an attitude on the part of those who are at present advocating one or another particular solution similar to that displayed by the real mother in the Biblical episode of Solomon's judgment. The false mother was willing to have the disputed child cut in two, so that half might be given each of the two claimants. The real mother preferred that the child be kept alive, even at the cost of seeing her rival get it.

Advocates of Esperanto, Ido, Interlingua, Basic English, the Bilingual World, or any of at least a dozen natural languages run the risk of seeing their candidate defeated in a world-wide choice such as has been outlined. Are they willing to run this risk in order to achieve what each of them says must be achieved—a world language for everybody?

27. Pro and con: the national languages present their candidacy

*Greek–Latin–French–English–Spanish–Italian–German–Russian–Chinese–Finnish–*Le Monde Bilingue–*The Devil's Advocate*

At the world linguistic congress that is to decide upon a language to serve as an international medium of communication, any language may be presented. Yet the candidates actually placed in the running will probably be relatively few. Still fewer will be the ones to outlast the first ballot or two. A handful of widely known natural languages, Classical and modern, an even more slender handful of constructed tongues, a dark horse or two, will be all that will survive the initial ballots.

Is it legitimate for us to allow our imagination to run riot and anticipate the nominating speeches and their rebuttals? Perhaps, and perhaps not. It will, at any rate, serve the purposes of recapitulation, and fix in the minds of the readers the main arguments, pro and con, that have been advanced each time one of these tongues has been named as a possibility. From a purely objective point of view, many of these arguments are without value, since any language, great or small, known or unknown, "easy" or "difficult" from adult standards, will serve the purpose, provided it is learned naturally and conversationally by the children of each land and is given a thoroughly phonetic written form. But it is adults, not children, who will make the decision, and the adult point of view, however subjective, is hard to eradicate, even among trained linguists, and must be taken into account.

We may therefore expect these arguments to be advanced, and the customary refutations to be made. It will not be amiss to listen in, as it were, on the proceedings of the linguistic congress in advance of its occurrence. Nor will it be amiss to personify each candidate as it is presented, and let it speak for itself, something that is not very likely to happen, but which injects a personal, warm note into the discussion.

Delegate X, being recognized by the speaker, rises and says: "I speak for Greek, and, for the purposes of this discussion, I am the voice of the Greek language, a tongue of great antiquity and high civilization, which has had uninterrupted use from the eighth century before Christ until the present day. Structurally and in vocabulary, I am highly representative of the great Indo-European family of languages, which includes fully half of the world's living populations. My power to express human thought, from the simplest to the most complicated, has been amply demonstrated during the three millennia that I have been in use. I am capable of giving voice to the most refined shades of meaning. Poets, statesmen, scholars, and philosophers have used me, and found me satisfactory. My scheme of sounds is easy to master by people of other tongues. My word-stock appears in all civilized languages spoken today, and has given rise to more than half of the international vocabulary of learning in all fields, from that of philosophy and abstract thought to that of physical science and technology. Having been internationally used in antiquity and during the Middle Ages, having achieved the greatest international use in modern times, I consider myself highly suited for the post of international tongue."

Delegate Y rises in rebuttal. "While all you say is true, it is undeniable that your ancient Indo-European grammatical structure is largely out of vogue today. Few people in the twentieth century are prepared to cope with your intricate system of noun declensions and verb conjugations. While your words are widespread in most modern tongues, the bulk of your vocabulary is unknown. The language we want is for practical, colloquial, not scholarly or philosophical use."

"I am the Latin language. Almost as ancient as Greek, equally representative of the Indo-European family, I am to an even greater degree a vehicle of civilized thought. For many centuries I was the world language, while the Roman Empire stood. Later, in the Middle Ages, I was the universal tongue of western scholarship, and all men who were literate used me in speech as well as in writing. I have many children in the world: French, Spanish, Italian, Portuguese are all sprung from me. Today, I am still used as an international tongue by the clergy of a Church that extends to all countries of the world. I, too, have been the expressive vehicle of literature, poetry, philosophy, and science. My vocabulary is international to an even greater extent than that of Greek, and I continue to be studied where Greek has gone out of fashion. I am a language of simple, yet majestic and sonorous sounds, which will not unduly disturb the speakers of other languages. I have within me, at the present time, the machinery for expressing the most complicated modern terminology. In asking to become the world language, I only claim what is my own."

"As a spoken tongue of common intercourse, you have been dying by inches, year by year, and you are becoming more and more dead. Your place has been usurped by the modern tongues, in diplomacy, in literature, in science. Grammatically, you are difficult to master and use, and your difficulty justifies the statement once made by Henderson in the language he had derived from you: 'Post decem annos de studere, pauces discipules pote, aut legere facile, aut scribere accurate, aut loquere aliquantulum i latine lingue' ('After ten years of study, few students can either read easily, or write accurately, or speak just a little in the Latin tongue'). Your complicated grammatical structure is accompanied by uncertainty as to your pronunciation, and the speakers of each modern tongue pronounce you in their own fashion."

"I am the French language, widespread and popular, elegant, clear, and expressive. For centuries I have been used as the world tongue of diplomacy and culture. No one who does not know me can consider himself truly educated. I am spoken today by no fewer than eighty million people, scattered all over the world. You will find me equally at home in Europe, America, Africa, and Asia. My grammatical structure, if not too simple, is at least definite and crystal-clear. I am thoroughly standardized, both as to grammar and as to pronunciation, so that people need not be in doubt as to whether they are using me correctly. My vocabulary is largely Latin, which gives it broad internationality, and my words have penetrated all other languages, most of all my great modern rival, English. When an official, authoritative text is wanted, I supply that text. As a tongue in full spoken use, I am not under the disadvantages of the Classical languages, yet I am Classical in the cultural and literary sense, with an uninterrupted tradition that goes back more than a thousand years. In the great political-economic controversy that agitates the present-day world, I am equally acceptable to East and West, for my history embraces both feudalism and the Jacquerie, absolutism and Jacobinism, the bourgeois industrial revolution and the Paris Commune."

"You are far less widespread than you formerly were. In recent years, you have lost a great deal of your old international prestige. Your sound-scheme is difficult for anyone not born to it, and lends itself to confusion and misunderstanding. Your grammatical structure is complex, particularly for what concerns the verbs. Your vocabulary may be Latin, but you have pushed the process of change to the point where far too many of your words are unrecognizable as stemming from their Latin ancestors. Your system of spelling is antiquated and misleading, and if it is phonetized, as it must be for international use, the abyss that separates you from your etymological origins will be deepened and broadened to the point where few of your words and forms will be recognized by those who today at least recognize them in writing. You may serve as an international language for an intellectual elite, but you are hardly suitable for the world's masses."

"I am the English language, second in number of speakers throughout the world, first in distribution, in commerce, in industry, in wealth, in economic power, in science and technology. My grammatical structure combines the features of inflectional Indo-European with those of isolating Chinese. My vocabulary is truly international, uniting Germanic, Romance, Greek, and Latin elements into an indissoluble whole, and affording the greatest freedom of choice to my speakers. I have spread with ease over the entire world, because practically everyone wants to learn me and use me. I am a thoroughly popular, colloquial tongue, yet I have proved my worth as an instrument of literature. I am direct and concise, yet quite expressive. More people want me as an international tongue than want any other."

"You are a tongue that is extremely confusing, not merely as to spelling, but also as to pronunciation and grammar. You have no standard form, and refuse to have any. Your sounds are among the most confusing in the world, with vowels and diphthongs that have bewildering glides when they are stressed and are completely unclear when unstressed. Your consonant clusters are harsh and unpleasant to the ear. Your stress is unpredictable. Your spelling is ghastly, and if it is phonetized, half of your word-stock, now perfectly recognizable in written form, will become a shrouded mystery. Your grammatical simplicity is a snare and a delusion. Your tricky auxiliary verbs, like *do* and *have* ('Do you have a book?'; 'Have you got a book?') are the despair of grammarians. Your system of functional change, whereby the same word may be used as any of three or four parts of speech ('Casualties from cold cut' says one of your newspaper headlines) leaves speakers of other languages breathless. You are much too given to slang and jargon, and you change far too fast to suit anyone but your own speakers."

"I am the voice of the Spanish language, a tongue of widespread use, ancient and honorable ancestry, ease of sounds and structure, long service in the fields of literature, commerce, exploration, and discovery. I am a friendly language, one that people fall into easily, as proved by the millions of non-Hispanic stock that today use me as their own. My word-hoard is abundant, for I have drawn freely from every source, and passed on to my sister languages of the West thousands of words from the Arabic of the Moors, the Indian tongues of America, the languages of the East. Yet I am basically Latin, and no one grounded in a Latin culture finds my words difficult. I have a free and easy interchange with the speakers of Portuguese on the one hand, those of Italian on the other. I am the leading language of a continent that may dominate the world's future, South America. My grammar has been deliberately simplified, to the point where it outstrips in logic and regularity all my sister tongues of the Romance family. My system of writing is so simple and phonetic that if I am chosen very little will have to be done to phonetize me."

"You are indeed widespread, but with uneven distribution. Outside of the western hemisphere and the isolated peninsula that is your original home, few people know you. You are not standardized as to usage or pronunciation, and each of the many countries that use you has its own special vocabulary, its own special slang, its own points of usage, which you have not succeeded in bringing under unified control. In some of your dialects, some of your sounds are too harsh; in others, too soft and relaxed. Your grammatical structure is simple in its early reaches, but it achieves great complexities of syntax and word arrangement, encouraging your speakers to be verbose and redundant."

"I am the harmonious tongue of Dante and Petrarch and Boccaccio and the *dolce stil nuovo,* a tongue so close to my ancestral Latin that for centuries my speakers referred to me not as 'Italian,' but as *il Volgare,* the Vulgar Language, Latin spoken without the rules of Latin grammar. Why seek a Latin without flexions when I am available? My sound-scheme is so perfect that I have been singled out as the language of song and music and fine diction. I am sonorous, and carry better than any other tongue on earth, with vowels that are clear-cut and distinct, consonants that are fully articulated and audible. I am the language of a great culture, whose continuity extends from the days of Romulus and Remus to the present, for between me and Latin there was never a clean break. I am the most worthy continuator of the Latin and the Roman tradition, which is universal, of the tradition of early Christianity, which is equally universal, of the tradition of the Renaissance, which first spoke in my words. I am the language of a nation that rises from its ashes each time it seems to die, and marches on to greater glory and nobler achievement in the fields that truly lead to everlasting renown—music, the arts, poetry, and literature, the things that enrich the life of man, not those that destroy it."

"You are the language of a land that has become backward in the modern march of science, technology, and industry. Your speakers are relatively few, and their ranks are cleft by dialects that are among the most divergent and complicated in the world of language. How many of your speakers really speak you? How many do nothing but pay lip service to you, and then go on to worship at other linguistic shrines? Your grammatical structure presents greater complexities than those of your sister Romance tongues, and your syntax is so elastic as to be baffling both to your own speakers and to others. You are restricted in territorial extent, and the millions you have sent out as emigrants have quickly lost you. You are pompous and verbose; you will never say in one short word what can be said in five long ones. Your vocabulary is indeed more Latin than that of any other living tongue, but by the same token it is far less international."

"I am the German tongue, purest and most typical of the languages of my Germanic branch, which is the most populous of the Indo-European family. I am not as conservative of ancient forms as is Icelandic, nor as revolutionary in my innovations as is English. My sound-scheme is not gentle, but it is manly, and my articulation is distinct. My vocabulary is extensive, expressive, and capable of infinite expansion, because I have retained, better than any other western tongue, the ability to form compounds. I abide in the pulsating heart of Europe, and have spread far beyond my borders. I am great in literary, musical, artistic, and cultural achievement."

"You are, despite your extent, a highly localized language. What overseas possibilities you once had you have lost. Your sounds are harsh and unmusical. You are given to consonant clusters that form the nightmare of people of other tongues. Your grammatical structure is both unnatural and illogical, as is your word-arrangement. How can you expect people with other language backgrounds to pronounce such incredible combinations of sounds as *Knechtschaft,* or manage such unmanageable compounds as *Kriegsgefangenenentschädigungsgesetz,* the sort of thing that your sister Germanic language English resolves into 'Law to provide compensation for war prisoners'? Your former scientific appeal is waning in a world in which every civilized nation devotes itself to scientific pursuits in its own language. You are a tongue of the past, not of the future."

"I am the voice of Russian, leading tongue of the Soviet Union, foremost among the Slavic languages, and the official tongue of the new world system, Communism. The territory over which I exercise full direct sway embraces one sixth of the earth's land surface, and my influence extends not only to all lands that have embraced the Communist gospel, but to all lands where there are Communists. Yet, while I represent a new philosophy of life, I am linguistically conservative, preserving the ancient Indo-European structure far better than any of my rivals. My sound-scheme is far from unpleasant to the ear; my grammatical rules, while complex, are no more so than those of Latin, Greek, or Sanskrit. I have served as the vehicle for some of the world's most important literature, and I am now developing into a language for scientific and commercial use. I represent both the past and the future."

"Despite your territorial extent, you are far more of an insular language than the tongue of the British Isles. You are landlocked and circumscribed. Around you there are two iron rings, one fashioned by your enemies, the other by yourself. While you claim to represent a new way of life and social order, the linguistic conservatism of which you boast, and your grammar and system of word-formation, represent a methodology that went out of style with the fall of the Roman Empire. Your words are excessively long, and weighted down with a mighty burden of endings. Your cases are bewildering to the speakers of most modern tongues. Your vocabulary is restricted, and departs from the Graeco-Latin norm that has been accepted by most western tongues. Your unstressed vowels are unclear, almost to the same extent as those of English, and your consonant clusters, while not as frequent as those of German, are equally bad when they occur. Your accentuation is capricious, arbitrary, and unpredictable."

"I am the Chinese language, a tongue of greater antiquity and more unbroken tradition than any language of the west, barring none. I have been in uninterrupted use since at least 2000 B.C., serving a population that achieved the arts of civilization long before your Greeks and Romans had issued from their barbarous nomadic state. This population today amounts to between 500 and 600 million—easily one fifth of the total number of the earth's inhabitants, and roughly double that of my nearest rival, English. In the course not of centuries, but of millennia, I have developed one of the simplest, most direct and concise grammatical structures on earth. With me, no one need worry about endings and cases and declensions and conjugations. My word-stock, composed of roots of a single syllable, is capable of infinite expansion by the simple process of composition. I can say in five words what it will take one of your western languages five sentences to achieve, yet I will say it in such a way as to bring out to the full the imagery and poetry of language."

"You, too, are a landlocked tongue, with little possibility of overseas expansion. Your speakers, while numerous, are mainly concentrated in one region of the earth, and you have done little to remedy their illiteracy. As a spoken tongue, you are broken up into numerous dialects, so different that they amount in practice to separate tongues. You are held together only by the artifice of a common written language, and once that fails you, as it must if you are to be phonetized, the number of your speakers will shrink, and your defects will become glaring indeed. Your sounds and tones are remote and unfamiliar to the majority of the other peoples of the earth. While you are the vehicle of an ancient and noble civilization, that civilization is too far removed from the main highways of culture, which have by-passed you to the east and to the west. You are not merely an isolating, but an isolated language."

"I am Finnish, an avowedly minor tongue. My speakers are no more than four or five million, and even if to them you add the speakers of related languages, like Estonian and Lapp, you do not go beyond a total of six or seven million. What, then, is my justification for presenting myself side by side with the giants of the language world? Simply this: in a world torn by fierce nationalistic jealousies and imperialisms, I am a thoroughly neutral tongue, partial to none of the great language groups, and representative of the numerous small languages whose speakers, summed together, are more numerous than those of any one of the world's greater tongues. I belong to a minor linguistic family, the Ural-Altaic, which does not seem linked to any of the others. My vocabulary and sentence structure are equally unfamiliar to the speakers of Romance, Germanic or Slavic, of Chinese or Semitic or Hindustani. All will have to make an equal effort to learn me. I represent no imperialistic tendencies whatsoever. I am not the carrier of any aggressive nationalistic tendencies or special political ideologies. I can be embraced with equal ease by the Americans and the Russians. My sounds are extremely simple and easy for the speakers of any other tongue, and my system of writing, even at present, is so thoroughly phonetic that little or no change will have to be made in order to phonetize me if I should be selected. My grammatical structure is logical; if it is complex, it is equally complex for anyone who has to learn me. If neutrality and impartiality are wanted in the international tongue, then I am the ideal candidate."

"You acknowledge your lack of speakers, distribution, and general importance, so nothing further need be said on that score. But you have other drawbacks. Your sounds are simple, but, as you admit, your grammar is hard. You have far too many cases and endings, and they are completely unfamiliar to all except your speakers. Your vocabulary is strange and difficult, and utterly uninternational. You will indeed have to be learned the hard way."

Jean-Marie Bressand, spokesman for *le Monde Bilingue,* now takes the floor:

"I am not one language," he says, "but a combination of two, the two that are most widespread over the earth's surface, both commercially and culturally–English and French. I shall not repeat what has already been said on behalf of each of my two components. What I wish to emphasize is that I offer a practical, acceptable compromise solution of the problem. Taken together, my two members are native to one human being out of seven. But if we consider the number of those who have some knowledge and understanding of both or either of them, or who can be easily, even though indirectly, reached by one of them, the proportion is roughly one out of two or three. What single tongue, natural or constructed, can make a similar claim? The Bilingual World represents not theory or hypothesis, but actual linguistic reality, and this gives it a tremendous advantage over all its competitors. Taken individually, English and French represent mankind's highest achievements, both in the past and in the present, both in the realms of science and commerce and in those of abstract thought and literature. The vast numbers of people of other tongues who have acquired these two languages are direct evidence of their individual power of attraction. Pooled together, they are irresistible, and are certain to lead mankind to ever loftier heights of progress and civilization."

The devil's advocate replies: "Your two languages are but two facets of a single form of thought, one that in the past has imposed itself not only by its civilizing influence, but also by brute force of arms. You represent a crystallization of the status quo, not an advance into the future. One of your members has already lost much ground, the other is barely holding its gains. Why should mankind accept you and your burden from the past? Why should it continue to bow forever to the type of civilization you represent? Why should it accept the added burden of language learning represented by two international languages where one would amply suffice?"

These are a few samples of imaginary nominating speeches and rebuttals by individual devil's advocates. For the purposes of our illustration, we may at this point conceive the closing of nominations for natural tongues (though many more will undoubtedly be presented if the linguistic congress ever meets) and pass on to a similar brief discussion of constructed languages.

28. Pro and con: the constructed languages present their candidacy

Basic English—Esperanto—Interglossa—Interlingua—The Devil's Advocate

As against a precise figure of 2,796 natural languages, all of which are potential candidates, the estimated maximum of constructed tongues is about 600. Of these, many are so far in the past that it will occur to no one to resurrect them. Yet a respectable group remains whose followers, many or few, still live and prosper. There is little point to presenting the hypothetical candidacy of numerous systems which, departing from the identical principles, are far too much alike (an excellent critical comparison of Esperanto, Ido, the old Interlingua, and Romanal appears in Guérard).

Four systems that differ radically, all of them advanced in modern times, may serve as samples of the arguments that will be advanced for and against the various constructed tongues that will pose their candidacy.

A delegate addresses the chair: "Mine is the voice of Basic English,* and the statement that I here make about myself is an example of that small-scale language at work. As a separate language system, I am the invention of one man (C. K. Ogden, 1890–1957), but as a part of English I am as old as the rest of the language. Man made though natural, springing from the mother tongue like Minerva from the head of Jupiter, I came into being armed with the powers—though wisely limited—of full English. Such skill has been used in the selection of my 850 words that with them man may say almost anything—in business, trade, industry, science, medical work—in all the arts of living and in all the exchanges of knowledge, belief, opinion, views and news which a general-purpose language has to take care of. Learning to do so is not hard because the rules for putting my words together have been made clear and simple and short. But there is nothing in good Basic which goes against the rules of good English. Great books have been put into me, as well as talks to men and women at the far ends of the earth. Because my word list is so short, all my sounds may be played on one recording, and teaching me with the help of sound motion pictures is becoming simpler and simpler. Moreover, my selection as servant of the earth's needs would give to men everywhere, if not

* This presentation, in Basic English, was supplied by Miss Christine M. Gibson of Language Research, Inc. It comes in part from the definition appearing in *Learning Basic English,* by I. A. Richards and C. M. Gibson, New York, Norton, 1945. Acknowledgment is gratefully made to the authors and publishers of *Learning Basic English.*

theirs by birth, use of one of the great living languages. I am a door opening on wider English."

The devil's advocate rises in rebuttal. "You are neither a natural nor a constructed tongue, but a distortion of a living language. The only improvement you offer over natural English is a restriction and limitation of vocabulary, which is no improvement at all, for the language of the future needs an abundant word-stock capable of taking care of all the needs of civilized living. Your claims are deceitful, since you permit the addition of special sets of words for special pursuits, thereby multiplying your vocabulary until it grows to be many times the 850 words with which you say you can achieve communication. You are bewildering to the speakers of English, who find themselves beset by restrictions at every step in the use of the tongue that is natural to them. You are offensive to non-English speakers, who find that you complicate their problems of translation far beyond the point of endurance. Your combinations of nouns and adverbs, nouns and prepositions, are highly idiomatic and highly tricky, as well as logically inaccurate. You do nothing to simplify the problems of English pronunciation or of English grammar, or to offer standardization of a tongue so highly unstandardized."

It is now the turn of a delegate who wishes to propose the candidacy of Esperanto: "I am the voice of Esperanto, the one and only constructed language that has a body of living speakers, the only language of my artificial family that has had the honor of a full, free discussion at international conferences and international bodies, and has been recommended by a consensus of such bodies to serve as the world language. Numerous nations have issued stamps in my honor, using me; even more numerous are the nations that use me officially over their air waves, and otherwise recognize me as a secondary language. I am neutral, since I belong to no nation. I am thoroughly international, yet quite familiar in spots to all who undertake to use me. My grammatical structure, while so simple that a child can learn me, has points of contact with the languages of the Indo-European group, with those of the agglutinative family, even with the isolating tongues. My vocabulary represents a blend of the two most numerous groups of the Indo-European stock, the Latin-Romance and the Germanic, but in me you will find Greek, Slavic, Oriental words. My system of suffixes and word-formation lends itself to infinite expansion of vocabulary and full-fledged literary use, and this I have proved by developing a flourishing literature, both original and in translation. My sounds are easy for all to pronounce, for I have taken only those sounds which most civilized languages hold in common, and my syllabic arrangement is open and clear, so that I vie with Italian in harmony and euphony. My system of spelling and accentuation is such that no one need ever be in the least doubt as to how any one of my words is pronounced when he sees it written, or how it is spelled when he hears it uttered. My career has not been ephemeral, like that of Volapük; despite oppositions and rivalries, I have survived and grown, and today my followers are more numerous than they have ever been. The smaller nations of the world favor me, as well they should, since I put their citizens on a plane of absolute linguistic equality with those of the larger and more powerful world states. When people hear the term 'international language,' nine out of ten think of me, and not of any other tongue, national or constructed."

The voice of the devil's advocate is heard: "You are an artificial, not a natural tongue. You are the product of one man's brain, not the outcome of a slow process of evolution. People who speak you are forever conscious of your artificiality, and consider you not so much a language as a game or a fad. You claim to be fully neutral and fully international, but your vocabulary, and even your grammar, lean heavily in the direction of the western tongues. The Slavic and Oriental elements you claim to possess are extremely scanty, and certainly not such as to predispose a speaker of those tongues in your favor. Being the product of a single brain, you are arbitrary in the extreme, and, in spots, unpredictable. What made you select the English *bird,* an isolated word that does not appear even in the other Germanic languages, in the place of the far more widespread *avis* or *avicellum* root of Latin, the *ornith-* of Greek, or even the *Vogel*-fowl of Germanic? Why do you turn to the German *Knabe* for 'boy' when *puer* and *paid-* are at your disposal? Why do you form your noun-plurals in the isolated Greek fashion, when *-s* is so much more widespread? Your sounds are monotonous and tiresome, and speakers of different languages tend to pronounce them in their own fashion, so that even now your pronunciation shows as many cleavages as does that of your predecessor, Latin. Your system of writing is phonetic, but your suprascript characters offer complications and often require substitution."

The nomination now shifts to Interglossa, presented perhaps by its distinguished creator, Lancelot Hogben: "I am a language that endeavors to combine western and Oriental elements, so that I may be equally acceptable to East and West. My vocabulary is largely that of international science, with a predominance of Greek roots, which are already familiar to most of the scientists of the West. My syntax is the isolating syntax of Chinese, a simple, resilient system that permits economy of words with a maximum of understanding. If I have not gained great favor, it is precisely because I have endeavored to achieve strict neutrality and a maximum of compromise."

The devil's advocate replies: "In your endeavor to achieve neutrality, you have turned into a system that pleases nobody. How can the speaker of Chinese, who might like your syntax, be expected to rest content with your vocabulary, which is totally unfamiliar to him? How can the western scientist, who knows your word-roots, be pleased with your syntax, to which he is not as accustomed? You have used Greek rather than Latin elements in your vocabulary. But does the average speaker of a western tongue, who knows the general meaning of 'microphone,' also know that the word's two elements mean 'small' and 'sound'? Does he know that *hetero-* is 'other,' and *dyne* is 'strength'? By endeavoring to be too neutral, you have ended by not being neutral enough, at least to the extent of winning acceptance from a considerable portion of the world's speakers."

Dr. Alexander Gode, greatest exponent of Interlingua, now offers his tongue: "I am the voice of Interlingua, the only scientifically constructed language in the world, the product of the labors of the world's greatest linguistic minds over a period of nearly thirty years. I am the language of international scientific congresses, because anyone who is scientifically trained can read and even understand me with ease. The principle that inspired my makers was that of maximum internationality of both words and grammatical forms, and this is reflected in my widespread acceptance in scientific circles."

An Esperantist rises to perform the function of devil's advocate: "Your rules of pronunciation and accentuation are delightfully vague, not fixed; this means that your chances of breaking up into various dialects are enormous. Your guiding principle is erroneous; because you used as your pilot languages a group of tongues in which Latin-Romance held an absolute majority, the outcome was a foregone conclusion; you are not so much an international as you are a Pan-Romance tongue. Of course you are easily understood by speakers of Romance or English. But what happens when a speaker of German, Slavic, or Chinese faces you? The scientist or scholar who can understand you could just as easily understand English, French, Spanish, or Italian, since they all hold the same scientific vocabulary in common. It is the little man who must be considered, the one whose linguistic and intellectual equipment is not vast. When your control tongues fail to show a majority, you arbitrarily use a Latin word. Why? You supply synonyms, but in haphazard fashion, instead of trying to utilize them to establish needed distinctions of meaning. You have no true speaking population, but only a reading public; and your reading public is such that it could read half a dozen natural languages as easily as it can read you."

These are some of the arguments, pro and con, that we might reasonably expect to hear advanced at a linguistic congress designed to select, from among the many natural and constructed languages, a single tongue for universal use.

Of great importance is the time limitation. Linguists (and we would hope that the delegates would be linguists, not politicians), if left to their own devices, would consume centuries. But with limited time for presentation and rebuttal, and with no more than one candidacy permitted to each delegate, the initial labors of the convention might be held to a reasonable limit. The runoff elections would be fully automatic, and consume one week at the most. At the end of a month, the international language would be selected. But this, of course, would be only the end of a beginning, not the beginning of the end.

29. What a world language won't do for us

The Lessons of History—The Abolition of War—A Millennium of Tolerance—The Era of Good Feeling—Dialectalization—Standardization—Eventual Disappearance of the National Tongues

Once the international language is selected, the real work of implementation will begin. But in its early reaches, it will hardly impinge upon the consciousness of the average man.

A five-year period of preparation is none too long for the double job that has to be done at this point. First will come the labors of a linguistic commission whose task it will be to smooth out the rough angles of the selected tongue. If this is a natural tongue, it must, first of all, be perfectly and fully phonetized. But this in turn means that it must be fully standardized. The task of standardization will be relatively easy in the case of a language, like French, which has a national academy and a generally recognized "correct" form; it will be difficult in the case of a language, like English, which displays important cleavages of a dialectal nature. It must be emphasized that the process of standardization and phonetization will apply to the language only in its international form, and that for purely internal use the speakers of the language will be left free to do what they choose. This will at once differentiate the national and the international language; the former will continue with its irregularities and antiquated spelling. The latter will be presented in invariable, prescribed, arbitrary form as to speech, with absolute correspondence of sound and symbol as to writing. If the speakers of the national language choose to adopt the new international variant for their own local use as well, so much the better for them; they will get rid of complexities of grammar and spelling that have been troubling them for centuries, and become at once the natural speakers of the international tongue. But this is not at all necessary or required.

If the choice happens to fall on a constructed tongue, a similar process of polishing will go on. Phonetization must be perfect and complete. Such points of grammar and vocabulary as have given rise to serious criticism must be carefully re-examined. Esperanto, for instance, might be required to get rid of its suprascript characters by the simple expedient of utilizing those letters of the standard western alphabet which it has discarded—*q, w, x,* and *y;* it might be requested to add to its word-stock a copious list of synonyms derived from the Slavic and Oriental tongues, so that its claims to neutrality and internationality may be strengthened.

This process of final revision of the international language should, however, be limited to one year, with the firm understanding that at the end of that year the commission will come up with a final draft of the language selected, and that this draft will, in effect, become final, and be subject in the future only to the natural processes of growth and development that at present characterize every living language.

Now comes the task of teacher training. Since the foundation of the entire system is that the international language be imparted, by natural speaking processes, to the world's future generations from kindergarten on, it is particularly important that the people who will devote themselves to this task be educational experts of the first order, and at the same time accomplished linguists in the spoken language field, with particular emphasis not on "linguistic science," general information about languages, philology, literary history, or even grammar, but on ability to learn and speak foreign languages with absolute purity of accent. The search for a large group of people of this description will not be easy, but the educational authorities of the various countries can accomplish it during the same year that the linguistic commission is putting the finishing touches to the international language. By the end of the year, both language and teaching staff should be ready.

A much smaller number of specially qualified teachers can be set apart to "teach" the international language in the upper elementary grades, high schools, colleges, and universities to those of the adult or near-adult generations who care to have it. It should be understood, however, that no one beyond the kindergarten years will be forced to learn the international tongue. This will be compulsory only for those who reach the kindergarten stage after the language enters into operation, which will not occur until five years after its selection and four years after it has been given definitive shape. Four years of training in the spoken language are not too many for those who are to impart it by natural methods as a spoken, natural tongue.

At this point, some adult readers will object: "But is not the international language for us?" It is, if you want it; it is not, if you don't. The international language should be viewed primarily as something for the world of the future, for those children and children's children concerning whom so many fine words flow, but on behalf of whom so little is ever done by each existing adult generation. The people of the world have waited many centuries, throughout many generations, which have grown old and died out without accomplishing anything about a world language. They can afford to wait a few years longer, with the absolute assurance that something will be done to smooth the way for their descendants. At any rate, there is nothing to prevent them from learning the new tongue at their own adult stage, the hard way, which is precisely the way in which they would learn any foreign tongue today. The real point is that if the world language goes into operation by, say, 1965, it will be spoken in the year 2000 by the younger adult generations of the entire globe, and by 2025 there will be few indeed who do not speak it.

It would be highly unfair, as well as highly illiberal, to try to force the international language upon all the adult generations of today. In addition, it would be highly impractical, not to say impossible. Let today's adults do what they want. The national languages will continue in full spoken use for centuries to come. The man who does not feel hampered today by his ignorance of foreign tongues will not feel hampered by his ignorance of the new, growing tongue that he hears spoken around him by the younger set, since the youngsters will also speak the tongue to which he is accustomed. If he is curious to know what goes on in their midst, he will learn it.

The educational means at our disposal today are such as the world has never before seen. Not only do we have schools and widespread literacy; we have radio, television, and spoken films. This on the one hand adds up to insurance that the international tongue will be readily learned by all who want it, as well as by the children who are absorbing it in kindergarten and elementary school; on the other hand, it means that there will be no dialectalization, no fractioning of the language into the multitude of local forms that characterizes almost every known language of today.

A unified language disintegrates into dialects when communications break down. The Latin language ceased to be Latin and became a variety of Romance tongues and dialects only after the Roman Empire, with its mighty network of roads and interchange of human beings, fell. So long as that Empire stood, language became more and more unified and standardized. American and British English diverged so long as communications were lengthy and difficult. Today, the two varieties of English are in the process of merging once more, with both British and American local dialects tending to die out and give way to a standard form of speech.

Those who claim that an international language, once established, would break up into a series of local speech-forms ignore the lessons of history. Language becomes united and standard when there is communication among all the speakers; it becomes a series of dialects when there is no such communication. Communications have never been so good as they are today. Only a catastrophe of major proportions, a full-fledged atomic war, or a mighty upheaval of nature, could break the communication links of today.

What of the problem of international conflicts and wars? Some of the advocates of international tongues optimistically assure us that an international language will abolish them forever. This is, of course, wishful thinking. History is there to recite to us a long list of civil wars among peoples speaking the same tongue. The most that we can claim is that the international tongue may succeed in removing such forms of national and racial antipathy as are engendered by linguistic lack of understanding. But, as aptly stated by Guérard, "sometimes people fight because they don't understand; sometimes because they understand each other too well." A man who walks along the street and is insulted by a hoodlum in a tongue he does not understand may blissfully continue on his way in the belief that the hoodlum has voiced a compliment; but if he understands the insult, he may put up his fists.

One problem that deeply concerns us all is the future of the existing national tongues. Will they be displaced by the international language, and eventually die out? Or will they forever continue to exist side by side with the new language for everybody?

Advocates of Esperanto, Basic English, Interlingua, etc. often assure us that their tongue is to be viewed "only" as an auxiliary language for international purposes, mainly commercial and diplomatic, that it will in no way affect the use of the national languages, that the latter will forever continue to exist and flourish despite the existence of the international medium.

This is again wishful thinking, but with the added feature that it is extremely doubtful whether even the wish should be there. The international language, valid at all times and in all places, will undoubtedly restrict the use of the national tongues, whose effective range is limited. In economics, bad money drives good money out of circulation because all want to hoard good money for future use. But language cannot be stored up for future use. Its utility is in the present. As time goes on, there will be less use of the national tongues, more use of the world tongue. Writers will prefer the new medium, which gives them access to world markets without the need of difficult and expensive translations. Advertisers will prefer it for the same reason. Dante once admitted that the main reason that had led him to write his *Divine Comedy* in Italian rather than the scholarly Latin of his day was that he wished to reach a broader public.

The final outcome seems clear. The national languages of today will live on for centuries, but their use will tend to become more and more restricted. Ultimately, they will turn into cultural relics, like the Greek and Latin of today. Should that prospect frighten us? Consider that language is forever changing, and that the English of the year 2500 would strike the present-day speaker as practically a foreign tongue. In five centuries the languages of today will be unrecognizable in any event. From our twentieth-century viewpoint, it would perhaps be better if they were embalmed in their present form, at their present stage of development.

Where the advocates of international tongues are undoubtedly right is in their assumption that the national languages of today will go on in full spoken use long after the present generations of speakers die out.

The people of tomorrow will evolve their own forms of life, political, economic, and cultural. The imperfections of our own present-day systems are glaring. Why should we wish to impose them unchanged upon the future generations? But a universal language is a tool, a means of rapid and easy communication. It is conceivable that some might not wish to pass on to their descendants some of our political and economic institutions, but few indeed would be those who would not wish to pass on to them the advances we have made in the fields of science, medicine, and technology, which are tools to human happiness and progress. To these, let us add one more tool—a tongue that will permit all of our descendants, regardless of color, race, nationality, or religion, to exchange their thoughts.

30. What we must do about a world language

Wishful Thinking About Our Own Language—Joining a Movement—Private Propaganda—Bringing Pressure to Bear on Governments—On Behalf of A World Language

The desirability of a world language is not seriously disputed by at least four people out of five. The fact that no one has yet fought a civil war over it need not preoccupy us. Civil wars are fought over issues that arouse great passions, either because great principles are at stake, or because people's economic, racial, social, political, or religious interests are involved. The international language is primarily a tool, not a principle or an interest. It is missed by a great many people on numerous and specific occasions, but seldom in such a way as to arouse fiery passion or fanatic zeal.

Yet the international language is, in its own way, an issue—one that we have temporized with for centuries, but which becomes more pressing with each new advance in technological science and the network of communications. In some ways, it resembles the ultramodern traffic problem in a great city, which grows and grows to the point of near strangulation. People worry along with makeshift temporary solutions, but the problem always keeps ahead of the solutions. "Some day," they say, "something will really have to be done."

The time is perhaps at hand when something will really have to be done about both problems. For what concerns the international language, the solution, while not easy, is clear. Let one language, natural or constructed, be selected by common accord, and let that language thenceforth be imparted in all of the schools of all countries, by natural speaking methods, on a par with the national languages. The machinery for both selection and implementation has been described. Details of both may vary, but the general line of action is unmistakable.

Those who have followed me in my exposition of the problem, and have found that the solution proposed is, in the main, reasonable and workable, will now come up with the sixty-four-thousand-dollar question: "What can I, as an individual, do to help bring about a world language?"

It is easier, in a way, to tell you what you should not do, or, to put it more squarely, what it is useless for you to do.

If you are convinced that there should be a world language (and four out of five people hold that conviction) here are a few things you should refrain from doing:

1. Do not indulge in self-hypnosis concerning the inevitability of your own language as the world tongue. This advice is particularly directed at speakers of English and French,

the two natural languages that are most often mentioned, at least by their own speakers, as likely candidates for the role. It is also directed at dedicated believers in certain constructed languages, notably Esperanto and Interlingua. If you, as a speaker of English, start out by saying, as do some of our leading exponents of so-called thought: "How wonderful it would be if everybody spoke English!" you at once run the risk of antagonizing the nine tenths of the world's population which does not speak English. You can impose English (or French, or Russian, or German, or any of a dozen other "big" languages) by force of arms, if you care to try that method; but in a world where the hydrogen bomb rules supreme, it is not advisable. Propaganda on behalf of the language of your choice is legitimate, provided it is carried on with an accurate knowledge of the facts and full consideration for the viewpoint of others; but the value of such propaganda is invariably diminished by more than half when it is carried on by native speakers of the language. Of course you would prefer English, which would call for no effort on your part; and equally of course, speakers of other languages would prefer their own.

If you are a partisan of a constructed tongue, remember that your particular solution is far from the only one, as evidenced by the few we have outlined above. You may think it is the best one; others may hold different opinions. At any rate, get rid of the attitude that "it must be my language—or bust!"

In sum, we must be prepared to accept another language than the one of our choice. If this language is selected by something approximating the democratic process, we should be prepared to go along with the choice of the majority, as we do in national and local elections where our side often loses out, but life goes on nevertheless.

2. "Joining a movement" (Esperanto, Interlingua, *Monde Bilingue,* etc.) is in itself innocuous, and may even be helpful,

to the extent that it fastens your own attention and that of others on the problem and the need for a solution. Do not, however, join the movement in the spirit in which you would join a religious group, since the triumph of one or another language system does not involve either your immortal soul or the fate of the world. Remember, too, that "movements" have displayed their inefficacy in the past, and that the conversion of all the world's individuals to the system of your choice is a practical impossibility. What the Christian, Moslem, and Buddhist faiths have been unable to accomplish (the unification of the entire world by persuasion) can hardly be accomplished by your "movement" or by any other.

3. There is an opposite vice to fanaticism, and that is excessive skepticism and experimentalism. A good many of today's interlinguists go to the extreme of casting doubt upon all languages, natural or constructed, and attempt to evolve new, more "scientific," more "logical" systems. The natural tongues have already proved their suitability as means of communication, by the very fact that they exist and are in use. The majority of constructed tongues, particularly those that have been advanced within the last century, are perfect enough to go into immediate use. All we need to do to make a successful international language out of any national tongue is to give it a fully phonetic system of writing, coupled with standardization of dialectal forms. In the case of the constructed tongues, a minor going-over to smooth out the angles that have elicited major criticisms is all that is needed. Any further "study" of the problem, as envisaged by UNESCO, is a pure waste of valuable time. Nor do we need another thirty-year study of the Interlingua type, in the course of which still another generation will die out without achieving anything.

These are the purely negative aspects of the situation. On the positive side, this much can be said: No language or system, nor even any survey or study, has the slightest chance of success unless it has on it the stamp of the official, *de facto* governments of the world, coupled with their powers of implementation and enforcement. We can never convince all of the world's people of the absolute superiority of one language or system over the others, and in this the world's people probably show their good sense, because no such absolute superiority exists. What we have instead is an entire series of workable languages and systems, any one of which, with a few minor retouches, applied for the most part in the field of writing and spelling, is competent to serve.

The world's governments must be induced to make up their minds that they are willing to accept one such language or system, as determined by a compulsory runoff vote of the members of a linguistic commission in which all the nations of the world will be equitably represented, and then put it into their school systems. The machinery for the original decision on the part of the governments to accept, in principle and in advance, the language that will be chosen is already there, in the form of UN and UNESCO.

People of all countries who are convinced that there should be a world language should bring pressure to bear upon their governments to bring up the issue in the only international bodies that we have at our disposal. This pressure, it must be emphasized, should not be directed on behalf of a particular language or system, but simply and merely on behalf of *a* world language, as yet undetermined. The languages and systems whose candidacy will be advanced will then rest upon their respective merits before a body that will include representatives of all nations on earth, chosen by their respective governments on any basis the individual government sees fit, but bound to a democratic process of majority rule.

The movement on behalf of *a* world language, as distinguished from movements on behalf of specific languages and systems, has a good chance of success. It can be carried on individually or in groups. It can and should attract all followers of specific movements who are genuinely interested in seeing one language for one world rather than the triumph of the tongue they happen to favor.

In all countries of the earth, totalitarian as well as democratic, there exists a limited right of petition in connection with things that are not considered subversive of the existing order. The international language tends to subvert nothing, but only to make communications easier and faster among the peoples of the world. Anyone can write a letter to his government, urging that steps be taken to bring about the same ease in human that exists in postal communications.

Wherever you are, if you believe in one language for one world, let your government, the UN, and UNESCO know it!

APPENDIX A: SAMPLES OF CONSTRUCTED LANGUAGES

Samples of constructed languages

In addition to the samples of constructed languages we have given in Part 2 of our discussion, it may be of interest to offer a few additional specimens, culled for the most part from the much larger collection given by Stojan. The first division consists of individual brief passages, for which a translation is offered. The second division consists of constructed-language translations of the first part of the Lord's Prayer.

LA PROMIERO LINIO DO SEZ FIGURO EZ LETANDUO POSIBLO DO TUTO LEZ FIGURO DO LA NATURO ("The first line of these figures is the possible extent of all the figures in nature"). Lango du Mondo, 1788, de Ria (This is largely a phonetically spelled French, in which the letter *o* is used to represent the French *e*-mute).

TIS AMBSATE UN PREM'QE M'AT DEBAT ("You dispute a prize which belongs to me"). Neo-Latin, 1885, Courtonne.

AK VOP SFERMED PRO SPES MANED, IF OM POBL TO POBL, NE EI MNOKA PFO AN AM LANK ("What an immense advantage for mankind, if from people to people we could communicate through the same language!"). Bolak [La Langue Bleue], 1899, Bollack.

CUJUS APPETAT BONUM ALIENUM, AMITTAT MERITO PROPRIUM BONUM ("Let the one who covets another's property justly lose his own property"). Linguum Islianum, 1901, Isly (This will be recognized as practically unchanged Latin).

IRGA CHANJO EN LA STATUTI DI L'UNIONO OD EN SA SKOPO DEVOS ESAR DECIDITA DA LA KOMITATO PER PLUMULTO DE SU TRIONI E SANCIONITA DI LA RIPREZENTANTI PER LA SAMA PLUMULTO ("Every change in the constitution of the union or in its purpose must be decided by the committee through the majority of its members and sanctioned by the representatives through the same majority"). Ido, 1908, De Beaufront and Couturat.

LINGUAS DE EUROPA, AB ANGLO AD ITALO, AB HISPANO AD RUSSO, HABE MAGNO VOCABULARIO COMMUNE, CUM ORIGINE IN LATINO, IN GRAECO, IN INDOEUROPAEO ("The languages of Europe, from English to Italian, from Spanish to Russian, have a great common vocabulary, with its origin in Latin, in Greek, in Indo-European"). Latino Sine Flexione, 1909, Peano.

LA CYENCO NO HAVAY DIRITE ANKORE LA ULTIMA PAROLO PRI LA TUBERKULOSO KAY LA KANCERO. MI OPINIAY KE LA PROJEKTO NO ESTAY KOMPLETA ("Science has not yet said the last word on tuberculosis and cancer. I think that the project is not complete"). Hom-Idyomo, 1924, Cardenas.

PATER NOSTER QUI ES IN COELIS, SANCTIFICETUR NOMEN TUUM, ADVENIAT REGNUM TUUM, FIAT VOLUNTAS TUA, SICUT IN COELO ET IN TERRA (This is the Latin version of the first part of the Lord's Prayer, as it appears in the Vulgate of St. Jerome, composed in 383 A.D.).

O BADERUS NODERUS KI DU ESSO IN SELUMA, FAKDADE SANKADUS HA NOMINANDA DUUS, ADFENADE HA RENNANDA DUUS, HA FOLANDA DUUS FIASSADE FELUD IN SELUMA, SIK KOKE IN DERRA. Carporophilus, 1734, anonymously published in Leipzig.

PATRE NOSTRI RESIDENT IN CELE, TEI NOMINE E SANCTIFICAT, TEI REGNE VOLE VENIR A NOSTRI, TEI VOLUNTATE E EXEQUER NE SOLU IN CELE MA ETI IN TERRE. Mundolingue, 1890, Lott.

PATRO NUE KVU ESTEN IN CIELO, SANKTE ESTAN TUE NOMO, VENAN REGITO TUE, ESTAN VOLO TUE, KOM IN CIELO SIK ANKU SUR TERO. Reformita Esperanto, 1894, Zamenhof.

VIO FADR HU BI IN HEVN, HOLIRN BI DAUO NAM, DAUO REIK KOM, DAUO VIL BI DUN AN ERD AS IT BE IN HEVN. Tutonish, 1902, Molee.

PATRE NOSTRO QUI ES IN CELOS, QUE TUO NOMINE FI SANCTIFICATO, QUE TUO REGNO ADVENI, QUE TUA VOLUNTATE ES FACTA SICUT IN CELO ET IN TERRA. Latino Sine Flexione, 1903, Peano.

PATRO NOSA QUA ESTAN EN CIELOS, SANTA ESTEN TUA NOMO, ADVENEN TUA REGNO, ESTEN FARATA TUA VOLO QUALE EN CIELOS TALE ANKE SUR LA TERO. Adjuvilo, 1910, Colas.

PATRO NOSTRI QUI EST EN CIELES, SANCTIFICAT ESTAS NOMINE TUI, ADVENIAS REGNE TUI, FIAS VOLITE TUI SICUT EN CIELE ET EN TERRE. Romanal, 1912, Michaux.

VATERO NIA KIU ESTAS EN COELUMO, HEILIGA ESTU NAMEO VIA, KOMMENU REGNEO VIA, ESTU WILLEO VIA KIEL EN COELUMO TIEL SUR ERDEO. Nepo, 1915, Cheshikhin. (Note the change from the earlier version, given on page 170, in which Slavic words were added to the Germanic and Latin-Romance.)

O MAISEN PARENTO KVI ESS IN ZOELI, VUN NOMI SAGITU, VUN REGNARI VENU, VUN BILI AGITU KVAM IN ZOELI TAM IN TERRI. Nov Latin Logui, 1918, Pompiati.

PATRO NOSYO QI E AN CIELUS, SANTIFITA ESAY NOMA TUYA, VENAY REGA TUYA, FACAY VOLUNTA TUYA QOM AN CIELU ETI SUR LA TERA. Uniala, 1923, Troost.

NIA PATRO KIU ESTAS EN HIMELO, SANTA ESTU ZIA NOMO, ZIA REGNO VENU, ZIA VOLO ESTU KIEL EN HIMELO TIEL SUR TERO. Esperido, 1927, Raymond.

PATRO NINA KAY ESTAS EN LA CIELO, SANKTA ESTOY VINA NOMO, VENOY REJECO VINA, ESTOY VOLO VINA KALE EN LA CIELO TALE SUR LA TERO. Nov Esperanto, 1928, De Saussure.

NOSTRO PATRO KI ES IN URANO, TUO NOMIN A SANKTIFIK, TUO VOL A ES, KUAM IN URANO TAM IN GEO. Etem, 1928, Yushmanov.

MEMS PATRO QWE ESIP IR CELESTII, TOM NOMINI SANTIFICATAP, TOM REGNI VENAP, TOM VOLITI FIATAP AQ IR CELESTII TALEQ OR TERRI. Qosmiani, 1928, Beatty.

PATRO NIA QUE ES NEL SIELI, VUA NOMO SANTIFICEVEU, VUA REGNO ADVENEU, VUA VOLO FAREVEU SUR IL TERO QUALE NEL SIELO. Novam, 1928, Touflet.

PATRO NIE QU ES IN CIELI, SANTIZAT EZ TUE NOM, ARIVEZ TUE REGN, TUE VOL EZ EXEKUTAT QUAL IN CIEL TAL ANK IN TER. Ido Reformita, 1928, Meazzini.

APPENDIX B: A LIST OF USEFUL ADDRESSES

A list of useful addresses

The following names and addresses will be of use to readers wishing to make specific inquiries about some of the constructed languages and other international language systems outlined in this work:

ESPERANTO. Esperanto Association of North America (G. Alan Connor, Secretary General), 114 West 16 St., New York 11, N.Y., U.S.A.

British Esperanto Association, 140 Holland Park Ave., London W. 11, England.

INTERLINGUA. Dr. Alexander Gode, 80 East 11 St., New York 3, N.Y., U.S.A.

ESPERANTO AND INTERLINGUA COMPARED. Ivy K. Reed, 315 Westbourne St., La Jolla, Calif., U.S.A.

IDO. Floyd Hardin, P.O. Box 393, Denver, Colo., U.S.A.

Uniono por la Linguo Internaciona, Case Champel 27, Genève, Switzerland.

INTERGLOSSA. Lancelot Hogben, Queen Elizabeth Hospital, Birmingham, England.

BASIC ENGLISH. I. A. Richards, Harvard College, Cambridge 38, Mass., U.S.A.

Christine Gibson, Language Research, Inc., 13 Kirkland St., Cambridge 38, Mass., U.S.A.

ZONAL LANGUAGES. Léonce Thommeret, Rue Cujas 18, Paris XV, France.

MONDE BILINGUE. Jean-Marie Bressand, Rue Racine 13, Paris VI, France.

American Bilingual Association, 895 West End Ave., New York 25, N.Y., U.S.A.

BASIC FRENCH. Georges Gougenheim, Université de Strasbourg, Strasbourg, France.

MONGLING. Kenneth Littlewood, Leeds, England.

COSMOGLOTTA. Interlingue-Institute, Cheseaux, Lausanne, Switzerland.

OCCIDENTAL. Institute Occidental, Chapelle (Vaud), Switzerland.

INTERLINGU. Thomas Wood, 39 Devonshire Road, Hazel Grove, Stockport, Cheshire, England.

SUMA. Dr. Barnett Russell, 1219 Gardena Blvd., Gardena, Calif., U.S.A.

LATIN. Mgr. Antonio Bacci, *Latinitas*, Vatican City.

PHONETICS (IPA). Daniel Jones, University College, London, England.

SPELLING REFORM. Godfrey Dewey, Simpler Spelling Association of America, Lake Placid Club, N.Y., U.S.A.

British Simplified Spelling Society, 34 Cranbourn St., London, W.C. 2, England.

B. Wrenick, Simplified Spelling Society, Ashley Rise, Walton-on-Thames, England.

Samuel Seegay, 107 University Place, New York 3, N.Y., U.S.A.

Phonetic Press, Pine Plains, N.Y., U.S.A.

Mont Follick, M.P., House of Parliament, London, England.

William Russell, Athens, Ga., U.S.A.

G. T. Wride, International Language League, 5306 Fifth Ave., Los Angeles 43, Calif., U.S.A.

Northwest Printery, 4617 W. Grace, Chicago 41, Ill., U.S.A.

Anglo-American Phonetics, Concord, Mass., U.S.A.

H. Porter Trefethen, Kent's Hill, Me., U.S.A.

GENERAL. Albert Guérard, Stanford University, Stanford, Calif., U.S.A.

Paul Mitrović, Namanjina Ulica 13, Sarajevo, Yugoslavia.

Theodore Andersson, Modern Language Association, 100 Washington Square East, New York 3, N.Y., U.S.A.

The Quarterly Review of Intercultural Communication (ed. Floyd Hardin). P. O. Box 393, Denver 1, Colo., U.S.A.

BIBLIOGRAPHY

Bibliographical Notes

Three essential source-books on the subject of the international language are: L. Couturat and L. Léau, *Histoire de la langue universelle,* Paris, Hachette, 1903; A. Guérard, *A Short History of the International Language Movement,* London, T. Fisher Unwin, 1922; and P. E. Stojan, *Bibliografio de internacia lingvo,* Genève, Universala esperanto-asocio, 1929. Unfortunately, all three books are hopelessly out of print, and copies are available only in major libraries.

Couturat and Léau restrict themselves to a discussion of constructed tongues up to 1903, save for a brief discussion of polygraphy (pp. 1–10; a brief bibliography of polygraphic systems devised for international use appears on p. 9), and a discussion of proposals to use dead languages (pp. 515–541). They subject each of the systems they discuss to a searching criticism after giving a detailed description. Their bibliography is scattered throughout the footnotes.

Guérard discusses not only artificial languages, but also proposals to use French, English, and Latin, and the possibility of an Anglo-French condominium. He gives a detailed, point-by-point comparison of Esperanto, Ido, the older Interlingua, and Romanal. His Appendix I (pp. 211–215, "Bibliographical Notes") presents a list of articles on the international language problem by renowned philologists and linguists (Bréal, Brugmann, Leskien, Courtenay, Jespersen, la Grasserie, Meillet, Meyer, Müller, Régnaud, Schuchardt, Sweet). His Appendix II (pp. 216–219) is entitled "A Tentative List of Artificial Language Projects (up to 1913)."

Stojan's work is a true bibliography, and makes a definite and almost successful attempt at completeness, listing no fewer than 321 artificial languages that had been offered up to the time of its appearance. It includes a section devoted to the polygraphists who tried to compose a "universal character" by which people of different languages might communicate their thoughts (Lull, Alberti, Trithemius, Nostradamus,

Porta, Campanella, Wilkins, Hartlib, Beck, Kircher, Becher, Besnier, Kochanski, etc.). Listed also are attempts at a "universal grammar" (Duns Scotus, Scaliger, Harris, Humboldt, Trombetti, etc.) and at universal alphabets (since 1412: Volney, Ellis, Lepsius, Bell, Rousselot, Passy, Viëtor, Jespersen, Marr), as well as international stenography since 1659, gestural languages for the use of deaf-mutes since 1614, and sign languages and symbolic codes since 1534 (including M. Dewey's *Decimal Classification,* Boston, 1885, now used by libraries). Cryptography and secret and commercial codes are also listed. Long sections are devoted to proposals to use Greek, Latin, French, English, and other languages for international purposes, and there is a listing of opinions expressed by famous philosophers, writers, and linguists on the subject of a universal language. Constructed-language projects are listed, but only occasionally and very briefly described.

I wish to express my grateful acknowledgment to these three excellent works, from which I have drawn copiously, particularly in connection with Part 2 of the present work.

My gratitude is also offered to the Reference Department staff of the Columbia University Libraries (and in particular to Mr. John M. Waddell) for the cordial and efficient cooperation they have given me in the preparation of this work.

Bibliography

(Note: Many of the works listed here are out of print, and a good number are not available even in major libraries. Where the publisher is not given, it is to be assumed that the author published his book privately. Considering the fact that Stojan devotes a book of 557 pages exclusively to bibliography, it is quite obvious that the list of works given here includes only a minute fraction of all the books and articles that have dealt with the problem of the international language up to this time. My criterion has been to include, in somewhat arbitrary fashion, those works which are mentioned or described in the course of our own discussion, plus a certain number of other works that have seemed to me, for one reason or another, significant. A conscientious effort has been made to include all works of note that have appeared since 1929, the date of appearance of the latest and most complete of our three major source-works. It must, however, be stressed that many worthy projects and works of all kinds dealing with the topic must inevitably have escaped my notice. My sincere apologies are tendered in advance to all recent authors and constructors of projects who may feel they have been slighted or ignored. An equally sincere request is made to them, and to all readers of this book, to send in to the author all relevant bibliographical information for possible inclusion in a later edition.)

American Association for the Advancement of Science, "Aims and Traits of a World Language," *Proceedings,* XXXVII, 1888, pp. 317–321.

American Philosophical Society, "Report of the Committee," *Nature,* XXXVIII, 1888.

Arnim, W. von, *Entwurf einer internationalen Verkehrssprache, genannt Veltparl,* Oppeln, Maske, 1896.

Baranyai, Z., *A Francia Nyelv,* Budapest, 1920.

Barral, J., *Elementos gramatikali dil linguo internacional e di sui dialekts,* Holzminden, 1914.
Barral, J., *La langue fédérale,* Nice, Visconti, 1923.
Bauer, G., *Spelin,* Agram (Zagreb), Suppan, 1888.
Baumann, A., *Wede,* Diessen-vor-München, Hüber, 1915.
Baumann, A., *Weltpitschn,* München, 1925–1926.
Baumann, A., *Oiropapitschn,* München, 1928.
Beatty, W., *Qosmiani,* Washington, 1922.
Beck, C., *Universal Character,* London, 1657.
Beermann, E., *Novilatiin,* Leipzig, Fock, 1895.
Bel, W., *De eerste proefbewijzen,* Amsterdam, 1869.
Bell, A. M., *World-English, the Universal Language,* London, Trübner, 1888.
Bellay, J. du, *Défense et illustration de la langue française,* ed. Humbert, Paris, Garnier, 1914.
Bernhard, S., *Grammatik der Lingua Franca Nuova,* Wien, 1888.
Beuthner, A., *Weltsprache Manbab und Weltschrift Mangif,* Marksneukirchen, 1912.
Bogdanov, A. (Malinovsky, A. A.), *O proletarskoy kul'ture,* Moskva, Kniga, 1925.
Bollack, L., *La Langue bleue,* Paris, 1899.
Boltz, A., *Hellenisch, die allgemeine Gelehrtensprache der Zukunft,* Leipzig, Friedrich, 1888.
Bolyai, F., described in Forti, A., "Intorno alla vita . . .", *Bullettino di bibliografia e storia delle scienze matematiche e fisiche,* I, p. 298, Roma, 1868.
Bond, S., *Omnez and Domni,* Wellington, Bryant, 1912.
Bond, S., *Optez,* Wellington, 1916.
Bond, S., *Meso,* Wellington, Bryant, 1926.
Braakman, J., *El Mundolinco,* Noordwijk, van Dillen, 1894.
Brackenbusch, W., *Is English Destined to Become the Universal Language?,* Göttingen, Kaestner, 1868.
Bradshaw, J., *A Scheme for Making the English Language the International Language,* London, Brain, 1847.
Braendle, F., *World-English (Veltlang),* Washington, 1910.
Bramwell, F. J., *Report to the British Association for the Advancement of Science, 1902,* London, 1903, p. 847.
Bravo del Barrio, *Europeo,* Madrid, 1914.
Brugmann, K. and Leskien, A., *Zur Kritik der künstlichen Weltsprachen,* Strassburg, Trübner, 1907.
Budilovich, A., *Obshcheslavyansky Yazyk,* Warszawa, 1891.

Cardenas, C., *Hom-Idyomo,* Wien, Manz, 1921.
Carus, P., "Esperanto, Ilo and Malay," *Monist,* Chicago, XIX, no. 3, July, 1909, pp. 430–432.
Chappaz, J. M., *Langage instantané,* Ville-la-Grande (Haute-Savoie), 1900.
Chappelier, P., *L'Esperanto et le système bilingue,* Paris, Grasset, 1911.
Chappelier, P., *Le français et l'anglais langues internationales,* Paris, Larousse, 1915.
Charpentier, *De l'excellence de la langue française,* Paris, 1683.
Cheshikhin, V., *Gram. Ideografiya i Neosinografiya,* Riga, 1913.
Christian, M. D., *Greek as an International Language,* New York, 1946.
Colas, J. (Esperema), *L'Adjuvilo,* Paris, Gamber, 1910.
Comenius (Komenský, J.), *Via Lucis,* 1641, Amsterdam, Cunradum, 1668.
Consoli, S., *Lingua nazionale della terra,* Catania, Nicolosi e Grasso, 1925.
Courtonne, E., "Langue internationale néo-latine," *Bulletin de la société niçoise des sciences naturelles,* Nice, Visconti, 1885.
Couturat, L. et Léau, L., *Histoire de la langue universelle,* Paris, Hachette, 1903 (see description in Bibliographical Notes, p. 265).
Couturat, L. et Léau, L., *Les nouvelles langues internationales,* Paris, Hachette, 1907.
Dalgarno, G., *Ars Signorum,* London, 1661.
Delormel, J., "Projet d'une langue universelle," *Moniteur,* 27 Brumaire III, Paris, 1795.
Descartes, J., *Lettre au P. Mersenne* (Nov. 20, 1629), ed. Adam-Tannery, I, pp. 76–79, Paris, Cerf, 1898.
Diels, H., *Volkslatein,* Leipzig, Teubner, 1901.
Diemen, J. van, *Nove-Latina,* Noorscharwoude, Keizer, 1921.
Dietrich, K., *Grundlagen der Völkerverkehrssprache,* Dresden, Kühtmann, 1902.
Donisthorpe, W., *Uropa,* Guilford, 1913.
Donoghue, T., *Geoglot,* Boston, International Geoglot Bureau, 1916.
Dormoy, E., *Le Balta,* Tours, Arrault, 1893.
Drezen, E., *Historio de Mondo-Lingvo,* Moskva, Hohlov i Nekrasov, 1928.
Drezen, E., *Za Vseobshchim Yazykom,* Leningrad, Gosudarstvennoe Izdatelstvo, 1928.
Durrant, E. D., *The Language Problem,* Rickmansworth, Esperanto Publishing Co., 1943.
Dyer, F., *The Lingualumina,* London, 1889.

Edmonds, G., *Universal Alphabet, Grammar and Language,* London and Glasgow, Griffin, 1856.

Eichhorn, N., *Die Weltsprache,* Bamberg, 1887.

Ellis, A., "On the Conditions of a Universal Language," *Transactions of the Philological Society,* 1888–1890, pp. 59–98, London, 1891.

Ernst, D., *La Novi Latine . . . de li Construende Interlingua,* Warburg, Werth, 1910.

Estienne, H., *La Précellence du langage françois* (1579), Paris, Delalain, 1850.

Faiguet, M., "Langue Nouvelle," *Encyclopédie* of Diderot and d'Alembert, IX, Paris, 1765.

Ferranti, M., *Simplo,* Roma, Tipografia Italia, 1911.

Fibula, *Latino Viventi,* Torino, Academia pro Interlingua, 1925.

Fieweger (pseudonym), *International-Verkehrssprache Dil,* Breslau, Aderholz, 1894.

Flach, J., *Der Hellenismus der Zukunft,* Leipzig, Friedrich, 1889.

Fonetik Crthografi, Northwest Printery, Chicago, 1944.

Foster, E. P., *Ro,* Cincinnati, 1908.

Foster, E. P., *Alphabet of Ideas,* Waverly, Roia, 1928.

Foulk, R., *Amxrikai spek,* New York, 1937.

Friedmann, P. L., *Pan-Arisch,* Altona, Bägel, 1908.

Fröhlich, K., *Reform-Latein,* Wien, 1902.

Gajewski, B., *Grammaire du Solresol,* Paris, 1902.

Gambatesa, G., *La lingua italiana lingua internazionale,* Palermo, L'Attualità, 1922.

Gigli, M., *Lingua filosofica universale pei dotti,* Milano, 1818.

Glubokovsky, M., *Vsemirno-Nauchny Yazyk,* Moskva, 1880.

Gode, A. and Blair, E., *Interlingua: a Grammar of the International Language,* New York, Storm, 1951.

Gode, A. and Blair, E., *Interlingua-English Dictionary,* New York, Storm, 1951.

Grasserie, R. de la, *De la possibilité et des conditions d'une langue internationale,* Paris, Maisonneuve, 1892.

Grasserie, R. de la, *Apolema,* Paris, Leroux, 1907.

Greenwood, F., *Excelsioro, Ulla,* London, Miller & Gill, 1906.

Grimm, J. von, *Ueber den Ursprung der Sprache,* Berlin, Abhandlungen der Kgl. Akademie, 1851.

Grosselin, A., *Système de langue universelle,* Paris, Roret, 1836.

Guardiola, J., *Kosmal Idioma . . . Orba genannt,* Paris, Schmidt, 1893.

Guérard, A., *A Short History of the International Language Movement,*

London, T. Fisher Unwin, 1922 (see description in Bibliographical Notes, p. 265).

Hale, H., "An International Language," *American Association for the Advancement of Science, Proceedings,* XXXVII, 1888; pp. 317–321.

Hamilton, J., *World-English (Cosmo-English),* St. Paul, 1924.

Hartl, A., *Lehrbuch der Perfektsprache (Lingua Perfect),* Linz, Zentraldruckerei, 1909.

Haugg, A., *Edilo,* München, Natur und Kultur, 1909.

Heimer, H., *Mondial,* Lund, Gleerupska, 1957.

Heintzeler, E., *Universala,* Stuttgart, Roth, 1893.

Hély, V., *L'interprète international,* Langres, 1908.

Henderson, G., *Lingua,* London, Trübner, 1888.

Henderson, G. (Hoinix), *Anglo-Franca,* London, Trübner, 1889.

Henderson, G., "Latinized English (Latinesce)," *The Referee,* London, Jan. 1901.

Henderson, G., *Phoenix and the Revival of Latin,* London, 1902.

Herkel, J., *Základy všeslovanského jazyka,* Wien, 1826.

Hilbe, F., *Die Zahlensprache,* Feldkirch, 1901.

Hoessrich, A., *Tal,* Sonneberg, 1903.

Hogben, L., *Interglossa,* New York, Penguin, 1943.

Holladay, L., *English as an International Language* (selected list of references), Chicago, Newberry Library, 1926.

Huart, A., *Le Median,* Cannes, de Guiglion, 1909.

Hume, D., Letter to E. Gibbon (Oct. 24, 1767), *Letters of D. Hume,* ed. J. Y. Grieg, II, p. 170, Oxford, Clarendon, 1932.

Hummler, J., *Mundelingua,* Saulgau, 1904.

Isly, F., *Langue Isly,* Paris, Richard, 1901.

Jacob, H., *A Planned Auxiliary Language,* London, Dobson, 1947.

Jespersen, O., *An International Language* [*Novial*], London, Allen & Unwin, 1928.

Kent, R. G., "Latin as the International Auxiliary Language," *Classical Journal,* Princeton, XVIII, no. 1, Oct. 1922, pp. 38–44.

Kerckhoffs, A., *Cours complet de Volapük,* Paris, Le Soudier, 1885.

Keyser, K. G., *Universalspraket,* Stockholm, 1918.

Kluyver, A., *Het Nederlandsch en de wereldtalen,* Hague, Volgers, 1924.

Kolkop, E., *Slovanština,* Jevíčko, Boháček, 1913.

Konečný, J., *Slavina,* Praha, Koníček, 1912.

Kornerup, T., *Gram. med faste Former,* København, 1917.

Kovalyov, A., *Samouchitel' mezhdunarodnago nauchnago yazyka,* Rostov na Donu, 1911.

Križanić, J., *Gramatično izkazanie o ruskom jeziku* (1666), Moskva, Chteniya Obsh. Istorii i Drev. Rossii, 1864.

Kuhlenbeck, L., *Das Problem einer int. Gelehrtensprache und der Hellenismus der Zukunft,* Leipzig, Friedrich, 1889.

Kunstovný, O., *Serve,* Praha, 1928.

Kürschner, F., *Die Gemeinsprache . . . Lingua Komun,* Orselina sur Locarno, 1900.

Lauda, E., *Kosmos,* Berlin, Hennig, 1888.

Lavagnini, A., *Monario, Unilingue,* Roma, Ars Nova, 1923.

Leavitt, J. E., *Universal Automatic Phonobet,* Cincinnati, 1933.

Leibniz, G. W. (ca. 1679): *see* Couturat, L., *La Logique de Leibniz,* ch. 3, Paris, Alcan, 1901; Couturat, L., *Opuscules et fragments inédits de Leibniz,* Phil. VII, B, III, Paris, Alcan, 1903.

Lenz, F., *Pasilingua Hebraica,* Neuwied, Heuser, 1887.

Leroy-Beaulieu, P., "L'abandon du latin et l'avènement du Volapük," *Economiste français,* Aug. 4, 1888.

Lesevich, V., "Vsemirny Yazyk i Narodnye Yazyki," *Russkaya Mysl',* XI–XII, Moskva, 1900; VI, 1903.

Letellier, C. L., *Cours complet de langue universelle,* Caen, Chesnel-Laporte, 1855.

Lévêque, T., *Ling Internacional Mondo,* Villejuif, 1910.

Liptay, A., *Langue catholique,* Paris, Bouillon, 1892.

Lockhart, L., *Everyday Basic,* London, Paul, 1934.

Lott, J., *Grammatik der Weltsprache, Mundolingue,* Leipzig, 1890.

Lull, R., *Ars Brevis,* Lyon, 1592.

Lundstrom, P., *Neolatino,* Milano, Schola et Vita, 1928.

Macauley, T. C., *Interlingua,* Oxford, Clarendon, 1930.

Maldant, E., *Chabé Abane, la langue naturelle,* Paris, Jouve, 1886.

Marchand, J. A., *Dilpok,* Besançon, Jacquin, 1898.

Martellotta, V., *Latinulus, grammaticas de latinula linguas,* Bari, 1919.

Max, St. de, *Le Bopal,* Paris, Val et Baudry, 1887.

Meazzini, G., "La lingua internazionale I.D.O." (reformed Ido), *Giornale del Jonio,* April 1928, Catania.

Menet, C., *Grammaire élémentaire de la langue universelle,* Paris, Bonhoure, 1886.

Meriggi, C., *Blaia Zimondal,* Pavia, Fusi, 1884.

Michaux, A., *Romanal, une langue internationale anglo-latine,* Boulogne-sur-mer, Boningue, 1917.

Mill, F., *Antivolapük, oder die Mezzofanti-Sprache,* Neuwied, Heuser, 1893.

Miller, A., *Extralingua,* Dartford, 1921.

Milner, H., *Cosman,* Karbitz, Beer, 1927.
Mitrović, P., *Les problèmes interlinguistiques,* Sarajevo, 1940.
Mitrović, P., *An Essay on Interlinguistics,* Sarajevo, 1954.
Mitrović, P., *Esay de un Inter-Sistemal Vocabular de Auxiliar Lingues,* Sarajevo, 1955.
Moeser, W., *Interlingua (Halblatein, Semilatin),* Linz, 1921.
Molee, E., *Altutonish,* Tacoma, 1912.
Molenaar, H., *Panroman,* Leipzig, Uhlig, 1903.
Moser, H., *Die Weltsprache, Pasilingua,* Praha, 1888.
Möser, W., *Universal-Latein,* Innsbruck, 1902.
Muttermilch, W., *W Kwestyi Wyboru Języka Pomocniczego Miedzynarodowego,* Warszawa, 1910.
Nesmeyanov, F., *Mezhdunarodny Yazyk,* Moskva, 1913.
Nicolas, A., "Spokil," *Mémoires de la société nationale d'agriculture, science et art d'Angers,* Angers, Lachèse, 1900.
Nield, G., *Loga,* Marseille, 1926.
Nietzsche, F., *Menschliches, Allzumenschliches,* Leipzig, Neumann, 1899.
Nilson, A., *Lasonebr,* Gefle, 1897.
Nodier, C., *Du langage factice appelé macaronique,* Paris, Techner, 1834.
Novikov, J., *La Fédération de l'Europe,* Paris, Alcan, 1901.
Ogden, C. K., *The Basic Dictionary,* London, Paul, Trench, Trubner & Co., 1934.
Ogden, C. K., *The ABC of Basic English,* London, Paul, Trench, Trubner & Co., 1936.
Ogden, C. K., *Basic English* (9th ed.), London, Paul, Trench, Trubner & Co., 1944.
Ogden, C. K., and Richards, I. A., *The Meaning of Meaning,* New York, Harcourt, Brace, 1952.
Oldfather, W. A., "Latin as an International Language," *Classical Journal,* XVI, no. 4, Jan. 1921, pp. 195–206.
Owen, R. L., statement in Charter of United Nations, pp. 534–549 (see also Senate Documents 49, 133, and 150 of the 78th Congress).
Parsell, J. R., *An Alfabet for the World of Tomorrow,* New York, 1945.
Parsell, J. R., *One Alfabet,* Kansas City, 1948.
Peano, G., "De Latino Sine Flexione," *Revue des Mathématiques,* VIII, 1903.
Peano, G., *Vocabulario Commune ad Linguas de Europa,* Torino, Bocca, 1909.
Pei, M., *English, a World-Wide Tongue,* New York, Vanni, 1944.

Pei, M., "A Universal Language Can Be Achieved," *Town and Country,* New York, Sept. 1944.

Pei, M., "A Universal Alphabet," *Free World,* New York, Nov. 1946.

Pei, M., "One World? One Language?" *Modern Language Journal,* Menasha, Jan. 1947.

Pei, M., "Is a World Language Possible?" *Tomorrow,* New York, Oct. 1949.

Pei, M., "For a World-Wide Second Language," *New York Times Magazine,* July 2, 1950.

Pei, M., "Six Languages for One World, *New York Times Magazine,* Feb. 24, 1952.

Pei, M., "Conquest of Babel," *New York Times Magazine,* May 24, 1953.

Pei, M., "Bilingualism: Facts or Fiction?" *Hommes et Commerce,* Paris, XXXV, 1956.

Peri, H., "Aspects de l'histoire de la langue universelle," *Actes du 7me Congrès int. d'histoire des sciences,* Jerusalem, Aug. 1953.

Perrier, Ferry G., *Parlamento,* S. Imier, 1918.

Petrashevich, V., *Osnovy mezhdunarodnago yazyka glot,* Petrograd, 1917.

Pirenne, H., *Mohammed and Charlemagne,* New York, Barnes & Noble, 1955.

Pirro, M., *Universal-Sprache,* Paris, Rétaux, 1868.

Pompiati, K., *Die neue Weltsprache, Nov Latin Logui,* Wien, Jasper, 1918.

Puchner, J., *Gramatica di Nuove-Roman,* Linz, 1897.

Raymond, H. E., *Elements of Esperido,* Kalamazoo, 1924.

Reed, I. K., *Esperanto and Interlingua Compared,* New York, Esperanto Association of North America, 1957.

Renan, E., *Vie de Jésus,* Paris, Michel-Lévy Frères, 1863.

Rethy, A., *Lingua Universalis Communi Omnium Nationum Usui Accommodata,* Wien, 1821.

Ria, J. de, *Palais de 64 fenêtres,* St. Petersburg, 1788.

Richards, I. A., *Basic English and its Uses,* New York, Norton, 1943.

Richards, I. A. and Gibson, C. M., *Learning Basic English,* New York, Norton, 1945.

Rivarol, *De l'universalité de la langue française,* Paris, Bailly, Dessenne, 1784.

Rosa, D., "Le Nov Latin," *Bollettino dei musei di zoologia ed anatomia comparata della R. università di Torino,* V, no. 89, Torino, Clausen, Oct. 15, 1890.

Rosenberger, W., *Grammatik und Wörterbuch der Neutralsprache (Idiom Neutral),* Leipzig, Haberland, 1902.

Rosenberger, W., *Reform-Neutral,* St. Petersburg, Rascher, 1912.

Rossello Ordenes, *Is (Interlingua Sistematic),* Palma de Mallorca, 1926.

Rothenbücher, A., *Prim Lektur in Universal,* Leipzig, Wiegand, 1909.

Rotter, M., "Tersboca," *Die Weltrepublik,* Zürich, Meyer, 1912.

Rovere, C. A., *Lingua e città internazionali,* Pinerolo, 1900.

Rudelle, L. de, *Grammaire primitive . . . Pantos-dîmou-glossa,* Paris, Delalain, 1858.

Russell, B., *Suma (the 1000-Word Universal Language),* Gardena, Calif., 1957.

Sapelj, G., Untitled report concerning an all-Slavic language, Ljubljana (Laibach), 1790.

Sarrauton, H. de, *Molog* (*Monos Logos,* telescoped Esperanto), Cannes, Analyse et Synthèse, 1911.

Scarisbrick, J., *Lips Kith,* Trowbridge, Lansdowne, 1919.

Scheefer, J., *Mondea,* Berlin, Korzeniewski, 1910.

Schipfer, J., *Versuch einer Grammatik . . . Communications-oder Weltsprache,* Wiesbaden, 1839.

Schleyer, J., *Grammatik der Universalsprache für alle Erdbewohner, Volapük,* Konstanz, 1885.

Schmelzeis, J., *Das Leben und die Werke der heiligen Hildegardis,* Freiburg, 1879.

Schuchardt, H., *Weltsprache und Weltsprachen,* Strassburg, Trübner, 1894.

Seidel, A., *Gramatic di Ile,* Steglitz, 1909.

Sivartha, D., *Visona, or Universal and Natural Language,* Chicago, 1887.

Slonimski, J., *Język Neoromanski,* Warszawa, Pomoc Szkolna, 1924.

Sondahl, M., "Altayko e El Esk," *Boletim Oficial da União Sociocrática,* Alagoinhas (Bahia), 1913.

Sotos Ochando, B., *Projet d'une langue universelle,* Paris, Lecoffre, 1855.

The Soviet Linguistic Controversy (translated from the Soviet press by J. V. Murra, R. M. Hankin, and F. Holling), New York, King's Crown Press, 1951.

Spitzer, L., *Parla,* Heidelberg, 1907.

Starchevsky, A., *Nastoyashchy (Zhivoy) Vsemirny Yazyk,* St. Petersburg, 1889.

Starrenburg, D., *Gramatico di la Mundolingua Menimo,* Valencia, Barranco Hermanos, 1924.

Steiner, P., *Elementargrammatik . . . Pasilingua,* Neuwied, Heuser, 1885.

Stempfl, J., *Myrana,* Kempten, Kösel, 1887.

Stempfl, J., *Communia,* Kempten, Dobler, 1894.

Stojan, P. E., *Bibliografio de internacia lingvo,* Genève, Universala Esperanto-asocio, 1929 (see description in Bibliographical Notes, p. 265).

Sudre, F., *Langue musicale universelle,* Paris, 1866.

Talmey, M., *Ido,* New York, Ido Press, 1919.

Talmey, M., "The Auxiliary Language Question," *Modern Language Journal,* Menasha, XXIII, no. 3, Dec. 1938.

Talundberg, M., *Perio,* Elberfeld, Wasserloos, 1904.

Tgransar, *Alphabetarion Ansailanzar Sehlerai,* Istanbul, Bizantio, 1921.

Thai, P. X., *Frater,* Saigon, Tu-Hai, 1957.

Thierfelder, F., *Deutsch als Weltsprache,* Berlin, Kurzeja, 1938.

Thommeret, L., *La paix? La voilà pour toujours,* Paris, Rodstein, 1945.

Thommeret, L., *Le Monde unique et sa paix,* Paris, Rodstein, 1946.

Thommeret, L., *Pour l'organisation linguistique universelle,* Paris, Rodstein, 1947.

Thomsen, V., *La langue commune de la science,* København, 1905.

Trischen, H., *Mondlingvo,* Dresden, Pierson, 1906.

UNESCO, *Scientific and Technical Translating and Other Aspects of the Language Problem,* Paris and Genève, UNESCO, 1957.

Urquhart, T., *Logopandecteision,* London, Calvert & Tomlins, 1653.

Verheggen, S., *Nal Bino,* Liège, 1886.

Vidal, E. T., *Langue universelle et analytique,* Paris, Sirou, 1844.

Voirol, S., *El Linguo Moderno Casuela,* Torino, Academia pro Interlingua, 1927.

Volk, A. and Fuchs, R., *Die Weltsprache,* Berlin, Kühl, 1883.

Voltaire, *Babel, Dictionnaire philosophique,* Oeuvres de Voltaire, ed. Beuchot, XXVII, Paris, Lefèvre, 1829.

Voltaire, "Letter to Catherine II," reprinted in *Le Temps,* Paris, May 20, 1869.

Vulda, L., *The Elements of Om,* Calcutta, 1925.

Wahl, E. de, *Radicarium Direktiv del Lingue International, Occidental,* Tallin, Uehiselu, 1925.

Wald, M., *Weltsprache Pankel,* Gross-Beeren, 1906.

Webster, N., *Grammatical Institute of the English Language,* Hartford, Hudson and Goodwin, 1782–1783.

Webster, N., *Compendious Dictionary of the English Language,* Hartford, Hudson and Goodwin, 1806.

Webster, N., *American Dictionary of the English Language,* New York, Converse, 1828.

Weferling, E., *Unesal Interlingu,* Braunschweig, 1923.

Weferling, E., *Panskrit,* Braunschweig, 1925.

Weisbart, J., *Europal,* Berlin, 1912.

Weisbart, J., *Medial,* Hamburg, 1922.

Wells, H. G., *Anticipations,* London, Chapman and Hall, 1901.

Wells, H. G., "La Langue Universelle," *Monde Illustré,* Montreal, Mar. 15, 1902.

Whorf, B. L., "Languages and Logic," *Technology Review,* Apr. 1941.

Wilkins, J., *Essay Toward a Real Character and a Philosophical Language,* London, 1668.

Wride, G. T., *Printing by Sound with the Roman Alphabet,* Los Angeles, 1946.

Zamenhof, L., *Lingwe Uniwersala,* Warszawa, 1878 (early attempt).

Zamenhof, L. (Doktoro Esperanto), *Langue internationale,* Warszawa, Gebethner & Wolff, 1887.

Zaslavsky, D., "Veliky yazyk nashey epokhi," *Literaturnaya Gazeta,* Moskva, no. 1, Jan. 1, 1949, p. 3.

INDEX

Index

M

N

Franklin Pierce College Library
00021471